Conversations with James Salter

Literary Conversations Series
Monika Gehlawat
General Editor

Conversations
with James Salter

Edited by Jennifer Levasseur
and Kevin Rabalais

University Press of Mississippi   Jackson

www.upress.state.ms.us

The University Press of Mississippi is a member
of the Association of American University Presses.

Copyright © 2015 by University Press of Mississippi
All rights reserved
Manufactured in the United States of America

First printing 2015

Library of Congress Cataloging-in-Publication Data

Conversations with James Salter / edited by Jennifer Levasseur, Kevin Rabalais.
    pages cm. — (Literary conversations series)
  Includes index.
   ISBN 978-1-4968-0357-3 (hardback) — ISBN 978-1-4968-0358-0 (ebook) 1. Salter, James—
Interviews. 2. Authors, American—20th century—Interviews. 3. Fiction—Authorship. 4.
Screenwriters—United States—Interviews. 5. Motion picture authorship. 6. Motion picture
producers and directors—United States—Interviews. I. Levasseur, Jennifer, 1977– II. Rabal-
ais, Kevin, 1976–
  PS3569.A4622Z46 2015
  813'.54—dc23
  [B]
                                  2015019110
British Library Cataloging-in-Publication Data available

Books by James Salter

The Hunters. New York: Harper & Brothers, 1956.

The Arm of Flesh. New York: Harper & Brothers, 1961.

A Sport and a Pastime. Garden City, NY: Doubleday (Paris Review Editions), 1967.

Light Years. New York: Random House, 1975.

Solo Faces. Boston: Little, Brown, 1979.

Dusk and Other Stories. San Francisco: North Point, 1988.

Still Such (Poem). New York: William Drenttel, 1992.

Burning the Days: Recollection. New York: Random House, 1997.

The Hunters (revised). Washington, DC: Counterpoint, 1997.

Cassada (rewritten version of *The Arm of Flesh*). Washington, DC: Counterpoint, 2000.

Gods of Tin: The Flying Years. Edited by Jessica Benton and William Benton. Washington, DC: Shoemaker & Hoard, 2004.

Last Night: Stories. New York: Knopf, 2005.

There and Then: The Travel Writing of James Salter. Emeryville, CA: Shoemaker & Hoard, 2005.

Life Is Meals: A Food Lover's Book of Days. With Kay Eldredge Salter. New York: Knopf, 2006.

Memorable Days: The Selected Letters of James Salter and Robert Phelps. Edited by John McIntyre. Berkeley: Counterpoint, 2010.

Collected Stories. London: Picador, 2013.

All That Is. New York: Knopf, 2013.

The Art of Fiction (Kapnick Lectures). Charlottesville: University of Virginia Press, 2016.

Don't Save Anything: The Uncollected Writings of James Salter. Berkeley: Counterpoint, 2017.

Contents

Introduction

There is your life as you know it and also as others know it, perhaps incorrectly, but to which some importance must be attached. It is difficult to realize that you are observed from a number of points and the sum of them has validity.
    —James Salter, *Burning the Days*

He may have struggled for years as the greatest unknown writer in America, but the beginning of James Salter's literary career sounds like a young novelist's dream. Even before he resigned from the Air Force in 1957 to write full time, Salter's ascent as a writer seemed to promise fame, fortune, and literary immortality. His debut novel, *The Hunters* (1956), sold twelve thousand copies and prompted the publisher to request another book. Salter then sold the film rights for sixty thousand dollars (equivalent to half a million today). Under Dick Powell's direction, Robert Mitchum and Robert Wagner embody characters first serialized in *Collier's*. Salter's 1961 follow-up, *The Arm of Flesh*, chronicles an American fighter squadron in 1950s Germany.

Then the West Point graduate who had logged more than one hundred combat missions in Korea in his twenties and published two novels while still in his thirties reinvented himself once again, this time as a screenwriter and filmmaker among such denizens as Robert Redford and Roman Polanski. Salter's co-made short documentary about football, *Team Team Team*, won a top prize at the 1962 Venice Film Festival. Four of his screenplays became feature films, among them *Downhill Racer* (1969), starring Redford, and *The Appointment* (1969), directed by Sidney Lumet. Before his forty-fifth birthday, Salter had written and directed a feature film, *Three* (1969), starring Charlotte Rampling and Sam Waterston.

Interviewing Salter in 1992 for the *Paris Review*, Edward Hirsch notes the success that *Three* experienced at the Cannes Film Festival. "It was a pleasant surprise," Salter says. "Finally, though, it was like everything I've done. It had its admirers, some of them ardent, but . . . the public displayed complete indifference."

Though lucrative, writing screenplays and making movies never brought

Salter the recognition he desired. It also diverted his time and attention from literary endeavors. Early in his 1970 interview for *Movie People*, he responds to a question about being "fairly well-known as a novelist" after the publication of his first two books: "First of all, I was not a fairly well-known novelist. I was unknown, and even today I am virtually unknown." More than forty years later, Nick Paumgarten echoes that sentiment in the *New Yorker*: "Salter is not famous." What matters, and what has kept Salter's work alive, Paumgarten makes clear in his next sentence: "Among many writers, and some literary people, he is venerated for his sentence-making, his observational powers, his depictions of sex and valor, and a pair of novels that, in spite of thin sales and obscure subject matter, have more than a puncher's chance at permanence."[1] Those two novels, *A Sport and a Pastime* (1967) and *Light Years* (1975), have enthralled generations of readers and divided critics.

For the majority of Salter's career, however, admirers have "pass[ed] his name along to the uninitiated with the trust of a personal secret."[2] His devoted readers, many of them also writers, speak with reverence about his two best-known novels, as well as *Solo Faces* (1979) and the short stories published in *Dusk* (1988) and *Last Night* (2005). As Adam Begley writes in his 1990 *New York Times* profile, "His readers, few in number but adamant in their conviction that he is a great writer, are confident that . . . [he] will eventually take his place in the canon of American literature."

The publication of *All That Is*—and the accompanying international publicity blitz—at last forged the audience Salter's early career promised. In an *Esquire* blog, Alex Bilmes describes a London book party: "He'd signed more copies of *All That Is* . . . than he'd sold of previous books."[3] With that novel, his first in thirty-four years, many first-time readers of Salter's fiction encountered an eighty-seven-year-old author with a biography (in capsule: Korean War fighter pilot turned novelist and filmmaker) that could have been scripted for Hollywood. Indeed, in his introduction to Salter's *Collected Stories*, Booker Prize–winning novelist John Banville writes, "Salter is that rarest of phenomena, a man of action turned successful, more than successful, artist—his is the career that Hemingway could only dream of."[4]

This volume collects twenty-two conversations with James Salter that span five decades. Several appear in English for the first time; others have not been previously published or were published in abbreviated versions. As a whole, they demonstrate the variety and scope of Salter's career along with the progression and solidity of his ideas about writing, reading, film, relationships between the sexes, and contemporary literature. They also demonstrate Salter's soaring, late-career popularity. After a shortage of early interviews, *All That Is* (2013) sparked worldwide interest in Salter's life and work. He granted interviews to journalists and writers from around the globe. This collection includes conversations published originally in Argentina, Australia, Canada, France, Sweden, and the United States.

While Salter corrects the misconception of his renown as a novelist in *Movie People*, the earliest conversation collected here, the most recent interview in this volume (August 2014) revisits that question. French journalist Arnaud Laporte asks whether fame has satisfied him. "Yes," Salter says, "but it didn't come at exactly the right time."

As a consummate prose stylist who persevered despite disappointing sales and the kind of negative reviews that indelibly mark a writer's psyche,[5] Salter has succeeded in fashioning "from the great heap of days . . . something lasting."[6] He enjoys a certain mystique among writers. David Bowman relays an apocryphal story in *Salon* about the difficulty of obtaining copies of *The Hunters* and *The Arm of Flesh*, both long out of print in the 1980s: "Salter had hired someone to physically drive a station wagon through backwater used bookstores and buy up any copies of those early books and then burn them." Salter revised *The Hunters* in 1997. In 2000, he published *Cassada*, a completely rewritten version of *The Arm of Flesh*—in effect reinventing his early career.

Because he attained a cult following before the mainstream media caught up and because of the long interim between his books, interviewers and critics tend to latch onto everything Salter writes and says, elevating his comments to the status of artist's statement—or gospel—as they repeat them back to him. After calling himself a *frotteur*—"someone who likes to rub words in his hand, to turn them around and feel them, to wonder if that really is the best word possible"—in the *Paris Review*, the term became a sanctioned definition for critics seeking to explain his method. In *Esquire*, Salter expresses regret for his "unfortunate choice" of phrase: "I meant that all I like to do is pick the right word, and rewriting is really one of the more pleasurable parts of writing for me. But I used that damn French and now it sounds self-indulgent: 'He's a frotteur! Oh, he is, is he? I've never seen one before.'"[7]

The same goes for statements written about Salter. The most persistent—that he is a "writer's writer"—recurs in the majority of these interviews. Though Salter can be quick to point out the pejorative in this tag (that it signals his lack of sales, or—as he tells Dexter Cirillo—that it's "just a cliché picked up by second-rate critics and passed along"), he cannot deny the long list of illustrious devotees, which includes Michael Ondaatje, Reynolds

Price, Edna O'Brien, Joseph Heller, Michael Herr, Susan Sontag, Frank Conroy, John Irving, Richard Ford, and Peter Matthiessen. About *Light Years*, Jhumpa Lahiri notes, "As a writer, I am shamelessly in its debt."[8] In their citation to the 2010 Rea Award, jurors Ann Beattie, Mary Robison, and Joy Williams conclude, "American short story writers hold no one in higher esteem than James Salter. . . . no one can match the beauty and precision of his prose."[9]

Nine of the twenty-two conversations collected here are conducted by published or aspiring novelists. "I went to see James Salter as one goes to see the wise man of the mountain," writes Andrés Hax. To mark the occasion, Jonathan Lee steals a menu from the restaurant where he interviewed Salter. David Bowman considers returning to Salter's house at night, hoping to exhume cast-off pages from the writer's garbage. Sonya Chung maintained a year-long correspondence with Salter before traveling to his home in Bridgehampton—or what might as well be Mecca for many of these novelist-interviewers. One of them, Thad Ziolkowski, writes: "In truth, he's the great American writer that most of America doesn't know it has produced."

This remark—that Salter has for too long been neglected—gives insight into the paucity of early interviews. Even after *Dusk* received the 1989 PEN/Faulkner Award, few interviews with Salter appeared. Reviewing *Burning the Days* in the *New York Times*, Dinitia Smith tells a story that hints at the distraction of outside disturbances and points toward Salter's redirection: "Ms. Eldredge [the author's wife] saw Salter's frustration with the film business and encouraged him to write full time. In 1980 she printed business cards for him that said: 'Mr. James Salter regrets he is far too occupied to: Write a Movie Script. Polish a Movie Script. Read a Movie Script. Take a Meeting.'"[10]

Many of these interviewers note Salter's generosity in conversation. His catholic curiosity and sincere interest in others can disarm but also deflect. He can halt or redirect questioning with a steely stare or a single-word response. "Salter, it pretty quickly turns out on meeting him, is a bit of a contrarian," Claire Allfree writes in the New Zealand *Listener*.[11] And Chung: " . . . with the recorder now on, I watch him lean back in his chair, and I perceive a kind of armor flip into place like a welder's mask." Hirsch relays what many of Salter's interviewers note: "His manners are precise and elegant; he has a splendid New York accent; he runs his hands through his gray hair and laughs boyishly. At sixty-seven he has the fitness of an ex-military man. He tells anecdotes easily, dramatically, but he also carries an aura of reserve about him. There is a privacy one doesn't breach."

While Salter remains guarded about his personal life (from *Narrative*: "I tend to be secretive . . . Even close friends say so."), readers of these conversations will encounter an author who speaks passionately about literature and his development as a writer. We discover the working methods of a revered prose stylist and are allowed into the presence of a *reader's reader* who speaks openly about literary influences such as Isaac Babel, Colette, Isak Dinesen, Marguerite Duras, and Thomas Wolfe. "Where other interviews, for any number of reasons, seem to be interminable, talking with Salter is like having a conversation with an old friend," Robert Burke writes. "His range and referents are both free-flowing and unassuming, and, when he is talking about writing and literature, he pays the interviewer the ultimate compliment of assuming that he or she is just as passionately concerned with these topics as he is himself." Salter scholars and readers will find in these interviews a wealth of stories about flying, filmmaking, climbing, writing, publishing, and the literary life.

After his promising beginning, the middle of Salter's career as a writer suffered because of long gaps between major publications, though he remained productive, writing stories, working as a journalist, and teaching. The real shift in popular and critical interest in Salter arrived with his long-awaited memoir, *Burning the Days*. Along with it, the number of published conversations increased. During the ensuing years, many of his projects reached fruition; since 2000, he has published eight books.

At the end of his long and diverse career, Salter has reached a pinnacle that few contemporary writers can envisage. Peers, along with a new generation of novelists, continue to seek direction and inspiration from his work—"a relatively small body of prose of uncommon subtlety, intelligence, and beauty," as Joyce Carol Oates writes.[12]

In the fall of 2014, at eighty-nine, Salter assumed a position as the inaugural Kapnick Distinguished Writer-in-Residence at the University of Virginia. The man who commenced mountain climbing in his fifties in order to write *Solo Faces* and in his early seventies taught his youngest son to play hockey[13] maintains an enviable energy that comes across in his work and in these conversations. And while Paumgarten calls *All That Is* "likely his last"[14] novel, Salter tells DeWeese in 2013, "I don't think I've used up even my own limited possibilities." This collection, fittingly, ends with the words: "I still feel a desire to write."

Salter's stamina, wit, depth of thought, and inquisitiveness infiltrate each of these conversations. Repeatedly, they return to his enduring pursuit to make art. "One puts everything into it, I mean everything you have," he says in *Movie People.* "You must give it all; that's the only way to replenish." Or, as he tells Hirsch about why he writes: "Because all this is going to vanish. The only thing left will be the prose and poems, the books, what is written down."

The editors thank James Salter and Kay Eldredge Salter for their invaluable help. Thanks, also, to Katie Keene at the University Press of Mississippi, William Dowie, Elizabeth Anglin, and all of the contributors and publications that allowed us to reprint their insightful interviews with James Salter.

JL
KR

Notes

Endnotes are given for interviews and articles not included in this book. Some introductions to interviews in this collection have been abbreviated to avoid repetition.

1. Nick Paumgarten, "The Last Book," 15 April 2013, 44.

2. William Dowie, "James Salter," *American Short-Story Writers since World War II*, vol. 130 of *Dictionary of Literary Biography*, ed. Patrick Meanor (Detroit: Gale Research Co., 1993), 282.

3. Alex Bilmes, "James Salter—The Greatest Writer You've Never Read," *Esquire* blog, 22 May 2013.

4. John Banville, introduction to *Collected Stories*, by James Salter (London: Picador, 2013), ix.

5. Towers in the *New York Times* calls *Light Years* "an overwritten, chi-chi, and rather silly novel" ("For Devotees of Scott Fitzgerald? Edward FitzGerald?" *New York Times*, 27 July 1975, web). Also in the *New York Times*, Anatole Broyard addresses the author: "Didn't you have something more in mind? Do you really feel that you have fulfilled your obligations?" ("Ending in the Middle," 25 June 1975, web).

6. James Salter, *Burning the Days* (New York: Vintage), 195.

7. Alex Bilmes, "Something Lasting: How James Salter Freezes Time," *Esquire*, June 2013, web.

8. Jhumpa Lahiri, "Spellbound," *Paris Review* blog, *The Daily*, 5 April 2011.

9. www.reaaward.org/Salter/Salter.html.

10. Dinitia Smith, "A Fighter Pilot Who Aimed for Novels but Lives on Film," *New York Times*, 30 August 1997, web.

11. Claire Allfree, "All That He Is: An Interview with James Salter," *Listener*, 14 June 2013,

web.

12. Joyce Carol Oates, "The Great Heap of Days," *New York Review of Books*, 14 July 2005, web.

13. Paul Grondahl, "State Author Bangs the Drum as Noisily as He Can," *Electric Times Union*, 1997, http://www.albany.edu/writers-inst/webpages4/archives/tusalter.html.

14. Paumgarten, 45.

Chronology

1925	Born James Arnold Horowitz, June 10 in Passaic, New Jersey, to L. George and Mildred Horowitz. Raised as an only child in New York City.
1938–1942	Attends Horace Mann School in Riverdale, New York, where he is an editor of the school's literary magazine. Has poems accepted by *Poetry* magazine.
1942	Reluctantly enters West Point. In his second year, he joins the Army Air Corps.
1945	Graduates from West Point and enters the Air Force as a pilot. On V-E Day, while on a navigation flight, he crashes into a house in Great Barrington, Massachusetts. No one is injured. Salter goes on to deployments in Manila and Hawaii.
1946–47	Writes a (never published) novel, which Harper & Brothers rejects.
1947	Promoted to first lieutenant.
1948–1950	Studies at Georgetown University, where he receives a master's degree in international affairs.
1950	First travels to Europe.
1951	Volunteers as a fighter pilot in Korean War. Marries Ann Altemus.
1952	Participates in more than one hundred combat missions.
1952–1953	Assigned to fighter squadrons in the United States.
1954–1957	Stationed in Germany.
1955	Daughter Allan Conrad is born.
1956	First novel, *The Hunters*, published.
1957	Daughter Nina Tobe is born. With the rank of major, resigns from the Air Force.
1958	*The Hunters* film directed by Dick Powell, stars Robert Mitchum. Salter receives $60,000 for the film rights.
1959	Father dies. Salter sells swimming pools. Meets Lane Slate. First visits Aspen.

1961	*The Arm of Flesh* is published. During the Berlin crisis, recalled to active duty in Chaumont, France. Makes first notes for *A Sport and a Pastime*. Meets Irwin Shaw.
1962	Legally changes name to James Salter. His wife and children also take the new name. Twins, Claude Cray and James Owen, born. *Team Team Team*, written and directed with Lane Slate, wins a first prize at Venice Film Festival.
1963–1964	Makes NET-TV documentary series *Circus* with Lane Slate.
1965	Writes screenplay *The Appointment*.
1967	*A Sport and a Pastime* published by Paris Review Editions. Sells three thousand copies.
1967–1969	Lives near Grasse, France.
1968	"Am Strande von Tanger" published in the *Paris Review* and selected for *The O. Henry Prize Stories 1970*.
1969	*The Appointment*—directed by Sidney Lumet and starring Omar Sharif and Anouk Aimée—and *Downhill Racer*—starring Robert Redford and directed by Michael Ritchie—are released. First feature film as writer and director appears. *Three*, based on a story by Irwin Shaw, stars Charlotte Rampling and Sam Waterston. Buys a house in Aspen. Robert Phelps sends Salter a fan letter. The two maintain a correspondence until Phelps's death in 1989.
1970	"The Cinema" published in the *Paris Review*.
1971	"The Destruction of the Goetheanum" published in the *Paris Review* and selected for *The O. Henry Prize Stories 1972*.
1972	"Via Negativa" published in the *Paris Review* and selected for *The O. Henry Prize Stories 1974*.
1975	*Light Years* published. Divorce from Ann Altemus.
1976	Begins living with writer Kay Eldredge.
1977	Takes up rock climbing after Robert Redford asks him to write screenplay about the subject.
1979	*Solo Faces* published. Makes first notes for novel that becomes *All That Is*.
1980	Daughter Allan dies in an accident. Moves to Long Island.
1981	"Akhnilo" published in *Grand Street*.
1982	Award from American Academy and Institute of Arts and Letters.
1983	"Lost Sons" published in *Grand Street* and selected for *The O. Henry Prize Stories 1984*. *Threshold*, starring Donald Suther-

	land (screenplay by Salter, directed by Richard Pearce), is released in the United States.
1984	"The Fields at Dusk" (later renamed "Dusk") published in *Esquire*. "Foreign Shores" included in *Best American Short Stories 1984*, edited by John Updike.
1985	Son Theo Shaw born in Paris
1986	Writer-in-residence at Vassar College. Writes an autobiographical essay, "The Captain's Wife," for *Esquire*, which prompts work on the memoir that becomes *Burning the Days*. Provides a foreword to the reissue of A. J. Liebling's *Between Meals: An Appetite for Paris*.
1987	Teaches fall semester at Iowa Writers' Workshop. "Akhnilo" anthologized in *American Short Story Masterpieces*, edited by Raymond Carver and Tom Jenks.
1988	"American Express" published in *Esquire* and selected for *The O. Henry Prize Stories 1989*. "Twenty Minutes" published in *Grand Street*. *Dusk and Other Stories* published.
1989	Teaches fall semester at Iowa Writers' Workshop. Original deadline for *Burning the Days* passes. Wins PEN/Faulkner Award for *Dusk and Other Stories*.
1991	Teaches spring semester at the University of Houston.
1992	*Still Such*, limited edition of prose poem about New York, published.
1993	"Comet" published in *Esquire*. "You Must" chosen for *Best American Essays 1993*.
1994	"My Lord You" published in *Esquire*.
1995	*A Sport and a Pastime* reissued by The Modern Library.
1996	Film *Boys*, based on Salter's story "Twenty Minutes," is released (directed by Stacy Cochran).
1997	Teaches fall semester at Williams College. *Burning the Days* is published. Counterpoint publishes revised version of *The Hunters*.
1998	He and Kay Eldredge marry in Paris. Awarded the New York State Edith Wharton Citation of Merit, the John Steinbeck Award, the PEN Center USA Award for Creative Nonfiction, and the English-Speaking Union Ambassador Book Award for *Burning the Days*. William Dowie publishes first full-length book on Salter, *James Salter* (Twayne Publishers).
1998–2000	Named New York State Author.

2000	The Ransom Center (University of Texas at Austin) acquires James Salter Archive. Elected to the American Academy of Arts and Letters. Rewritten version of *The Arm of Flesh* published as *Cassada*. Provides a foreword to the reissue of Irwin Shaw's *The Young Lions*.
2002	"Last Night" is published in the *New Yorker*.
2003	*Light Years* wins the Mercantile Library-Clifton Fadiman Medal. "Bangkok" published in the *Paris Review*. "Give" published in *Tin House*. *Bangkok* (six stories) and *L'Homme des Hautes Solitudes* [*Solo Faces*] published in French translation by daughter Nina's publishing company, Éditions des Deux Terres.
2004	Publication of *Gods of Tin*, selections from Salter's writing about flying from *The Hunters, Cassada, Burning the Days*, and his previously unpublished Korean War journal. Short film released based on "Last Night," starring Frances McDormand (directed by Sean Mewshaw). "Such Fun" published in *Tin House*. "Eyes of the Stars" published in *Zoetrope. Soldiers Once and Still: Ernest Hemingway, James Salter, and Tim O'Brien* by Alex Vernon (University of Iowa Press) is released.
2005	*Last Night: Stories* and *There and Then: The Travel Writing of James Salter* published.
2006	*Life Is Meals* published. PEN/Faulkner finalist for *Last Night*.
2007–2008	Penguin Modern Classics reissues *The Hunters, Light Years*, and *Solo Faces*.
2010	*Memorable Days* published. Receives the Rea Award for the Short Story and PEN USA's Lifetime Achievement Award.
2011	Receives the *Paris Review*'s Hadada Award, which honors "a distinguished member of the writing community who has made a strong and unique contribution to literature." Documentary *James Salter: A Sport and a Pastime* (directed by Sandy Gotham Meehan) is released.
2012	"As They Were: American Masters through the Lens of James Salter" (photos 1962–1963), the Armory Show, Pier 94 Manhattan. PEN/Malamud Award for "excellence in Short Fiction." Atlantic Fiction for Kindle releases "Charisma," which is also published in the *Telegraph* (UK), 2013.
2013	*All That Is* published. Awarded a Yale University inaugural Donald Windham–Sandy M. Campbell Literature Prize

($150,000) for "outstanding achievement in fiction." *Collected Stories* is published in the United Kingdom.

2014   Becomes the inaugural Kapnick Distinguished Writer-in-Residence at the University of Virginia. Receives the F. Scott Fitzgerald Award for Achievement in American Literature.

2015   Agrees to write a memoir for Knopf. Dies on June 19 in Sag Harbor, New York, at age ninety.

Conversations with James Salter

James Salter on the Screenwriter

Fred Baker with Ross Firestone / 1970

Extracts from *Movie People: At Work in the Business of Film*, edited by Fred Baker with Ross Firestone, The Douglas Book Corporation, New York, 1972. Reprinted courtesy of Lucia Douglas Rubenstein and Ross Firestone.

Q: Was there a conscious decision on your part to begin an active film career? About what point in your life did you decide you wanted to make films?
A: I was living in the country, and I had a friend named Lane Slate. We wanted to become famous. He claimed to know something about the making of films. We joined forces. He was a writer also. And we set about to make three short films. Of those, only one was ever completed; that's *Team Team Team*. We borrowed the money from everybody to make the films; a banker, various relatives, dentists: the classic story. When *Team Team Team* was finished, we took it to George K. Arthur, who was one of the best distributors of small films in New York; there were not many then, and there are not many now. And he said, Well, yes he would look at it. He looked at it, and his comment was, "It would be better if it were shorter." It was twelve minutes long. Nevertheless it won a certificate from CINE and was sent to the foreign festivals. One day in July we received a letter from Venice written in Italian which said that we had won first prize. This news was staggering to us. Of course we felt it opened the door to everything we dreamed of. But we were the only ones who felt this. The film opened in New York during the newspaper strike of 1963, and it had the misfortune of being booked with something called *No Exit*, made by a South American. This film was very poorly attended, and consequently ours went virtually unseen, and in six weeks the glory had all vanished, and we were back where we began.

Q: How did you approach the writing of *Team Team Team*? Did you wing it with an eventual script in mind? Or was there a script already written from the start?

A: Yes, of course there was. As a matter of fact, we had a very elaborate script. But it turned out we never got anything on film that was in the script. And so consequently we arranged, we wrote a new film, so to speak, in editing, with what we had. The original script was called *Beat Notre Dame*. It was to be a film of what goes on backstage in football in the days when there wasn't so much coverage on television. It was to show what went on from Monday to Friday with a big college team. However, the team we picked never played Notre Dame, and so our original idea didn't make much sense. We then changed the name of the film to *Goodbye, Louis Heyward, and All That*, and we called Heyward out on the coast one day to get permission to use his name, on the CBS tie-line or something, and Heyward was very uncommunicative.

When he answered the phone our knees were shaking, that's all I know. And we lost our courage, so we abandoned that title, and the film took a different form. Anyway, we finally cut a film out of what we had. Of course we did have a storyline at the beginning, and we did try to shoot according to it, but we didn't get the things we felt we needed. We devised a new film, and that film was called *Team Team Team*.

Q: Did that indicate to you anything about the relationship between script and film?

A: Well, either before or during that period I had what for me was an unforgettable interview with Adolfas Mekas, who was the only film director I had met at the time. He was fresh from *Hallelujah the Hills*, or it was in production, I forget. And he told me that he had a script, but that he very seldom showed it to the actors because it only served to confuse them. He would certainly not let them read ahead in the script; at most he would give them what they were shooting right then, and frequently they'd even change that. And then following that he said—he impressed me very much, he had a cigarette holder and he was wearing the coat from one suit and the pants from another, we were upstairs in Carnegie Hall—he said that the most a director could hope to do was influence the flow of the film since it would never turn out exactly as he intended. So for a long time, that having been an exposure which was very strong, and of course my experience with *Team Team Team* confirmed it, I thought that no matter what you wrote, the film was going to turn out different. And I must say that even now, the greatest problem, my biggest obsession, is how close will it be to what I imagine it's going to be, because I've done a lot of work since then and I know there are a lot of difficulties. Of course Mekas happens to be . . . his position is an extreme one. But Truffaut once quoted, perhaps it was Renoir, who said, and this quote is not exact, "I am like a young man going to his girlfriend to propose. I pick up a small bouquet of flowers which I carry in my hand, and as I go over to her place I rehearse in my mind all the things I am going to say and exactly how it is going to be. But of course when I arrive there and start to talk something entirely different happens." And this does go on in the making of the film.

Q: What prompted you to undertake to document circuses for educational TV? You made . . .

A: Ten films. Well, someone had seen our film at NET and offered Lane the opportunity to produce and direct ten films on the American circus. He invited me to participate with him, and so with his cousin, who had never held a tape-recorder in his hands, as our sound man, and a few others, we undertook to make a series of ten documentaries on the history of the American circus. At the same time it was the largest single commitment NET had ever made. These films were half-an-hour long, and they were budgeted at $7,500 each. We traveled all around the country. In the end, of course, we ran out of money before the films were finished; we were obliged to pay very low prices for everything and also to do things ourselves. We made the titles ourselves. We sent away for something in the back of *Photography Magazine* which claimed it could make stop-images for motion picture film for $2.98 or something, and it came and it worked, and we made them. Of course the films are not . . . Technically they leave certain things to be desired. But those films were undertaken with a great deal of affection, and a considerable amount of research went into them, and I think that of all the things I've done—in the end I did five of the films and Lane did five—among those five I did I think one of them is probably the best film I've ever done.

The terms "writing" and "directing" when applied to documentaries are perhaps a little overblown. One does not really direct a documentary, one makes a documentary. There are two aspects to the writing. The first is writing down beforehand or perhaps during and in some cases after the filming exactly what you are trying to film and in general show; and the second part of it is the narration. Some documentaries are live-voice, that is to say, only the participants speak and nothing is explained. However, in ours there was a great deal of narration, and we wrote the narration. Lane wrote five and I wrote five.

Q: Did you write the narration post-shooting?

A: Yes, the narration was done after the shooting was finished, although naturally we were taking notes continually. We interviewed literally scores, perhaps even a hundred or more, circus people. We read everything there was, and we reached a position where, although we didn't know all there was to know, we knew more than the audience.

Documentaries are virtually the only training open for filmmakers. Unfortunately there's a limited amount of documentary film being made, and it's terribly difficult to have it shown. There's a limited audience for it. It's a shame because of films that have moved me greatly, certainly two or three of them have been documentaries. I would definitely list Pare Lorentz's *The River*, which I saw literally dozens of times, and also, for instance, William Klein's *Cassius Le Grand* [released as *Float Like a Butterfly, Sting Like a Bee* by Grove Press Films], a documentary in a very courageous and different form, and I think a dazzling and impressive film. But as I said, it's very difficult to show a documentary. Few people see it. And worse, much worse, to the people who can give you the opportunity to make a film, a documentary counts for very little.

Q: During this time, you were becoming fairly well-known as a novelist. You were still to write your third novel, I believe, *A Sport and a Pastime*, but here you were, a novelist getting into the film game. Did you feel the intrigue or the occupation of being a novelist not enough? I mean, accomplished novelists are few and hard to come by, and . . .

A: First of all, I was not a fairly well-known novelist; I was unknown, and even today I am virtually unknown. Furthermore, there is no scarcity of novelists . . . The point is that we have novelists who are also essayists, critics, playwrights, and poets; some of our greatest have had that breadth of interest. And it seems to me if a writer can be a playwright as well as a novelist he can certainly be a film writer. Writing films is a dramatic form although unfortunately, I think, an inferior one. It doesn't seem to me that it was a giving up of one thing. It was merely a question of trying something else, of putting one's hand to another kind of task in the same field. It's writing; filmmaking is writing. You hear all the time that filmmaking is writing with a camera. Certain filmmakers say that they are only completing the writing when they actually direct and shoot the film. So I don't think it represents taking another road.

I was always dismayed at the slaughter of books by Hollywood. And consequently I never wanted to be involved in these atrocities. It's terrible to have people call you up and say, "Hey, I saw your movie on television last night." And of course it's not your movie at all, it's something somebody else has written, possibly based on a book of yours. I hate those moments; one experiences them all the time. I sold my first book to the movies because I had a letter from the producer which said earnestly that he *had* to make this film—I recognize today that this is just a stock phrase all producers use no matter what their interest in a film is—and also because it enabled me to live for a few years.

Q: What was your first dramatic screenplay? Was it *The Appointment*?
A: No. Like so many things in life, it happened by accident: my agent introduced me to Irwin Shaw. Shaw is a man who has an enormous affection for football, which he played at college. So, when he saw *Team Team Team*, it was a film about something very dear to him. He was interested at that time in producing films from his own stories, and he commissioned me to write and direct a film made from one of them. It was a short story that he selected. I read it and was not pleased with it, whereupon he challenged me to pick any story I liked if I didn't like that one, they were all good, he said. He frightened me a little bit. I asked someone's advice and they said, "Take the chance and do what he wants; you can make a good film out of it." And that's how the script got started. The story was called "Then We Were Three," and the film which came to be made four or five years later was called *Three*. That was my first . . .

Oh no, I made a mistake. I'm sorry. My first script was one a producer asked me to write, an original film about New York. He had asked me to submit some story ideas. I did, and he liked one of them, and I wrote a script from it. It was called *Goodbye, Bear*. It was never produced. *Three* was the second film I wrote. Apparently, it was not going to be made either. Shaw didn't like the script, and the movie companies didn't like the idea of making films from Shaw's stories because Shaw had already produced one. It was called *In the French Style* and it didn't do well, and they lost interest. So there, two scripts and neither of them produced; that was about 1964.

I was in a state of great excitement and elation merely to be talking to people who actually had the power to make a film or claimed they had the power. To think that I would be involved in the making of the film was enough to give me the energy and the courage to do all kinds of writing. As a matter of fact, in *Goodbye, Bear* I had written the entire thing with detailed camera directions, working out every scene. And the director read it and said, "Well, that's very nice, but you haven't left anything for me to do. Why don't you do it over again and leave all that stuff out?" So without the slightest bit of anger or disappointment I went right back and wrote the whole thing over again, merely describing what the scene was in general and indicating nothing of camera shots, I had all kinds of energy and enthusiasm. The actual possibilities of having something produced have very little connection with it.

It's only really later when you've made a couple of films that you're demoralized when you do a piece of work and it doesn't get done or it vanishes. However, in reading Renoir and the list of projects that he began or became involved in or even wrote but never made, it certainly strengthens your patience and your humility. I had written books no one had published, stories that nobody accepted, so I wasn't too astonished to find that a film I had written was not made. Of course, it is a disappointment, but I was busy writing a novel, and also at this time I met Peter Glenville.

Glenville asked me if I would be interested in writing a film for him. Eventually he sent me a story treatment, what I felt was a very melodramatic piece of not much value, an Italian confessional opera that he said, to my great surprise, he was interested in directing. He invited me to write a letter to the producer giving my opinion of it. I said, in short, that no matter what was done with it that it could never be a film of any real merit, and consequently I recommended that they forget about it. Of course, in those days I didn't realize how much they both had involved. The producer had already bought the story rights and had flown here and there to talk to people, and they were in a sense already committed. The difficulty in the way our system works is that one often becomes committed to a completely worthless thing but pursues it with just as much ardor as if it were something good. And that was what was happening here. At any rate, the letter only served to convince the producer and Glenville that I was exactly the man to write the film, and they asked me to.

Q: Was this a script from a book?
A: No, it was an original story outline by an Italian writer.

Q: This was eventually to become *The Appointment*?
A: Yes; I later met the writer in Rome when we were shooting the film, and I noticed that he affected the same style of dress as Adolfas Mekas.

Q: So you eventually wrote this.
A: The irony is that it turned out to be the best script I had written.

Q: Why did you write it if you didn't like the material you had to work with? Did you feel that you could improve on it that much so that it was a challenge, or was it money?

A: It was partly money, partly the fact that Glenville was a man of greater reputation than anybody I had had a chance to work with. [. . .]

I went to Rome and spent three months there walking the streets and talking to people. Then, as I say, I wrote the script, which was the best I had ever done. The excellence of a script, however, has only a limited relationship to whether a film will get made and how it will get made. The producer then began a long two-year struggle trying to get the film mounted, in the course of which he would telephone me frequently with the latest changes in casting. And so forth. The film was written about a twenty-two, twenty-three-year-old Italian girl, and he would telephone me with news that Metro would make the picture if Sophia Loren played the lead or that they would make it if Natalie Wood was playing it. I even made a trip to California to attempt to explain to an actress exactly what the role was since many things in it were implicit and one had to have an understanding and a certain knowledge of Europe. These explanations were tragic. They were received with what I felt to be complete indifference. And the questions themselves were, for me, dumbfounding. In some cases they were very complicated psychiatric questions dealing with father relationships . . .

Q: These were from the actresses who were considering the role . . .

A: And also undergoing deep analysis.

Q: Was Glenville still involved by now?

A: In the way of film, he had long since parted and we were seeking a director as well as a cast.

Q: But the money was up, so to speak?

A: No, the money was not up, that was the problem. It was in an effort to get money that this odyssey by the producer and, to a lesser degree, by me, was made. I experienced a lot with this film, most of it sorrowful. Anyway, many casting configurations were considered, and also from time to time the producer would call me to tell me that something was absolutely set, oh, say, William Wyler as director, if I would only write a memorandum to William Wyler explaining what the film was really about. And then I would do this, but I would never hear anything. Then the next call would come, Wyler was out, somebody else was in. Also, after about eighteen months of this, I suppose the script itself was becoming somewhat shopworn from having been passed around, and there began to be some suggestions as to how it could be improved.

There's one suggestion that I remember. The producer called me one day. I was fortunately lying in bed. He said that Paramount would definitely do the film; there was just a question of making some small modifications in the story. Until this point we had never changed a word of it. And in fact the way things finally turned out, we never did change a word from beginning to end. But Paramount had sent him a memorandum about some small changes they were interested in. He said he would like to read it to me. And he began to read a really terrible document that compared the film to Shakespeare, saying that what it really needed was an Iago. And then it identified one of the minor characters as being a potential Iago, and suggested how his role could be made a more important part of the film. And while he was doing this I kept interrupting him. He often called to make a little joke about one thing or another; humor was the one thing which sustained us, and I really thought he was putting me on about the whole thing. I thought either he had written the memorandum himself or he was making it up rather than reading it, because it was so absurd. But then he reached a point where the absurdity was so frightening I realized it must be the truth. Paramount had suggested that Iago was motivated in his hatred of women and in many of his sinister characteristics by the fact that he had been castrated in a Volkswagen accident three years before the film began. He said, "Well, why don't you think it over for a few days?" Fortunately, as in most other cases the whole thing vanished for some reason, and he was into another company, another cast, and so forth. [...]

Q: Do you feel you will now reject writing screenplays for others? Have you reached the point where you will only concentrate on making personal, original films?
A: I wrote films as I made documentaries. It was the only thing open to me, and having taken those steps forward I don't want to retrace them. Of course there are always exceptions: the documentary you are really interested in or the film for a director or an actor that you really want to write. But in general, no, that's something that I like to think I've gone through and am finished with. I would like to write films for myself.

Q: You're a writer and now a writer-director, and you've taken a short story by Shaw and made a film, writing it yourself and directing it. *Three.* [. . .] What's your feeling about [collaboration]?

A: I myself prefer to work alone because that's always been my habit, and I have difficulty working with people I'm not extremely close to and affectionate toward. But if there were no possibilities or precedent for working alone in film, if it were only possible to work in collaboration with other writers or the director, I suppose I would accept that. Fortunately, it's not the case. I think it depends on what you can do and what you would like to do. I don't think a film must necessarily be written by a single man to be good; I don't think these things are related. A group of people could easily write a wonderful film, and perhaps things like comedy—in comedy, particularly, a number of people might be able to react to each other and stimulate each other to a point where they might do a better job. As for myself, I find it hard to imagine a writing collaboration. [. . .]

I have talked to screenwriters who tell stories about slipping the producer three pages a day from under their door at the Excelsior Hotel, or something like that. Every day they produced three pages, and every day he read them, and they were three pages closer to a finished script, presumably. That alone is something I can't do because some days I only write a half a page, some days six, and I'm often correcting what went before.

The writer, like the producer and the director and I suppose eventually the actors, operates under the illusion that he is Olympian in his powers, and he hates to be broached in the exercise of them. And naturally it is difficult to have to explain your work or alter it or have it questioned by somebody as mortal and as fallible as a producer. I prefer to do all the talking in the beginning and then go off by myself and write the film. But that again is a matter of what I've struggled for because it's necessary for me. If it's not necessary for another writer, then there's no reason why he should do it, why he would want to.

I want to say something about screenwriters, because we talked about them and went on to something else. The notion of a screenwriter is, or has been historically, either a failed or an inadequate writer or a captive writer, frequently a drunken writer or weak writer, generally speaking one exiled to that place in California, who never comes east again except to see old friends at the Algonquin or whatever. The onus has been somewhat taken over now by television writers, but I think anyone with the courage and sense not to be one will resist it to the end. This is a big difficulty in films and one that limits the possibility of writing for films, this contempt in which you are obliged to hold yourself if you work for films as a writer, and I think it has kept a lot of writers out of films, although the number of important writers who have worked at one time or another in films is astonishing. Steinbeck and Faulkner wrote for films; Fitzgerald, of course, Nabokov, Dos Passos, Thornton Wilder. James Agee wrote films, produced and unproduced. Generally speaking, they did not stay. Fitzgerald went at the tail end of his life, when he was a wreck. Faulkner went and left immediately. His writing for films was kind of a sinecure. It's very hard to identify a good writer who has had a continued association with films. Again, there are always exceptions or possibilities which force you to change your mind. Pinter has written a number of film scripts and one cannot call him anything but a writer of major rank. But I think in Europe you find it a little more often, the process of making films is different. Of course, in France you have somebody like Jacques Prévert, poet and writer who is equally well known as a film writer, who wrote among other things *Les Enfants du Paradis*. Cocteau is a writer and a filmmaker. But in America it's as I described it, and unless I'm paranoiac about it, and I don't think I am, most writers don't want to have anything to do with it. It's changing, though.

Q: Ultimately, what do you feel goes into making good screen writing or a good screenplay, and how do you relate to the fact that [. . .] the actual script itself is only a small percentage of what gets onto the screen? What is involved in the creation of a good screenplay?

A: James Jones once told me he was writing a screenplay. He treated the fact with a certain disinterest and even contempt. I asked him how he could feel that way, and he said, well, it really didn't matter because his reputation was a literary reputation and this other stuff was just something he was doing. I don't know what happed to that screenplay and whether it was good or bad. I would like to think that it was inadequate, but I could be absolutely wrong. It's possible I suppose for a man of talent to be not completely committed and still do a script from which a director or actor will make an extraordinary film. The fact is that a film goes through so many stages in its creation, from the original idea, a book or a concept, through the writing, the director and actors, the editor, that some inadequacy along the line may easily be remedied by excellent work later. This applies right up to the very end. I like to think that a good script will generally lead to a good film. But I know of at least two or three cases which are contrary. I said earlier that the best script I had done at that time was *The Appointment*, and yet I think it's the worst film I have ever been connected with.

So what is one to assume from these things? We know that film is a collaborative affair, frequently geography—real or figurative—intervenes; the producer, the director, and the writer may be worlds apart or may not even have met one another yet. The amount of politics and negotiation and conciliation and reconciliation and adaptation and changes that go on is great. You asked me earlier, do I want to write any more scripts and what do writers feel about writing films. Well, in a way this answers that.

Q: Right now let's consider a very successful film from a screenplay you did, *Downhill Racer*, a very exciting film.

A: By the time I started on *Downhill Racer* I had already written a number of films, and I had reached that exalted position where somebody called me up and asked me if I was interested in writing a film; in this case, Roman Polanski's producer. I went to see Polanski and his producer, and they proposed a film about the making of a champion. They wanted a very hard, lean, a very different film. Polanski himself was a skier and was very interested in making it. Robert Redford was involved in the film from the start, and it was he who had suggested me. So, really, the three of us began together.

There existed a book called *The Downhill Racers* and a script written from that book. Paramount had bought these, and the book and script were the seeds that started the whole project. At the very beginning I said I was not interested in reading or adapting a book, I would rather start from scratch. Polanski said, okay, and that's the way it was done. I spent about two months traveling with the US team and going to Europe to see—at the time he was not the triple medal winner—Killy, and the French coach, Bonnet, and many other people. I did an enormous amount—for me, at any rate—of research. I had a fantastic researcher helping me, Jeanine Johnson, and at the end of that time I had written an outline of the film Polanski and I had talked about.

Naturally Paramount was horrified. They said, what is this? This is no film. There has to be more conflict, more motivation, more dialogue, more fucking. I didn't know what to say except to say they didn't understand. A crisis resulted. Finally after a lot of arguing we received permission to go ahead and write the script. They said they probably wouldn't make it, but there was a chance, and I went ahead and wrote the script, and they didn't like it. Polanski, meanwhile, became involved in another film.

So Redford was left with this script which he liked and which I liked very much, and he eventually took it to Bluhdorn of Gulf and Western, who'd broken his leg at St. Moritz, or something like that. So he knew something about skiing. Redford got Bluhdorn to read the script, and Bluhdorn claimed he liked it and invited us to his office, talked to us in his shirtsleeves, clapped us on the back, called me Jimmy, said we were going to make . . . he described a film to us which I did not recognize as being the film I had written, but apparently that's what he thought it was. And so we went ahead. Redford struggled and finally received permission to make the film after a lot of difficulties. [. . .] I was rewriting things until the day shooting started.

There were some significant changes in the film; the end was changed. My original ending was different. They are probably right. We argued for three days, and in the end I wrote something more in line with what they wanted. I didn't like it as much, I thought it destroyed the whole motion of the film, but perhaps they were right. The film seems to make sense to me.

Q: What was the ending you had?
A: Well, the film I had written originally was even harder than the film that exists now, and the central character was considerably less admirable. The essence of the film was that a coach who had struggled for years to try and have a champion finally found himself close to his lifelong goal but having to work with an instrument he despised, that's Redford. And in the end it was a question of *hubris*. Redford lost the race. Now, that's an entirely different film, and, I don't know, maybe not as good a film. Anyway, different.

Q: Most people, Jim, love that film. How do you feel about it?
A: Well, I like it. There's a great deal that's omitted from it, that is to say things that were written were omitted, some things were not shot, some were shot but did not turn out as they should, and lastly some things were sacrificed in editing for a certain kinetic power. And some of these I missed. All I'm saying is *I* would have made a slightly different film. But as I look at the film that they made, I admire it. I've seen it three or four times, and find I even like it a little more as I see it again. There's been a lot of discussion about *Downhill Racer* and the fact that it is, some say, underwritten, some say not written at all, as a matter of fact. That's not the case because most of the images were written. It isn't words, dialogue, but it's writing a film. Of course, it goes without saying, the director and the actors invented and created things in the course of shooting. Some things were written; some things were not.

Q: Let's talk about *Three* now. How did it happen that you came to make it finally?
A: Well, eventually everyone had turned down the script, and I'd forgotten

about it. Then Bruce Becker, a producer I know, came to me and asked me if I still had the script because he had always liked it and perhaps he now had an opportunity to get it made. He took it to United Artists. Meanwhile I went to Europe. I was going to live there for a year or two; I was still working on *Downhill* at the time. He wrote to me and asked if I had any notions about casting. I had a magazine with a picture of Charlotte Rampling in it. Of course I had seen her in *Georgy Girl* and *Rotten to the Core*. And I read his letter and looked at the magazine. I thought, well, why not? I wrote him back. I think I enclosed the photo. The next thing I knew he was calling me or wiring to say United Artists liked Charlotte Rampling and that if we could get her we could make the film. So I went to London to talk to her agent and eventually to her, some weeks later. She was interested in the film, and she conditionally agreed to make it. Then she went off to Sardinia to work in an Italian film, *Sequestro di Persona*. While she was there we were still fixing things with United Artists.

Finally it reached a point where I came to New York to cast the two male leads. While I was there we received word that Charlotte had changed her mind and didn't want to do the film. We immediately jumped on an airplane for Rome, went to dinner with her, spent the evening, and persuaded her to give her definite agreement to do the film. From that point the film was really authorized and in progress. We had some difficulties because it was all done in Europe and everybody on the crew was European. I had never worked there; the producer knew nothing of Europe. But eventually we put it all together and began shooting the film. [. . .]

Q: Was there any discussion of the fact that you wanted to direct your own script?
A: No, it was understood right from the beginning it would be me. That was part of the arrangement. In the meantime, of course, I had certain other credentials, things had happened that I suppose made me, not really more acceptable but more visible. I mean, there are always people making their first film.

Directing a film is not the most difficult thing in the world by any means. As a matter of fact, it's a very simple thing. Of course, directing an extraordinary film is a little more difficult. But many very ordinary people have directed not only one but literally scores of films, and I would say that any intelligent person who wanted to could direct a film. Of course I'm not saying direct Elizabeth Taylor or some of the great dreadnoughts of cinema, but anyway make a film. They're made at home all the time. They're made by college students, high school students, even illiterates. Directing films is nothing mysterious. [. . .]

Q: How did you as director relate to the script you had also written?
A: Well, I respected it. I said: here's a good writer and I must make this film the way he wrote it. There was no conflict. I rewrote a few small portions of it, two or three, in cases where the weather or circumstances did not allow us to do what was written. Generally speaking, those portions turned out to be some of the best parts of the script.

Q: How did you handle it when an actor couldn't really get one of your lines or wanted to have a change? Did you look to have your script read pretty much as you wrote it?
A: Well, there were some lines they couldn't get or they could not get them the way one heard them in one's imaginary ear. In those cases I did a number of things. I was never sure what to do, this being a first film. In some cases, the happiest ones, I rewrote the line, found something they could deliver well, frequently a thing they suggested. And those were always the best solutions. Robie Porter added a number of lines. Sam Waterston suggested several scenes. Both of them turned out to be better than whatever I had imagined. So that's very pleasant when that happens. In other cases I insisted on the line as it was written and worked until we got to a point where it was fairly satisfactory, and of course in a few cases we never could reach even that, and the line is just delivered badly. For instance, there's a line in there, "Poor baby," Charlotte says to Sam, with a faint American sarcasm. You know how they say, "Poor baby." Well, she couldn't deliver that line. Maybe because those words don't mean exactly the same thing in England, the expression is not used the way it is in America. She couldn't pick up on it, and in the film when she says it, it's sort of a meaningless line because I was never able to explain to her exactly what it was, how it should be done.

There were other cases. Robie delivers a little piece in dialect about his learning to juggle, and it should have been left out. He never quite . . . it's always getting away from him. He never gets close to it. It should have been rewritten. But I didn't do it. That was a different matter. Rod Steiger says that a director is first of all a father, and I failed in my fatherly duties in that instance. Sam Waterston I knew could deliver the lines far better than Porter, in fact he had done it for me. And I thought the intelligent thing is to have him do it. But of course the actors are disappointed to have their lines given away, I hadn't realized how disappointed they can become. And we ultimately got into a terrible mess which I could only resolve by letting Robie give his lines badly. It sounds foolish, doesn't it? It sounds foolish, but when you're involved it's astonishing how complicated these things can be.

I didn't want a heavily acted film. We rehearsed, the dialogue was always written, but I tried to direct in a way that made it seem to have been invented on the spot. I personally like that quality of it. That appeals to me. I know many people, critics, object to it. They say the acting is atrocious or nonexistent. Of course that's intentional. If you like it . . . I don't propose that all films be less acted than they are, but frequently the acting interferes between me and what's going on. I prefer under-acting to over-acting. And I think American films generally are heavily over-acted. Perhaps the public is not accustomed to seeing a film that is made with a kind of innocence of acting, and maybe they won't become accustomed to it.

The schedule was a big problem. The terrible thing about a film, the biggest difficulty for me, is getting up in the morning, facing people right away, and saying things to them. My life is one of little contact before noon, with the exception of a small argument over breakfast. I found it very hard to get up early and start working like that. Another thing was the schedule always pressing so that you have very little time to try things in different ways, in other words, to discover things. There's very little room for that when your schedule is tight. I wouldn't want to work that way again. I would much rather do less and have more time to do it. We trimmed a lot out of the script as we went along, ultimately ten or fifteen percent of what was originally written. But if I were making the film again, not talking about changing characters or concepts, I would definitely cut out more of the film and try to have more time for the things that we did do. I would cut out another ten percent, and we would have shot only seventy-five percent of the original script, but have given ourselves more time in which to do it.

I learned three things from the film. One of them Lumet showed me: when an actor is nervous or you're dealing with a non-actor, don't use the clapsticks before the take. Of course, it's really simple, but when we had a tough time with a non-actor we used to clap after the take, and he didn't jump and freeze up. I thought that was valuable. Having people there to take care of the actors, and having time for the actors is another thing. The third is having the time to be able to work within the schedule because if you are too squeezed . . . It depends on the film you're making. I'm only talking about myself. I need a little more time.

I felt at the beginning that I could make a good film, an extraordinary film, about almost anything, regardless of the subject or the story or the characters. But I now see it's not exactly that way. Something almost chemical occurs at the very first instant which colors and influences the film despite anything one can do. That happened with Shaw's story. I was not deeply interested, I did not think it was a particularly good story, nor well told, and perhaps in a way that is revealed, it contaminates the film. I don't know. You never know what you are revealing and what you have succeeded in hiding.

Q: But you liked your script enough to proceed.

A: Yes, I did. I wasn't ashamed of the script. Quite the contrary. But what I said a moment ago, almost at the beginning, in some germinal way what you're working with defines the film. I don't know how. Maybe it's in a way I cannot explain. I liked the script, and I made the film without reservations. I never said this is a weak film, but we'll go ahead anyway. On the contrary. One puts everything into it, I mean everything you have. As Gide said—he was talking about writing—write this book as if it were your last, he said. Into it put everything you have been saving, everything you have withheld. You must give it all; that's the only way to replenish.

Circling Important Themes:
An Interview with James Salter

Robert E. Burke / 1988

From *Bloomsbury Review* 8 (May/June 1988), 3, 6, 18. © Robert E. Burke. Reprinted with permission.

Interviews can be—and all too frequently are—tedious, nerve-wracking experiences. This is due, in part, to the entirely artificial nature of the situation: Two complete strangers, author and interviewer, find themselves in cramped quarters, accommodating one another's schedules, trying to say something interesting while a micro-cassette is indifferently catching every cough and "uh." James Salter is, however, the rare exception. Where other interviews, for any number of reasons, seem to be interminable, talking with Salter is like having a conversation with an old friend. His range and referents are both free-flowing and unassuming, and, when he is talking about writing and literature, he pays the interviewer the ultimate compliment of assuming that he or she is just as passionately concerned with these topics as he is himself.

This interview was conducted by Robert Burke in San Francisco in February 1988.

The Bloomsbury Review: Your previous publisher of *Light Years* made a point on the dust jacket that you were retired military . . .
James Salter: Not quite. I *was* in the Air Force.

TBR: The reason I ask is that there seems to be something incongruous about the idea of a military person describing your characters in *Dusk* as well as *Light Years*, most of whom are affluent and professional. I guess I would think of them as East Coast "country club" set.
JS: Don't be misled by that. I am not a military person. I had some connec-

tion with it, but only in the sense that I belong to the generation—and even the locale—of Salinger, Kerouac, and Norman Mailer. The war [World War II] was a big part of life, and I was in the service at the end of the war and for a few years after, but I'm not a career military person. I stayed in because it was thrilling, so I stayed longer than I should have. I would like to have those years back, but in any case, I don't think that it's significant. Getting back to your original question, that "country club" set might have been accurate in O'Hara's time, but I don't think they are significant anymore in New York life, or at least the part of New York life that I know. I was born in New York, in Manhattan, and went to school there, and I still think of myself as a New Yorker after all these years. New York life really doesn't revolve around country clubs. Importance isn't commissioned that way, nor is social life defined that way. I agree with you, though, that they [my characters] are people who are educated, able to support themselves, and lead a certain kind of life. What can I say? It's just the kind of life that interests me.

TBR: Do you write with a particular audience in mind?
JS: My favorite short story writer is, I think, Babel. He said that he wrote for an ideal audience of one or two people. And his ideal audience was an educated woman, perhaps in her thirties. I like his feeling about that. I write for a few people who I think will like it. Beyond that, you can't imagine who your audience is.

TBR: One of the things I noticed in the first story in *Dusk*, "Am Strande von Tanger," is that you seem to have an impulse towards a particular technique where the point of view is refracted. And when you employ that technique, it feels somehow disjointed, that one is following the story but not the characters.
JS: I wrote that story so long ago—it was the first story that I ever had accepted and published—that I cannot remember my impulses. Let me say that it was the first story of any merit that I had published. I had, in fact, written stories earlier, but they weren't any good. I have had comments about the point of view a number of times, that I'm not being faithful enough to the idea of a single point of view, perhaps a well-defined point of view. That may be true, I really don't know. I don't think of point of view when I'm writing. I don't mean the act of writing, but when you're looking at a story and working it out and reworking it, the idea of point of view really doesn't enter into my thinking. I'm thinking in more primitive terms: Is this interesting? Is this the way it should be told? Is this what I want, one way or another? That

particular story may be more deficient than the others, I don't know. I put "Am Strande von Tanger" in there because I liked it, because it was the first successful story I had written, and I put it first because I didn't want to put what I felt was the strongest story first.

TBR: You seem to have, especially in *Dusk*, an incredible empathy for your female characters. There is something very special in that. Do you attribute your empathy for women to anything in particular? There are really so few male writers who write convincingly about women.

JS: Well, there is Tennessee Williams, of course. In my view, women are my real heroes, and I like to write about them. Whether I know more about them, I don't think I know more than other people. In fact, I'm convinced that men who have never written a word know far more than I do about them. I'm attracted to writing about them, and I admire them greatly. *Light Years* is really more about a woman than anything else, in my view anyway, which is no better than anyone else's. What the writer thinks about the book is often ridiculous compared to what the book turns out to be. Let me say, and I may be way off the mark, that *A Sport and a Pastime* is about a heroic girl. I think of it that way. That's not the only thing that it's about. Since you only have one or two themes in your life—even great writers only have one or two—you keep circling them one way or another, closer and closer. I would say that it seems to be one of the things that interests me, whether consciously or not. It is conscious, but on the other hand it must be something that I really don't understand perfectly.

TBR: How do you feel about the idea of classifying writers by region? Do you feel it's valid?

JS: Well, it's valid insofar as it works. I come from the East. All of my associations are with the East, but I'm not a regional writer. Geographical classification is one classification, and a very convenient one, or it used to be. For instance, Dreiser was thought of as the first important American writer who didn't come out of the educated—I don't want to say patrician—he was the first writer from the "gutter," so to speak, from the proletariat. So, before then it would be ridiculous to say that there were these two classes, because nobody from the other class was writing. Now there was Dreiser, and many other writers followed him. You could break it down that way. You could legitimately say that there are "gay" writers whose concerns, whose method of writing, whose stimulus, whose everything is "gay." Or as Gore Vidal put it, who deal in "homosexual matters." But for a long time we've spoken of writers in a regional sense. It's only one of a number of possible classifications. I think that you can do it. The real question, though, is what use do we want to make of these classifications? It used to be a matter of affinities. Europe had been closer to the East Coast, or had been for many years, than any other part of the country. Just as the Pacific and Asia were much closer to California. But now, modern times have made it possible for you to cross these regional lines very quickly. And, in addition, a more terrible thing has happened: Television, and modern life, in a way, have come along and obliterated these distinctions. I was recently at a dinner party in Chicago, and an architect, a very interesting man, said, "What cities of America do you like best?" And I tried to think of a good answer for him, but I was really stumped. The answer is that there is very little to distinguish many of these cities from one another. I mean there are the same shops, the same shopping centers. So these regional things, which used to be very distinct in America, have gradually been modified, and, in a sense, we're looking at one big society without a very powerful culture.

TBR: Was there ever a time in your life when you just decided to write, to the exclusion of everything else?

JS: Yes. Well, I mean there had to be. When you're young, you want to do a lot of things. But when you grow older, by virtue of time, you must begin to make choices. I'd always written, even as a child, but there did come a time when I did decide to pull it all over and do nothing but write. I recently read something by Laclos, who wrote *Les Liaisons Dangereuses*: "Écrire, quelque chose de merveilleux!"—"To write, what a marvelous thing!" And it's so true. I imagine that painting or music is the same way, but for me nothing else gives the same sort of gratification—not every minute, of course—but there is something so special about writing. And if you're fortunate, people will read your work. And if you're very fortunate, people will continue to read you for a long, long time.

A Few Well-Chosen Words

Adam Begley / 1990

From *New York Times* (28 October 1990). © Adam C. Begley. Reprinted with permission. Adam Begley is the author of *Updike*.

"Somewhere," James Salter once wrote, "the ancient clerks, amid stacks of faint interest to them, are sorting literary reputations. The work goes on endlessly and without haste. There are names passed over and names revered, names of heroes and of those long thought to be, names of every sort and level of importance." Salter was writing about his friend Irwin Shaw, whose name, once renowned, has slipped quietly from the first rank. Where will the tireless, indifferent clerks file the name James Salter? His readers, few in number but adamant in their conviction that he is a great writer, are confident that the author of *A Sport and a Pastime* and *Dusk: And Other Stories*, the collection that won him the 1989 PEN/Faulkner Award (perhaps this country's most prestigious literary prize), will eventually take his place in the canon of American literature.

He is a writer's writer—in the words of the critic James Wolcott, our most underrated underrated writer. With hardly a dissenting voice, critics have praised his manifest devotion to craft, the acuity of his observation, the maturity of his vision. Jaded editors and aspiring writers alike speak his name with reverence. And yet, of his six books, only one has sold better than 10,000 copies in hard cover. *Solo Faces*, a taut novel about a rock climber who tests the limits of his courage, sold about 12,000 copies when it appeared in 1979. His admirers insist that all this will soon change; the PEN/Faulkner Award, the brilliant critical reception of *Dusk*, the busy proselytizing of his fans and the publication (possibly in 1992—Salter writes very slowly) of an eagerly anticipated memoir will push him at last into the limelight.

Even those skeptics who think his work is too refined, too poetic ever to win a wide audience believe Salter's is a name that will endure long after the

23

names of many best-selling literary novelists have passed from memory. Joe Fox, his Random House editor, suspects that Salter would agree: "Jim knows that over the long haul he will be considered an important author. I think he has a fatalistic belief in his talent, and all the rest is just temporary." Salter himself has written: "Life passes into pages if it passes into anything."

At age sixty-five, he has been a writer and nothing else for nearly twenty years, and that's how he'd like to be known. His polished manners and easy gift for anecdote are well suited to the task of defining and protecting his writer's persona. He's precise and gracious in his gestures (and even more so in his writing), but his elegance seems somehow manufactured, an armature designed to conceal a core of enigma.

He's cut himself off from the past. He simply cast aside two very different careers that might have amply satisfied anyone less single-minded about pursuing the literary life. Friends who have known him for several decades confess that they've heard him say very little about his early years. "Well, he was in the Air Force," one friend offers vaguely. In fact, he served as an officer for a dozen years and flew more than a hundred combat missions as a fighter pilot during the Korean War. A West Point graduate, he's left that behind, too. "I've done my very best to forget almost everything they taught me," he says.

Ask him about his ten years in and out of the movie business and he'll discourage the topic. Push him a bit and he'll say, "It's not worth talking about . . . it was all wasted time." Some might consider that writing the screenplay for *Downhill Racer*, an early Robert Redford movie that's now a favorite of film students and movie buffs, is hardly wasted time. Salter also wrote and directed *Three*, starring Charlotte Rampling and Sam Waterston. Released in 1969, *Three* closed almost as soon as it opened, but managed to make the "Ten Best" lists of two prominent critics, Rex Reed and Archer Winsten, and met with considerable success at the Cannes Film Festival. Despite his disdain for the movie business, Salter has recently completed a screenplay based on one of his own stories, "American Express," which PBS plans to broadcast in its "American Playhouse" series.

What Salter really likes to talk about is books and writers. On a pleasant day you might find him out on the patio behind his Bridgehampton, L.I., house, sitting at a picnic table, small, strong-looking hands curled around a glass of iced tea. As he talks, he'll sometimes close his eyes for a few beats; as he listens, he may slowly nod his head or run a hand through his grizzled, close-cropped hair. When he mentions favorites—Isaac Babel, André Gide, or William Faulkner—he's likely to slip into anecdote, a way of avoiding more personal conversation. Faulkner, he says, "used to get up in the night and write on the walls of his bedroom in pencil; now there's a writer." *Tropic of Cancer* comes up and he provides a virtuoso imitation of Henry Miller's recorded voice, a thick Brooklyn accent enumerating the joys of Paris. Only reluctantly, and with many a disclaimer, will Salter discuss his own work.

His first two books—*The Hunters*, published in 1957, the year he resigned from the Air Force, and *The Arm of Flesh*, which appeared in 1961—are both suspenseful novels about flying and fighter pilots. Neither, according to Salter, merits much attention. North Point Press, which has done much to sustain his modest following by keeping his other novels in print in handsome paperback editions, offered several years ago to reprint the two apprentice works; Salter said no. Yet they were greeted with lively acclaim when they first came out—*The Hunters* was even made into an undistinguished 1958 movie starring Robert Mitchum. Though clearly inferior to his more recent work, both books remain eminently readable.

As far as he's concerned, Salter's writing career began some twenty-five years ago. By that time, he says, "I thought I could sit down and show what I could do." The result was *A Sport and a Pastime*—"the first good thing I wrote, my first acceptable book," he says. In a less dispassionate vein, the author Reynolds Price announced in the *New York Times Book Review*, "Of living novelists, none has produced a book I admire more than James Salter's *A Sport and a Pastime*."

The content of the novel is extraordinary in its own right: Salter records every last erotic detail of the love affair of an eighteen-year-old French shop girl and a Yale dropout determined to know "the real France." But it is the beauty of the writing that has kept the book alive and vibrant for the last quarter-century. In this slim volume, he's able to build from the ground up an entire, ageless provincial French town (nominally Autun, in Burgundy) and fill it with abundant life: " . . . those small epiphanies of which the town is comprised. The clink of spoons as they dine, unseen, behind the shutters of the girls' school." He has given Autun seasons, moods, and the impalpable quality of time passing: on a winter afternoon, "The air is thin as paper. The day is raw"; on a late summer morning, "The air is lucid and sweet." Details like these, unobtrusive in themselves, conspire to create an atmosphere so real that the love affair—agonizing, inevitable—seems to break out from the comforting confines of the imaginary. A slightly contrived ending spoils nothing—the book feels utterly true.

Doubleday published *A Sport and a Pastime* in 1967 under the imprint of Paris Review Editions. According to Salter, Doubleday felt "ill at ease" with the book, printed only a small number of copies and was "quite happy to see it disappear without a trace." Eight years would pass before the publication of his next novel, *Light Years*.

"The notion came from a remark by the film maker Jean Renoir," says Salter. "'The only things that are important in life are the things you remember.' I wanted to write a book that was like that." *Light Years* is the record of a marriage and a way of life that seems, at first blush, whole and perfect, the bright flower of a peculiar American hybrid, bohemian bourgeoisie; later, the illusion of harmony, like the marriage, decays. The things remembered in this deeply sad life are often just that—things; and so the narrative reads at times like a lush mail-order catalogue, a dazzling display of polished surfaces. Although this exurban household on the Hudson River seems at times to prefigure the yuppie ostentation of the 1980s, Salter has no intention of trivializing the search for a beautiful life. His characters, even when half-submerged by the dross of good living (a pet pony, handmade shirts, fine wines), retain a dignity that lends weight to their destiny.

Like *A Sport and a Pastime*, *Light Years* had its fervent admirers. A perfect match for the Reynolds Price encomium came from Brendan Gill of the *New Yorker*: "Among contemporary novelists, I can think of none who has written a novel more beautiful than *Light Years*." But mixed with the raves were two disastrously negative reviews, both in the *New York Times*. Anatole Broyard, writing in the daily *Times*, described the main characters as "insulting to our patience and our expectations." Robert Towers concluded his review in the *Book Review* with a lacerating appraisal: "an overwritten, chi-chi, and rather silly novel." The barrage was sufficient, Salter believes, to cut sales drastically; only about 7,800 hardcover copies of *Light Years* were sold.

Looking back on the early fate of his two best-loved books, he wonders: "Could those coincidences be enough to keep one from having readers? I don't know. I can't answer that." As though reciting a universally acknowledged axiom, he says, "You can't be admitted to the ranks of writers of importance unless you have sales." He pauses, as if to consider the consequences. "I'm doing what I can." Another pause, then, "I guess I could do more."

Born in 1925 and raised in New York City, Salter graduated from the Horace Mann School in Riverdale. His father, an engineer who had graduated first in his class at West Point in 1918, arranged a second alternate's appointment for his only child. "That's like a fifty-to-one shot in the third race," says Salter. But the principal failed the mental exam, the first alternate failed the physical, and a seventeen-year-old Salter, who had planned on going to M.I.T., found himself a cadet. He chose the Army Air Corps—partly, he maintains, because pilots in training were exempt from summer maneuvers. Instead, the future airmen were shipped off to flight school in Arkansas, where they were taught to fly tiny, open-cockpit planes by a watermelon farmer.

The first time Salter mentions his only airplane disaster, which occurred on V-E Day, May 8, 1945, after a late-evening flight in a T-6 trainer, he says merely that it was "One hundred percent pilot error." Asked to elaborate, he reveals some mitigating circumstances and, at the same time, his talent for storytelling. He talks slowly, in a gruff but soft voice: "The winds aloft we were given were completely wrong. Everybody from the squadron got lost (except for one pilot, and he probably figured his winds out wrong so they turned out right). I was the only one who got lost and couldn't find himself. At about midnight, attempting to land in what I took to be a big park in the middle of a town, I hit a tree, tore a wing off and went into a house directly across the street.

"The lucky part—aside from surviving at all—was that the family in the house was celebrating the return of their son, who had just arrived home that afternoon after being a prisoner of war in Germany. They were having a party for him in the house. I'd been flying overhead for some time trying to see through the ground fog, trying to find a field or anywhere to land, and they thought it was some kind of official salute and they'd gone out into the street to see what it was. They were all standing there when I passed over their heads and into the house, right into the kitchen. There wasn't a drop of gas left in the airplane—that's why it didn't explode and burn."

Salter had a tooth knocked loose.

He also risked being washed out of the program. But he was merely assigned to fly B-25 bombers, a subtle demotion; it wasn't until 1952, six months before he was sent as a volunteer to Korea, that he finally managed to wangle a transfer into a fighter unit. "Where I always wanted to be," he says.

Three chapters of Salter's memoir have already appeared in print: two articles in *Esquire* and "A Single Daring Act," which came out in the spring issue of the literary quarterly *Grand Street*. As an eyewitness account of aerial warfare, "A Single Daring Act" is understated and breathtakingly effective; as autobiography, it's guarded, self-effacing, measured in tone; as descriptive writing, it's unremittingly lucid. Here, for example, is the one "crucial" difference between the Russian MIG-1 and the American F-86: "They had a cannon—the maw of a MIG seemed swollen and menacing. We had machine guns that were almost feminine in comparison. . . . It was the sledge-hammer versus the hose. The hose was more flexible and could be adjusted quickly. The slower-firing cannon could not; you could almost say, oh, God, between the heavy, glowing shots."

At the end of his tour of duty in Korea, Salter had shot down one MIG and damaged another—well shy of the five kills necessary to become an ace. In "A Single Daring Act," he writes, "Later I felt I had not done enough. . . . I had not done what I set out to do and might have done. I felt contempt for myself, not at first but as time passed, and I ceased talking about those days, as if I had never known them." These lines, the most personal and revealing in the essay, reflect the fierce rigor of the standards he imposes on himself, standards he refuses to relinquish in his life as a writer.

He served in the Air Force for five more years, stationed in various countries in the Pacific, in Germany, in France. He led an aerial acrobatic team, rose to the rank of major, became a squadron operations officer. All the while, on weekends and at night, he worked on his fiction, finishing one manuscript that was later rejected and a second that became *The Hunters*. Married, with two small children, he was in line to become a squadron commander when he abruptly resigned.

"In 1957, I decided: write or perish." So Salter claimed on an unsuccessful 1971 Guggenheim grant application. Asked if this was not an uncharacteristic flash of melodrama, he replies with calm assurance: "There came a time when I felt I was not going to be satisfied with life unless I could write. So I did what was essential for me, or else perhaps the most important part of me would have perished."

Frank Conroy, director of the Iowa Writers' Workshop, where Salter taught in the fall of 1989, marvels at the jump from military man to pure writer. The transformation was thorough. "The man's an artist," says Conroy emphatically. "That's what drives him, that's what gives him his power." Few lives are marked by sudden and absolute turning points. Salter became a published author while still a fighter pilot, and he continued to fly in the reserves for several years after deciding to dedicate himself to writing. In 1961, during the Berlin crisis, his unit was called up and transferred overseas to a base in France. But his resignation in 1957 nonetheless signaled a profound metamorphosis.

Born James Horowitz, he retired from the Air Force as Maj. James Horowitz. But he began his writing career as James Salter, and eventually, in the early '60s, took Salter as his legal name, as did his wife and children. This is not a fact that he discusses willingly. Though some friends who met him as Jim Salter have heard it rumored that he was born with another name, he himself never mentions it. Asked directly, he declines to elaborate on why he changed his name.

In the late '50s and early '60s, Salter lived in the Hudson Valley, in Grandview, then in New City, New York. Twins were born into the family in 1962. To supplement his income, he tried selling swimming pools—with indifferent success. It was while pursuing this unwanted occupation that he met a television writer named Lane Slate. The two men decided to collaborate on a documentary. Antonioni, Godard, Truffaut, and others were just beginning to develop a following in America; it seemed that Hollywood, which for the most part Salter held in derision, might soon be able to accommodate serious filmmakers at work on important films. The first Slate and Salter collaboration, a short film about collegiate football practice sessions called *Team Team Team*, won first prize in 1962 at the Venice Film Festival. This success led to a series of documentaries, including a ten-part work on the circus for public television and a film for CBS, which Salter shot and Slate directed, about fifteen contemporary American painters. Hollywood producers, always eager to find writers who understand film, began asking him to work on screenplays.

"A film writer is very much like a party girl," says Salter. "While you're good-looking and still unlined, the possibilities seem endless. But your appeal doesn't last long and you're quickly discarded." He never approached that last sad phase. Although many time-consuming projects came to nothing, four of his scripts were made into full-length films, the most successful of which was *Downhill Racer*. And though *Three*, his directorial debut, was a commercial flop, he was immediately offered the chance to direct another movie. He declined. "My weakness in life," he explains, "has always been lack of absolute commitment to writing. Unlike Faulkner, I don't write on the walls of the bedroom. Consequently, I find myself essentially an enemy of film."

In 1977, Robert Redford approached Salter and asked him to write a screenplay about rock climbing. He agreed, but before he sat down to write, he felt he had to know his subject. He took up climbing. Always an avid athlete (he likes to ski and play tennis and touch football), he mastered at fifty-two a sport many feel compelled to abandon at a much younger age. He climbed at Yosemite, in Colorado and at Chamonix in the French Alps.

But Redford didn't like the script. "I guess he didn't see himself in it," says Salter. But Salter's old friend, Robert Emmett Ginna Jr., who was at that time editor in chief of Little, Brown, read the script and thought he had discovered a way to find a wider audience for Salter's work. Ginna offered him $50,000 to turn the script into a novel. The result, *Solo Faces*, is perhaps too dark, its hero too tongue-tied and solitary to appeal to a popular audience. Rock climbers, however, revel in the meticulously observed depiction of their sport; admirers of exact prose are similarly impressed. The writer Peter Matthiessen, a friend and neighbor, considers it Salter's best novel.

After *Solo Faces*, Salter had a card printed up rejecting every kind of Hollywood overture: "James Salter regrets that he is unable to . . ." He marks a check in the appropriate box and sends off the rebuff by return mail.

Salter's marriage fell apart in the early '70s. For the past fourteen years, he has been living with Kay Eldredge, a journalist and playwright. In theory, they divide their time between Aspen, Colorado, and Bridgehampton, but their life is considerably more peripatetic than that. Grants, teaching jobs, and lecture tours take them to Europe or Iowa or Japan. France, which figures prominently in much of Salter's fiction, is a constant draw. "Recently, we've been moving three or four times a year," says Eldredge, who describes their life as "luxurious without money."

Eldredge and Salter have a five-year-old son, who until this year was free to wander with his parents; now that he'll be in school, the family will have to settle down somewhat, possibly in Bridgehampton. Eldredge hopes that fewer dislocations will mean that both she and Salter will get more work done. In the past few years, Salter's writing has advanced slowly. His two-book contract with Random House specified that the first manuscript, his memoir, was due in January 1989; his editor hopes to have it by early '91.

An autobiographical article Salter wrote for *Esquire* in 1986 inspired him to begin the memoir. Although he says he had no model in mind, he mentions Vladimir Nabokov's *Speak, Memory* and Isak Dinesen's *Out of Africa*. He praises Nabokov for his "irreplaceable sense of detail" and Dinesen for "the courage she had in what she omitted." Salter's book will be composed of self-contained chapters organized around specific themes or phases in his life, some of which may overlap chronologically.

Why would a man who has always been loath to talk about his past, even with his closest friends, agree to write a memoir? One answer is that James Salter is a writer, and no writer would pass up the opportunity to tell such a rich and varied story. But if his habitual reticence and the three chapters already published are any indication, Salter will be as selective in his reminiscence as Dinesen was.

"He thinks it's important not to reveal everything," says Eldredge, "in part so the mystery of things won't dissolve. I'm closer to him than anybody, and there are still great pockets of isolation and privateness." Nonetheless, Eldredge feels that in the last few years Salter has made a conscious effort to drop his reserve. Friends agree that since he began work on the memoir he's been more willing to talk about previously unmentioned subjects—he tells stories about flying, refers casually to his days at West Point. It's as if, in writing about his past, he is at last beginning to loosen its hold on him.

Publication of the memoir may also announce to a much wider audience the existence of this well-kept literary secret. "Remember," says Frank Conroy, "we're talking about a mature writer working at the peak of his power." Ben Sonnenberg, former editor of *Grand Street*, agrees: "The memoir will be the coming together of it all."

As for Salter, he feels he had better have vast ambitions. "I haven't yet achieved much," he says. With a dismissive wave of the hand he forestalls objection. "My ideal is a book that is perfect on every page, that gives you tremendous aesthetic joy on every page. I suppose I am trying to write such a book."

Interview with James Salter

William Dowie / 1992

Previously unpublished interview. Printed with permission. William Dowie is the author of *James Salter* (Twayne Publishers, 1998).

The interview from which these excerpts are taken was done by mail in early 1992, with Salter responding in his own hand to my printed questions. The motivation came from my having agreed to write an entry on him for the *Dictionary of Literary Biography* (1993). I had already had several conversations and exchanged many letters with him after receiving his note of thanks for my essay on *Solo Faces* that had appeared in Armand Singer's *Essays on the Literature of Mountaineering* (1982).

I first met Salter in 1985 when I drove from Boston to his summer place in Sag Harbor, a rented house since he was building a home in nearby Bridgehampton. That night before dinner Jim asked me, "Is this going to be an interview with a tape recorder, or are we going to have martinis?" I opted for the latter.

William Dowie: I think you said World War II became "the reality against which all future things would be judged." Is there a war book for you that says it all?

James Salter: The war was the great forge of my time. It was the reality of the grown-up world when I entered it (that world) and its indelible imprint has never gone. No single book contains it all. I was stunned by Malaparte's *Kaputt*. I admired James Gould Cozzens's *Guard of Honor*, John Horne Burns's *The Gallery*, Michener's *Tales of the South Pacific*, Lewis's *Naples '44*, Toland's *The Rising Sun*. Also James Jones's *From Here to Eternity* which, though barely touching the war, seems the truest and most accomplished novel.

WD: How did you start writing your first novel?

JS: First awkward attempts to write, to begin a novel, Honolulu, 1946. I showed it to two friends a year or two later when it was well advanced. One said it was rubbish. The other didn't like the title. I finished it in about 1949 and it was turned down by publishers although Harper Brothers said they admired it and would like to see my next.

WD: When did the interest in writing begin?
JS: In grammar school I suppose. At prep school I was on the literary magazine, won mention in a national poetry contest, and had things published in *Poetry* magazine.

WD: Did you first want to be a poet and write poetry?
JS: I won a graduation award as school poet. John Simon, a classmate, won the Latin scholar award. As we left the stage, Salter: I didn't know you were a Latin scholar, John. Simon: I didn't know you were a poet.

WD: Is there a story that typifies the way you get inspired to write? A couple of stories that exemplify different ways?
JS: This is a difficult question since writing doesn't generally reveal its—let's use the word—backstage unless very hastily done. "Am Strande," for example, came from several specific instances and circumstances. "American Express" evolved from long days spent in the trash heaps of things heard, known, imagined, etc. "Foreign Shores" was based on an incident. "Akhnilo" is all imagination. And so forth.

WD: What's your pattern of writing?
JS: A lot of scribbling, overlaying, inserting. I think of things and then write them down. I don't think by writing.

WD: The cadences, sounds, chasms of *Dusk* are breathtaking, on a different level than contemporary writers I'm most familiar with. I read an Updike story and it looks slack by comparison. I need to see your work in the right context, but if that context is mainly European, how can I take its measure without reading it in the original French?
JS: I'm not really a European. I'm American from the ground up. I can't say whether or not I always feel like one. My roots—the ancestral—are European, between Frankfurt and Moscow, all that in there. *Light Years* is domestic, so are "Twenty Minutes," "Dusk," "Dirt," "Foreign Shores," "Akhnilo," "Lost Sons," "American Express." I could never write in French—I don't know it

well enough, and literary French, the written language, is intolerant in the extreme.

When I read, I read "aloud" to myself, and the writing I like best has the finest music. As Babel said, he didn't write, he composed.

James Salter, The Art of Fiction No. 133

Edward Hirsch / 1992

James Salter interview by Edward Hirsch. Copyright © 1993 by James Salter, originally appeared in *The Paris Review*, The Art of Fiction No. 133, used by permission of The Wylie Agency LLC.

James Salter is a consummate storyteller. His manners are precise and elegant; he has a splendid New York accent; he runs his hands through his gray hair and laughs boyishly. At sixty-seven he has the fitness of an ex-military man. He tells anecdotes easily, dramatically, but he also carries an aura of reserve about him. There is a privacy one doesn't breach.

Salter was born in 1925 and raised in New York City. He graduated from West Point in 1945 and was commissioned in the US Army Air Force as a pilot. He served for twelve years in the Pacific, the United States, Europe, and Korea, where he flew over one hundred combat missions as a fighter pilot. He resigned from the Air Force after his first novel came out in 1956, and settled in Grandview on the Hudson, just north of New York City. He has earned his living as a writer ever since. He has three grown children, a son and two daughters, by a previous marriage. He lives with the writer Kay Eldredge and their eight-year-old son, Theo. They divide their time between Aspen, Colorado, and Bridgehampton, Long Island.

Salter has published five novels: *The Hunters* (1956), *The Arm of Flesh* (1961), *A Sport and a Pastime* (1967), *Light Years* (1975), and *Solo Faces* (1979). He received an award from the American Academy and Institute of Arts and Letters in 1982. Five of his stories have appeared in O. Henry collections and one in the *Best American Short Stories*. His collection *Dusk and Other Stories* (1988) received the PEN/Faulkner Award.

It rained continuously during the four days I visited Bridgehampton in August of 1992, but I scarcely noticed the weather, so content was I to sit at the dining room table asking questions and listening to Salter's carefully considered answers. Even on gray days the traditional, cedar-shingled two-floor house with its many French doors and windows seemed bathed in light. We drank ice tea by day, and one exquisitely made martini each night (Salter at one point estimated that he has had eighty-seven hundred martinis in his life). Afterward, company came for dinner; many bottles of wine were consumed; the interviewer wandered off to examine the framed menus on the wall, the etching of two bathers by André de Segonzac, the miniature painting by Sheridan Lord of the landscape near the house.

Salter writes in a study on the second floor, a small, airy room with a peaked ceiling and a half-moon window. His desk is a large wooden country-trestle table made of old pine. Everywhere there are telltale signs of the memoir he has been working on for the past years—envelopes that have been scrawled on, scraps of paper that have been entirely covered with his minute handwriting. On the morning that I was left alone in the study I found well-thumbed copies of Nabokov's *Speak, Memory* and Isak Dinesen's *Out of Africa* resting on a map of France with places circled and marked. I discovered an aeronautical chart, a sheaf of twelve extremely detailed pages of notes in red, blue, and black ink, a journal from 1955 with the sentence written across the front: "Every year seems the most terrible." On the small wooden table next to the desk lay a group of *cahiers*, little soft-covered gray-numbered notebooks, each containing a possible chapter of the memoir. These homemade workbooks are dense with notes—the author's instructions to himself, quotations from other writers, entries that have been color-coded for the place where they might be used. "Life passes into pages if it passes into anything," Salter has written, and to read through these notes is to reconfirm what one knew all along: how meticulously each of his pages is written, how scrupulously each of his chapters constructed. Everything is checked and rechecked, written and revised and then revised again until the prose shimmers, radiant and indestructible.

Coming down the stairs past the photograph of Isaac Babel I grew once more wildly excited about Salter's work-in-progress. He demurs: "Hope but not enthusiasm is the proper state for the writer."

INTERVIEWER: How do you actually write?

JAMES SALTER: I write in longhand. I am accustomed to that proximity, that feel of writing. Then I sit down and type. And then I retype, correct, retype, and keep going until it's finished. It's been demonstrated to me many times that there is some inefficiency in this, but I find that the ease of moving a paragraph is not really what I need. I need the opportunity to write this sentence again, to say it to myself again, to look at the paragraph once more, and actually to go through the whole text, line by line, very carefully, writing it out. There may be even some kind of mimetic impulse here where I am trying to write like myself, so to speak.

INTERVIEWER: So it is crucially a process of revision?
SALTER: I hate the first inexact, inadequate expression of things. The whole joy of writing comes from the opportunity to go over it and make it good, one way or another.

INTERVIEWER: Do you revise as you go?
SALTER: It depends, but normally, no. I write big sections and then let them sit. It's dangerous not to let things age, and if something is really good, you should put it away for a month.

INTERVIEWER: Do you think of the sentence or the paragraph as an organizing unit?
SALTER: Normally I just go a sentence at a time. I find the most difficult part of writing is to get it down initially because what you have written is usually so terrible that it's disheartening, you don't want to go on. That's what I think is hard—the discouragement that comes from seeing what you have done. This is all you could manage?

INTERVIEWER: You give a lot of attention to the weight and character of individual words.
SALTER: I'm a *frotteur*, someone who likes to rub words in his hand, to turn them around and feel them, to wonder if that really is the best word possible. Does that word in this sentence have any electric potential? Does it do anything? Too much electricity will make your reader's hair frizzy. There's a question of pacing. You want short sentences and long sentences—well, every writer knows that. You have to develop a certain ease of delivery and make your writing agreeable to read.

INTERVIEWER: I find your prose style wholly distinctive, beautiful and implacable. How did you hit upon it?
SALTER: I like to write. I'm moved by writing. One can't analyze it beyond that.

INTERVIEWER: Do you write every day?

SALTER: No, I'm incapable of that for various reasons. It's either because of the press of affairs or I just haven't brought myself to a position where I'm ready to write anything down.

INTERVIEWER: Do you need a lot of solitude to write?
SALTER: Complete solitude. Although I've made notes for things and even written synopses sitting in trains or on park benches, for the complete composition of things I need absolute solitude, preferably an empty house.

INTERVIEWER: In those circumstances, does writing come easily?
SALTER: Important novelists often say that writing a novel is hard. I think Anthony Powell said it was like conducting foreign policy—that you have to be prepared to go and do it every day no matter how you feel. But in general, I am unhappy writing something I am not terrifically interested in. Waiting for that interest to be there probably slows down writing a bit. And also my life, which I like, has a lot of travel. It usually takes a while to go somewhere, get organized, sit down, start working.

INTERVIEWER: Does the travel help your writing?
SALTER: It's essential for me. There is no situation like the open road, and seeing things completely afresh. I'm used to traveling. It's not a question of meeting or seeing new faces particularly, or hearing new stories, but of looking at life in a different way. It's the curtain coming up on another act.

I'm not the first person who feels that it's the writer's true occupation to travel. In a certain sense, a writer is an exile, an outsider, always reporting on things, and it is part of his life to keep on the move. Travel is natural. Furthermore, many men of ancient times died on the road, and the image is a strong one. Kings of Arabia, when they are buried, are not given great tombs. They are buried on the side of the road beneath ordinary stones. One thing I saw in England long ago struck me and has always stayed with me. I was going to visit someone in a little village, walking from the railway station across the fields, and I saw an old man, perhaps in his seventies, with a pack on his back. He looked to be a vagabond, dignified, somewhat threadbare, marching along with his staff. A dog trotted at his heels. It was an image I thought should be the final one of a life. Traveling on.

INTERVIEWER: You once said that the word *fiction* is a crude word. Why?
SALTER: The notion that anything can be invented wholly and that these invented things are classified as *fiction* and that other writing, presumably

not made up, is called *nonfiction* strikes me as a very arbitrary separation of things. We know that most great novels and stories come not from things that are entirely invented, but from perfect knowledge and close observation. To say they are made up is an injustice in describing them. I sometimes say that I don't make up anything—obviously, that's not true. But I am usually uninterested in writers who say that everything comes out of the imagination. I would rather be in a room with someone who is telling me the story of his life, which may be exaggerated and even have lies in it, but I want to hear the true story, essentially.

INTERVIEWER: You're saying it's always drawn from life?
SALTER: Almost always. Writing is not a science, and of course there are exceptions, but every writer I know and admire has essentially drawn either from his own life or his knowledge of things in life. Great dialogue, for instance, is very difficult to invent. Almost all great books have actual people in them.

INTERVIEWER: Would you describe your prose style as impressionistic?
SALTER: To be technical, impressionism means outdoor subjects with a lot of color and a breaking away from classicism, isn't that it? Someone said that I write the way Sargent painted. Sargent based his style on direct observation and an economical use of paint—which is close to my own method.

INTERVIEWER: Your work seems unique in the way it brings together a set of apparently masculine concerns, ordeals, initiations, with an exquisite prose style. Is that how you see it?
SALTER: I've made an effort to nurture the feminine in myself. I don't mean overtly, but in terms of response to things. Perhaps that's what we're talking about. I am happy with my gender, but pure masculinity, which I have been exposed to a lot in life, is tedious and inadequate. It's great to listen to men talk about sports or fights or war or even hunting sometimes, but the presence of the other, the presence of art and beauty, which crude masculinity seems to discount, is essential. Real civilization and real manhood seem to me to include those.

INTERVIEWER: Some readers complain that your work is too male oriented, yet you have said that women are the real heroes. Why?
SALTER: I deem as heroic those who have the harder task, face it unflinchingly, and live. In this world women do that.

INTERVIEWER: In "A Single Daring Act" someone says, "You're going to hit the glory road here." There are still heroes in your work.

SALTER: I believe there's a right way to live and to die. The people who can do that are interesting to me. I haven't dismissed heroes or heroism. I presume we're talking of this in the broadest sense and not merely in the sense of goal-line stands or Silver Stars. There is everyday heroism. I think of Eudora Welty's "A Worn Path," about a black woman walking miles to town on the railroad track to get some medicine for her grandchild. I think real devotion is heroic.

INTERVIEWER: What do you mean when you say that there's a right way to live? Do you mean to be discovered by each of us?

SALTER: No, I don't think it can be invented by every one; that would be too chaotic. I'm referring to the classical, to the ancient, the cultural agreement that there are certain virtues and that these virtues are untarnishable.

INTERVIEWER: A lot of your stories are about people being tested—They're men mostly—but I'm also thinking of the ordeal of Jane Vare in "Twenty Minutes." Does the drama reside in the ordeal?

SALTER: Well, life is an ordeal, isn't it? You're continually being tested. It doesn't seem unusual to me to pick an apex or a dramatic instant of this testing. It's a conventional device of storytelling. And, of course, courage is in there sometimes.

INTERVIEWER: Do you think your sensibility is French?

SALTER: Not particularly. Ned Rorem said that it is. I like France, and I like the French, but no.

INTERVIEWER: Is Colette a figure who has meant anything to you?

SALTER: Oh, yes. I don't remember when I first came upon her. Probably through Robert Phelps, although I must have read scraps here and there. Phelps was a great Colette scholar who published half a dozen books about her in America, including a book I think is sublime, *Earthly Paradise*. It's a wonderful book. I had a copy of it that he inscribed to me. My oldest daughter died in an accident, and I buried it with her because she loved it too.

Colette is a writer one should know something about. I admire the French for their lack of sentimentality, and she, in particular, is admirable in that way. She has warmth; she is not a cold writer, but she is also not sentimental. Somebody said that one should have the same amount of sentiment in writing that God has in considering the earth. She evidences that. There's one story of hers I've read at least a dozen times, "The Little Bouilloux Girl" in *My Mother's House*. It's about the most beautiful girl in the village who is so much more beautiful than any of her classmates, so much more sophisticated, and who quickly gets a job at a dressmaker's shop in town. Everyone envies her and wants to be like her. Colette asks her mother, Can I have a dress like Nana Bouilloux? The mother says, No, you can't have a dress. If you take the dress, you have to take everything that goes with it, which is to say an illegitimate child, and so forth—in short, the whole life of this other girl. The beautiful girl never marries because there is never anyone adequate for her. The high point of the story, which is marvelous because it is such a minor note, comes one summer when two Parisians in white suits happen to come to the village fair. They're staying nearby in a big house, and one of them dances with her. That is the climax of the story in a way. Nothing else ever happens to her. Years later, Colette is coming back to the village. She's thirty-eight now. Driving through town she catches sight of a woman exactly her own age crossing the street in front of her. She recognizes and describes in two or three absolutely staggering sentences the appearance of this once most beautiful girl in the school, "the little Bouilloux girl," still good-looking though aging now, still waiting for the ravisher who never came.

INTERVIEWER: When did you get to know Robert Phelps?

SALTER: It must have been in the early 1970s. A letter arrived, a singular letter; one recognized immediately that it was from an interesting writer, the voice; and though he refrained from identifying himself, I later saw that he had hidden in the lines of the letter the titles of several of the books he had written. It was a letter of admiration, the most reliable form of initial communication and, as a consequence, we met in New York a few months later when I happened to be there. He was, I discovered, a kind of angel, and he let me know, not immediately, but over a period of time, that I might belong, if not to the highest company, at least to the broad realm of books and names—more was entirely up to me.

Phelps introduced me to the French in a serious way, to Paul Léautaud, Jean Cocteau, Marcel Jouhandeau, and others. His life in some respects was like Léautaud's—it was simple. It was unluxurious and pure. Léautaud lived a life of obscurity and only at the very end was rescued from it by appearing on a radio program that overnight brought him to public attention—this quirky, cranky, immensely prejudiced, and educated voice of a theater critic and sometime book writer and diarist who had unmercifully viewed life in the theater for some fifty years and lived in a run-down house with dozens of cats and other animals and, in addition to all this, carried on passionate love affairs, one for years with a woman that he identified in his diaries as The Scourge. Phelps had some of that. He lived a very pure life. Books that did not measure up to his standards he simply moved out into the hall and either let people pick up or the trashman take away. He did this periodically. He went through the shelves. So on his shelves you found only the very best things. He believed in writing. Despite every evidence to the contrary in the modern world, he believed in it until the very end. Phelps died about three years ago. I said I thought of him as an angel. I now think of him as a saint.

INTERVIEWER: It seems as if André Gide was a major influence on you at one time.

SALTER: He was, but I cannot remember exactly why. I read his diaries when I first started writing in earnest, and then I read, and was very impressed by, *Strait Is the Gate*. I had an editor at Harper Brothers, Evan Thomas, who asked me what I was interested in, and I told him I was interested in Gide. A look of bewilderment or dismay crossed his face, as if I'd said Epictetus, and he said, Well, what book of his are you reading? I said, *Strait Is the Gate*. It's simply a terrific book. Have you read it? He said, No. I could tell from his tone that it was not the sort of thing he read or that he approved of my reading. My impression of Gide, looking back, is of an unsentimental and meticulous writer. I would say my attentions were not drawn to the wrong person.

INTERVIEWER: Are there other French writers who particularly influenced you?

SALTER: I've read a lot of them. Among those who are probably not widely read I would say Henry de Montherlant is particularly interesting. Céline is a dazzling writer. Here we have a disturbing case. Certain savage works of his have been stricken from the list. We know his views. The French almost executed him themselves. So we are talking about a dubious personage who is now deemed, I think correctly, as one of the two great writers of the century in France. It's a perfectly valid nomination. Even his last book, *Castle to Castle*, is tremendous. It must have been written in the most trying circumstances imaginable. When you read something good, the idea of looking at television, going to a movie, or even reading a newspaper is not interesting to you. What you are reading is more seductive than all that. Céline has that quality.

INTERVIEWER: What about Ford Madox Ford? I see a tonal similarity between *The Good Soldier*, which has been called "the best French novel in English," and *A Sport and a Pastime*.

SALTER: I admire Ford Madox Ford and probably never admired him more than when Hemingway thought he was cutting him to ribbons in *A Moveable Feast*. I don't know the details of his life. I do know that when he was a little boy he was counseled by an uncle, Fordy, always help a lame dog over a stile. Ford behaved that way during his life. I just admire him greatly. He must have been in his late thirties when the First World War broke out and he volunteered and went and served. Along about that time, either just before or after—he had already written a number of books—he sat down to write *The Good Soldier*. He said it was time to sit down and show what he could do. I think that's wonderful and, of course, the book itself is not bad.

INTERVIEWER: How do you feel about Hemingway?

SALTER: I feel about Hemingway the way most people feel about Céline. He's a powerful writer, but personally, I find his character distasteful. I know a lot of people who met him—they all say he was wonderful. I don't think so. A nice thing about life is that you can rearrange the pantheon and demote certain figures you are dissatisfied with. It doesn't hurt anybody. So I've moved him down; he's gathering dust in the basement.

INTERVIEWER: Do you ever think of what you're doing as revising or rethinking a Hemingway ethos?

SALTER: I don't . . . I've never considered that. Of course, you never know what you're really doing, do you? Like a spider, you are in the middle of your own web. People have pointed out to me certain ideas and themes of Hemingway's in my writing. Each time I thought I was coming to it for the first time. There's a terrible temptation—I confess to it—that sometimes when you're sitting, trying to write something, you think, how would someone else do it? In the beginning I hadn't reached a point where I'd completely eliminated Hemingway from such consideration. You say, How would Yukio Mishima or John Berryman have written this, for instance? What kind of phrase would they use to describe such a thing? It opens the door to different approaches that might not be close at hand though you probably don't want to use them once you've thought of them. It's a weakness that arises when you are hesitant, when you cannot go on. Your mind wanders to these things.

INTERVIEWER: What about Henry Miller?

SALTER: Glorious writer. I would be very disappointed in a future, which is going to tell us which things are worth something and which aren't, that didn't treat him considerately. I find him irresistible. There are no distractions when you are reading Miller for the first time. I don't think you should read all his books—many are repetitious. Once you're in the thickets of *Sexus*, *Plexus*, *Nexus*, and *Black Spring* you're staggering around as if people are beating you with newspapers, like a dog. But when you read *Tropic of Cancer*, you're reading a wonderful book. There's life, irreverence, esprit in it. I don't write anything like him. I can't. You'd have to *be* Miller, that's what's magnificent about it. It seems to me that when you read, what you are really listening for is the voice of the writer. That's more important than anything else. And it's Miller's voice, of course, which is the thing that makes you linger at his elbow until long past closing time, and you absolutely want to go home with him and keep talking, even though you know better.

INTERVIEWER: In "Winter of the Lion" you said that Irwin Shaw was the first writer of distinction you ever met—a father figure, a friend, an enormous voice. He seems an unlikely Virgil to your Dante.

SALTER: What I admired in him was he seemed to know how to behave. He was courageous. He embodied a lot of things that I respect, but perhaps hadn't explicitly put a name to before. I met him in the early 1960s, I believe. We rarely talked about books or writing, principally because he was overly generous, I thought, in his estimation of writers. He would frequently praise writers who might merely be good fellows or that he thought were decent. He was very prickly about his own work.

INTERVIEWER: His first *Paris Review* interview is one of the most pugnacious interviews I've ever read.

SALTER: He was that way, discussing his own things. You quickly learned that. We were sitting somewhere in Paris, which was where I first met him, and I questioned something about a story of his. Experience had not yet taught me whether to do this or not. Immediately his tone and general demeanor changed, and he said, Well, they're all good stories, something to that effect. He said some people liked some of his stories and some liked others and that there had been stories that he thought were not particularly good that had gone on and won prizes, so how did one know? You said to yourself, Let's skip this.

INTERVIEWER: It seems as though you took from him not so much a model of how to write, but how to live as a writer.
SALTER: The income. The income.

INTERVIEWER: What did he talk about?
SALTER: He would drift into the past sometimes. I remember one night particularly when he was talking about the great moments of his life. He said something like the greatest moments of his life were being called onto the stage the night that *Bury the Dead* opened and the audience was shouting, Author, author! Another was the liberation of Paris. The third was catching a pass in a football game when he was playing for Brooklyn College years ago. There were some other things. Marian, his wife, was there, and I think his son, Adam. They probably felt a bit slighted, though they must have been used to it by that time. But I liked his categorization of things that were great.

INTERVIEWER: What did you mean when you said that he saw in you the arrogance of failure?
SALTER: He probably saw in me what one sees in any unrecognized but ambitious person.

INTERVIEWER: What do you think of Shaw's designation that you were a lyric and he was a narrative writer?
SALTER: Rather accurate. I've tried to rely less on lyricism because, having been stung by comment that it was unearned, I've come to the conclusion that I should pare down a bit, perhaps distill a bit more. That does have the effect of giving lyric things greater power.

INTERVIEWER: Did you ever think of yourself as an expatriate writer?
SALTER: No. I have lived in Europe, the longest period when I was in the Air Force and stationed there, but we were visitors essentially. The other long period was living in Magagnosc, a little village down near Grasse. I went over because Harvey Swados suggested it. He was a charming man, very handsome, with a luxurious beard, a full head of hair, a wise face with generosity and intelligence shining from it. In a moment of candor, he once remarked that he possessed every quality of genius except talent. He had talent, but he didn't feel it was of the highest level. He had a sabbatical from Sarah Lawrence and was going to France for the year with his family. He said, Why don't you come along, and in essence we said, Why not? The vil-

lage was one that Auguste Renoir had lived and worked in for a while, and the house was an old stone farmhouse that had been occupied the previous year by Robert Penn Warren and his wife, Eleanor Clark. I'd written and asked about the house and she wrote back and described it in some detail—the views of the sea, the goat that came with the house, the eucalyptus trees. The description was perfect and she concluded by saying, You will have the most wonderful year of your life if you don't freeze to death. There was no heat in the place. And so we went to France for a year and a half, but with no intention of remaining there. John Collier had a house in the vicinity, and we became friends too. *Expatriate* is too serious a word.

INTERVIEWER: There are American writers who go abroad to Europe and become more entrenched as Americans, like Hawthorne and Twain, and those who long to fit in and become more European. How do you see yourself?

SALTER: Completely American. But I admire European ways.

INTERVIEWER: Do you think of yourself as a late bloomer?

SALTER: More or less. I'm hoping that a few green sprigs are still going to appear.

INTERVIEWER: It seems as if your experiences in the military totally propelled your first two books, *The Hunters* and *The Arm of Flesh*.

SALTER: The first two books, yes. Things that have come afterward, not much. There's only one short story that has anything to do with the military, and now this memoir that I'm writing has chapters about the military. I was in for twelve years, thirteen if you count being recalled, and a lot of things happened in that time.

INTERVIEWER: Did you learn anything from flying that helped you in writing?

SALTER: The time flying, that didn't count. It's like the famous eight or ten working in the shoe store. You deduct that from your literary career.

INTERVIEWER: You began writing in your mid-thirties. That's a late start, isn't it?

SALTER: Well, I began publishing in my mid-thirties. I was writing before that.

INTERVIEWER: When did you start?

SALTER: I wrote as a schoolboy. I was able to devote a little time to it when I was in the Air Force. In 1946 and 1947 I wrote a novel, and it was terrible. I didn't realize that then. Harper Brothers turned it down, but said they would be interested in seeing anything else I wrote. That was enough encouragement. I wanted to write another book anyway, and when I did, I submitted it to them, and they accepted it. That was *The Hunters*, the first thing I had published.

INTERVIEWER: What was it that kicked in that got you writing that first novel?

SALTER: It was an impulse I had from the beginning. I didn't know what made me write at the beginning, but later I understood. It's simple: the one who writes it keeps it. I suppose I felt that, though I wouldn't have been able to say it.

INTERVIEWER: How do you feel about those first two books now?

SALTER: Youth.

INTERVIEWER: You've spoken about your military experiences as the great days of youth when you were mispronouncing words and believing dreams. It must have been difficult for you to resign your commission in 1957 in order to make your way as a writer.

SALTER: I've managed to forget how difficult it was. I do remember when I heard my resignation had been accepted. We were in Washington with a young child in a borrowed apartment that looked out over the city. It was night, and there it was spread beneath me the way Paris is spread beneath you when you see it for the first time. Everything that meant anything to me—the Pentagon, Georgetown, flying out of Andrews, everything I had done in life up to that point, I was throwing away. I felt absolutely miserable—miserable and a failure.

INTERVIEWER: I've heard that you said "write or perish."

SALTER: Yes, it was one or the other. I wanted to be a writer, but on the other hand I had given everything to this other. I wasn't a rebellious officer. I had given everything, and I had gotten a lot in return. It was precisely like divorce. The sort of divorce where two decent people simply cannot get along with one another; it's not a question of either of them being at fault; they just can't continue. And if they've been married for a while and have children and everything else that's involved, it's difficult. That's how it felt. I knew I had to get divorced, but I wasn't happy about it. I was very apprehensive about the future, what lay beyond.

INTERVIEWER: The painter in the story "Lost Sons" is certainly an outsider, but he feels a residual nostalgia for the military life he might have had. Do you still feel that?
SALTER: Well, there are moments, as the poet said, when the blind captain dreams of the sea. When the geese fly over in the autumn you think of it, but that's all long gone. That sawed-off limb has grown over and healed.

INTERVIEWER: "That person in the army, that wasn't me," John Cheever wrote after the war, but you didn't feel that.
SALTER: No, like many prisoners, you come to love the prison and the other inmates. Cheever simply hadn't paid enough to have that feeling.

INTERVIEWER: If you could choose to be remembered by two books of your own, which two would you choose?
SALTER: I would think *A Sport and a Pastime* and *Light Years*.

INTERVIEWER: When did you first start writing *A Sport and a Pastime*?
SALTER: The first notes for it, probably in 1961; I began seriously writing it in 1964 or 1965.

INTERVIEWER: Where were you?
SALTER: At that time, I had a studio in the Village. We were living in the suburbs, and I went into the city to work.

INTERVIEWER: Was it dislocating to be living in New York and writing about France?
SALTER: Not particularly. It takes a few moments perhaps to disassociate yourself from quotidian life, but afterwards you are completely with the book. In any case, my method is to go in with a lot of ammunition. I had a lot of notes.

INTERVIEWER: It's almost as if in writing that book a cluster of notions or terms came together at once, about sensuality and eroticism, food and alcohol, the landscape and culture of France?
SALTER: I suppose so. Despite what I said earlier, the cities of Europe were

my real manhood. I first saw them in 1950. Apart from New York, a bit of Washington, and Honolulu, I had lived in no other cities, and Europe's were a revelation to me. I liked living in them. I like Europe because the days don't punish you there.

INTERVIEWER: I wonder how you came up with the title, which is taken from the Koran.

SALTER: I've read the Koran, but I saw the phrase in an article.

INTERVIEWER: The narrator treats "green bourgeoise France" as a secular holy land. That part seems autobiographical.

SALTER: It's possible not to like France. I know that Kerouac, whom I knew slightly, went to Paris once and came back after a couple of days with the memorable comment that Paris "had rejected him." But he's an anomaly. If your eyes are open, you will see how attractive France can be.

INTERVIEWER: When *A Sport and a Pastime* came out you were hailed as "celebrating the rites of erotic innovation" and yet also criticized for portraying such "vigorous 'love' scenes." What did you think of all that?

SALTER: The eroticism is the heart and substance of the book. That seems obvious. I meant it to be, to use a word of Lorca's, "lubricious" but pure, to describe things that were unspeakable in one sense, but at the same time, irresistible. Having traveled, I also was aware that voyages are, in a large sense, a search for, a journey toward love. A voyage without that is rather sterile. Perhaps this is a masculine view, but I think not entirely. The idea is of a life that combines sex and architecture—I suppose that's what the book is, but that doesn't explain it. It's more or less a guide to what life might be, an ideal.

INTERVIEWER: People seem to have different opinions of what the book is about.

SALTER: I listen occasionally to people explaining the book to me. Every few years there's an inquiry from a producer who would like to make a movie of it. I've turned the offers down because it seems to me ridiculous to try and film it. To my mind the book is obvious. I don't see the ambiguity, but there again, you don't know precisely what you are writing. Besides, how can you explain your own work? It's vanity. To me it seems you can understand the book, if there's been any doubt, by reading the final paragraph:

"As for Anne-Marie, she lives in Troyes now, or did. She is married. I suppose there are children. They walk together on Sundays, the sunlight falling upon them. They visit friends, talk, go home in the evening, deep in the life we all agree is so greatly to be desired."

That paragraph, the final sentence, is written in irony, but perhaps not read that way. If you don't see the irony, then the book is naturally going to have a different meaning for you.

INTERVIEWER: It has been said that Dean's desire for Anne-Marie is also a desire for the "real" France. It's a linked passion.
SALTER: France is beautiful, but his desire is definitely for the girl herself. Of course she is an embodiment. Even when you recognize what she is, she evokes things. But she would be desirable to him even if she didn't.

INTERVIEWER: There's a postmodern side to the book. The narrator indicates that he's inventing Dean and Anne-Marie out of his own inadequacies.
SALTER: That's just camouflage.

INTERVIEWER: What do you mean?
SALTER: This book would have been difficult to write in the first person—that is to say if it were Dean's voice. It would be quite interesting written from Anne-Marie's voice, but I wouldn't know how to attempt that. On the other hand, if it were in the third person, the historic third, so to speak, it would be a little disturbing because of the explicitness, the sexual descriptions. The question was how to paint this, more or less. I don't recall how it came to me, but the idea of having a third person describe it, somebody who is really not an important part of the book but merely serving as an intermediary between the book and the reader, was perhaps the thing that was going to make it possible; and consequently, I did that. I don't know who this narrator is. You could say it's me; well, possibly. But truly, there is no such person. He's a device. He's like the figure in black that moves the furniture in a play, so to speak, essential, but not part of the action.

INTERVIEWER: He's like a narrator on a stage.
SALTER: Exactly. He stands in front of the curtain.

INTERVIEWER: It gives an almost voyeuristic feel to the novel.
SALTER: But that's its appeal, don't you think? I'm speaking of voyeurism not in the sense of being satisfied to look at life and not act in it. I'm speaking in the Peeping Tom sense, which is immensely exciting. You are seeing

something forbidden, something absolutely natural and unrehearsed; someone unaware of being observed. As we know from physics, observed things are not the same as unobserved things. So, I like the idea.

INTERVIEWER: Is it possible to say how much of the book is invented and how much is real?

SALTER: Well, I've been to France, and I've been to Autun, and I do know people like that. I usually write, if I can, by preparing some things in advance. I don't like to step on the podium, as it were, with nothing. There are performers who can do that, but I can't. So when I sit down to write a page, I like to have some things that I've thought up in advance. And for a book, a lot of things. I'd jotted down a lot of things before I wrote that book and some were from life; some of them were quasi life; a few were invented.

INTERVIEWER: *Light Years* is an epiphanic book; in a way like *A Sport and a Pastime*. It consists of a series of luminous moments.

SALTER: In *Light Years*, these moments, let's say these scenes, are themselves the narrative. They serve as the narrative. *A Sport and a Pastime* has erotic moments that overshade everything else and in a way comprise the book. Perhaps it's the same method in both.

INTERVIEWER: What do you think *Light Years* is truly about?

SALTER: The book is the worn stones of conjugal life. All that is beautiful, all that is plain, everything that nourishes or causes to wither. It goes on for years, decades, and in the end seems to have passed like things glimpsed from the train—a meadow here, a stand of trees, houses with lit windows in the dusk, darkened towns, stations flashing by—everything that is not written down disappears except for certain imperishable moments, people, and scenes. The animals die, the house is sold, the children are grown, even the couple itself has vanished, and yet there is this poem. It was criticized as elitist, but I'm not sure this is so. The two of them are really rather unexceptional. She was beautiful, but that passed; he was devoted, but not strong enough really to hold onto life. The title was originally "Nedra and Viri"—in my books, the woman is always the stronger. If you can believe this book, and it *is* true, there is a dense world built on matrimony, a life enclosed, as it says, in ancient walls. It is about the sweetness of those unending days.

INTERVIEWER: One critic said that life's imperfections or impurities are rarely illumined in your fiction. That seems patently wrong to me, although there is a struggle for perfection in the lives of the characters, but it's a surface perfection, isn't it?

SALTER: Well, it's only shallow people who do not judge by appearances, as Wilde said. Frivolous, but it touches an important question of the times, which is the relation of appearance to substance, of the perceived to the true.

INTERVIEWER: I've read that the notion behind *Light Years* came from a remark by Jean Renoir.

SALTER: "The only things that are important in life are the things you remember." Yes, I like that idea. I came across it after I was working on the book. But no matter, it authenticated something I felt. I wanted to compose a book of those things that one remembers in life. That was the notion. I suppose that the plot of the book is the passage of time and what it does to people and things. Perfectly obvious again, but combining those two ideas gave me the feeling of what the book should be. That still doesn't displease. I find it satisfying.

INTERVIEWER: Viri, in the book, seems deeply dependent on the love of a woman for his happiness. It's the sanctuary for his feeling. Nedra, on the other hand, seems happiest when she's apart from men.

SALTER: Women are stronger in this as well as other regards. Women can graze and be happy, but men have no object other than women.

INTERVIEWER: At one point Viri says, "There are really two kinds of life. There is the one people believe you're living and there is the other. It is this other which causes the trouble, that other we long to see."

SALTER: Isn't this like that very small book that Poe said could never be written, "My Heart Laid Bare." There is a socially acceptable, let us say, conventional life that we live and discuss and pretty much adhere to, and there is the other life, which is the life of thought, fantasy, and desire that is not openly discussed. I'm sure, the times being what they are, there are people who do talk about it and probably on television, but in general, in most lives, these two things are completely distinct. I am conscious of them and attempted to write a little about it.

INTERVIEWER: The cover of the North Point edition features Bonnard's painting *The Breakfast Room*. That painting seems to capture the atmosphere of the novel.

SALTER: I sometimes write thinking of a certain painter, and I wrote *Light Years* thinking of Bonnard from the very beginning. He is a painter of intimacy and solitude, he was not part of any school, and his life was spent, generally speaking, away from the brilliance of the lights and out of the mainstream. Not only his pictures but his persona appealed to me.

INTERVIEWER: There was an enormous leap in subject matter from *Light Years* to *Solo Faces*. What happened?

SALTER: *Solo Faces* was not a book I thought of myself. It has a different paternity. I was asked to write it. I had written a script about the same people, not quite the same series of events or details. Robert Ginna, a very close friend and then editor in chief of Little, Brown, liked the script and asked me if I wouldn't write it as a novel. At first I was uninterested but he persuaded me to do it. That explains why it seems a bit off my beaten path.

INTERVIEWER: I wonder how it changed from script to novel?

SALTER: It had to be considerably more realized as a novel. The central figure is based on a real man, Gary Hemming, who was a climber in the 1960s, very well-known. He was one of those figures that friends and people came into contact with and never quite forgot. His background is somewhat mysterious. I did a lot of research on it, including reading his letters. He was a lone wolf and somewhat offhanded in his actions, but he handled his correspondence very carefully. I had a pretty fair idea what he was like from interviewing his friends and from reading. Major events in the book are based on events in Hemming's life. He did lead a remarkable rescue on the Dru. He was in *Paris Match*; he became famous. He was dead by the time I thought of writing about him. Actually, the thing that persuaded me to do it was a piece of film that had been on French television. It was about ten minutes long, an interview with Hemming. In it he was sitting in a meadow near Chamonix in a long winter undershirt, and when I saw him I suddenly realized what everyone had been talking about. There was this quality in him that was remarkable. He was a bit like Gary Cooper, to go to the commonplace, in the honesty of his face. There was something about him that was speaking to you from the center of his being. When I saw those ten minutes I became intrigued by the idea and felt that I could write about it.

INTERVIEWER: If Hemming is a model for Rand, I wonder if you had a model for Cabot?

SALTER: Oh yes. John Harlin was the other climber, the companion and rival. We didn't know one another, but we were pilots in Germany at the same time. He died on the Eiger.

INTERVIEWER: How fully did you rely on your own experiences of mountain climbing?

SALTER: Some. I always took a pencil and notebook with me, but I rarely made a note. I was far too occupied. What I heard being with climbers, the confessions and anecdotes, was more important to me. I climbed with Royal Robbins, who was and probably remains the most important moral force in American climbing. I went to Europe with him, and Yosemite. He was a stern, somewhat laconic figure, but very decent to me. One time we climbed something, not particularly trying for him, of course, but terrible for me. We were going up a pair of cracks and had to traverse over to another pair. The traverse was probably six or seven feet. You could almost span it with your arms. He went across—he was leading, of course—and then it came my turn. It was at the very limit of my abilities. I remember the moment well because I was looking down—height at that time was still a consideration to me—and I thought, I'm not going to make this, I'm going to fall here. That wasn't so alarming—we were roped—but what was really causing despair was the thought that after falling I was going to have to climb up and do it again anyway. That evening we were having a drink, and I told him what I had felt. I asked him if he ever felt anguish of that kind in climbing. All the time, he said. I felt he was telling me the truth.

INTERVIEWER: What do you remember most emphatically about climbing?

SALTER: That you come to these places and say to yourself, I can't do this, I know I can't do this, I'm certain I can't do it, but I have to do it, I know I have to. You would give anything to be somewhere besides there, but there's no use thinking about it. You have to go on. In the end it uplifts you somehow.

INTERVIEWER: The stories in *Dusk* were written over a fairly long period of time, but there are some persistent concerns and structures. What's your idea of a short story?

SALTER: Above all, it must be compelling. You're sitting around the campfire of literature, so to speak, and various voices speak up out of the dark and begin talking. With some, your mind wanders or you doze off, but with others you are held by every word. The first line, the first sentence, the first paragraph, all have to compel you.

Further, I think, it should be memorable. It must have significance. Merely because something has been written is not adequate justification for it. A story doesn't have to surprise—Mishima's "Patriotism" disdains surprise. It needn't be dramatic—Peter Taylor's "A Wife of Nashville" has no drama. What it must do is somehow astonish you, and what it must be is somehow complete.

INTERVIEWER: Who is your favorite short-story writer?

SALTER: I would say Isaac Babel. He has the three essentials of greatness: style, structure, and authority. There are other writers who have that, of course—Hemingway, in fact, had those three things. But Babel particularly appeals to me because of the added element of his life, which seems to me to give his work an additional poignancy. He lived in difficult times; he was murdered in the end by the state. He disappeared in the camps. We don't know what happened to him. He was the one who said, "I wasn't given time to finish." I've always been surprised that he hasn't had more recognition here. Of all the stories I have read, the greatest number that are near the top come from Babel and Chekhov.

INTERVIEWER: I've heard you say that Babel was a hero in the world.

SALTER: He is heroic to me. My idea of writing is of unflinching and continual effort, somehow trying to find the right words until you reach a point where you can make no further progress and you either have something or you don't. Babel was such a writer. He worked on manuscripts for a long time; there was a trunk full of them that just disappeared with work in it that he simply wasn't ready to have printed yet. His remarks, those that have been translated—various speeches or talks at symposiums between about 1930 and 1936—give you the impression of someone who is not without confidence, but by no means arrogant or proud. He said at one point that he wished he had never taken up anything as difficult as writing but instead had become a tractor salesman like his father. At the same time you know that in the final account it's not what he was going to do. He made a remark about Tolstoy that is very touching. He observed that Tolstoy only weighed three poods—a Russian weight measurement—but that they were three poods of pure genius.

INTERVIEWER: There's something about Babel's work that strikes me as similar to yours. In Babel there's a terrific sensitivity that is shaped or meets the forge of Cossack military conduct.

SALTER: I suppose you tend to take as models and admire people you are able to feel close to in a certain way. I feel many of the things I believe he felt. I would say the difference is that Babel rode with the Cossacks; I was one.

INTERVIEWER: Is Babel's argot something that has influenced you?
SALTER: You mean the unexpected slangy word, like a knuckleball. I steer away from it because a master, Saul Bellow, has appropriated that. Perhaps that's unfair—he may have come upon it himself, but in any case, it's similar to Babel's and you don't want to be the third party.

INTERVIEWER: What's your favorite book of Bellow's?
SALTER: *Henderson the Rain King* is a book that if you make a little tick beside things worth noting, you'll end up with page after page of them. It's a spectacular performance. Bellow once urged me to write about the horse country in Virginia. It was when I was telling him about my wife's family and my land-owning father-in-law. I told him I didn't know enough about the horse country in Virginia to write anything, I'd only been there a dozen times. Then he amazed me. He said, Yes, well, I'd never been to Africa when I wrote *Henderson*.

INTERVIEWER: Almost all of your stories have been published in the *Paris Review, Esquire*, and *Grand Street*.
SALTER: I've responded in some cases to invitation. Rust Hills at *Esquire* has been very encouraging; Ben Sonnenberg when he edited *Grand Street* was a wonderful editor. And of course the *Paris Review* published my first three or four stories, and George Plimpton also published *A Sport and a Pastime* when he first started Paris Review Editions. Although I have never managed to appear on the masthead, which has innumerable people on it, I feel I am a member of the family.

INTERVIEWER: What about the *New Yorker*?
SALTER: I've never had a story in the *New Yorker*; everything has been re-jected. At one point I came close. I had written a story called "Via Negativa," and I had a note from Roger Angell who said, please come in to talk about it. I sat in a little gray office with him, and he told me that he liked the story very much. He said, This is really quite good, but I'm afraid we can't take it. I was stunned. I said, Why is that? He said, At the *New Yorker* we have two rules we never violate. The first is that we never publish anything with ob-scenity in it. Second, we never publish any stories about writers or writing.

I hardly knew what to say. What about the Bech stories by Updike? I asked. He said, Well, that's another matter. A year or two later I was talking to Saul Bellow about this, and he said, I tried to get them to publish a section of *The Victim*, but they didn't accept it. They said they had two rules that they never violated. One, they never published anything that had obscenity in it. Two, they never published anything about death or dying.

INTERVIEWER: What do you think is your best short story?
SALTER: I like "American Express." It's the most recent story, and I think the most accomplished. It has a lot of levels. It is not simply what it appears. I like that aspect of it. It has a certain reach that I respond to, and I like the ending. Lastly, it's about lawyers, which is something I wanted to write about for a long time.

INTERVIEWER: What was the first story you ever wrote?
SALTER: The first published story was "Am Strande von Tanger," and oddly enough, that's probably the one I like next best. What I like about that story is it seems to be very carefully observed. When one reads it, I think there is the feeling of yes, this is exactly so, this is exactly how it was. I admire that in others.

INTERVIEWER: One of the things that figures into your fiction is money. Or maybe it is the absence of money that sometimes crushes your characters.
SALTER: I think the major axis of life is a sexual one. You know—the music changes but the dance is always the same. You could easily say, however, that wealth and poverty are an axis, and of course in America we have magnified that. We make no distinction between status and money. The real event of the 1980s was not the national debt or self-indulgence or any of these things; it was the emergence of great looting fortunes, the likes of which we hadn't seen for a hundred years and which threw the moral equilibrium completely out of balance and made us revise the value of everything—not to the benefit of society, though of course society will heal itself. And with of all that money, how pathetic that none could be found for a distinguished publishing house like North Point Press, to allow it to go on as it had. Well, what can you expect?

INTERVIEWER: It's struck me how often the deaths or failures of artists—Gaudí, Mahler—figure in your work.

SALTER: We were talking about the dissatisfaction of poets, their feeling that the culture, the nation, did not give them the honor or respect they deserved, though half of that comes afterwards. Ours is a culture that enshrines the ephemeral, and that leaves certain things and people out. The deepest instinct, I think, is to want to do something enduring, something worthwhile, and to be engaged by that, whether one achieves it or not . . . So perhaps that's how artists figure in.

INTERVIEWER: Have you ever written poetry?
SALTER: I wrote it in school, and I've written it episodically after that. I like brevity, the power of names.

INTERVIEWER: I wonder if poets in particular have influenced you as a writer?
SALTER: Very much. You have to like Berryman; you have to like Lorca, Larkin, Pound. *The Cantos*, unfathomable, a lot of it. When I was a child in school, we were made to stand up, at the rear of the class as I recall, and recite poems we had memorized. That anthology stays with one, even though it's largely just of verse. Like the shreds of popular songs and advertisements, they stay with you the rest of your life, you simply can't get rid of them. Then there were poets one was taught in English class. Keats and Shelley—I never liked them, possibly because we were instructed to admire them. I liked Byron, Tennyson . . . there's a simple sort of schoolboy poet. I remember Housman fondly. I said, Ah, now here's a poet that strikes my nature, and I like his language. I've since learned that Housman is not that important but I still have an affection for him as you do for someone you knew when you were young. You realize that perhaps your feelings were impetuous.

INTERVIEWER: Pound had the idea of structuring *The Cantos* around luminous moments. That doesn't seem far from what you were after in some of the novels.
SALTER: No, it doesn't.

INTERVIEWER: I wonder when Nabokov became an influence on your work.
SALTER: Oh, I forgot to mention him. Admirable writer. One of a kind. When did he write *Speak, Memory*? I read chapters in the *New Yorker* and was struck immediately by the voice. Of course, here's a poet. You say to yourself, Vladimir, let's be honest. You are a poet, and you're just writing

a lot of prose. It's quite good, but we know what you're really interested in. *Speak, Memory* seems to me eminently that kind of book. I think, all in all, it's his best. The first half of *Lolita* is very strong. *Pale Fire*, Mary McCarthy's favorite, is quite a strong book as well. However, *Speak, Memory* is indelible. It can be read and reread. The notions in it, the leaps of imagination and the language are essentially poetic. When I first read him I said to myself, Well, you might as well quit. But you forget about that after a while.

INTERVIEWER: He spoke of combining the passion of the scientist with the precision of the poet. I wonder if you feel that he has influenced you at the stylistic level?

SALTER: I don't have his nimble kind of mind. It would be useless for me to attempt to dance by putting my feet in his chalk marks on the floor, but I find him inspirational.

INTERVIEWER: Didn't you interview him?

SALTER: It happened that one of the first pieces of journalism I did was an interview with Nabokov. They said, First of all, he only gives written interviews. You must send in your questions in advance. So I sat down and wrote ten we assume penetrating questions, which I wouldn't like to see again, and sent them to him. No response, of course. But it was arranged that if I went to Europe I would be able to meet and talk to him. I reached Europe and was in Paris, it was in the winter, and I was in one of those hotels where they still had telephones with a separate piece you held to your ear, the old French phones. I got hold of the *Time* man in Geneva who had arranged the meeting with Nabokov, and he gave me the distressing news that the interview was called off. Nabokov had changed his mind. I said, How can he do that? I've come to Europe. Well, he's called it off. I didn't know what to do. He said, Why don't you call him? The idea was unthinkable. It was like somebody saying why don't you call the Pope? There seemed to be no alternative, so I called. A voice said, Montreux Palace Hotel, and I said, Mr. Nabokov, please. The phone was ringing and, of course, I didn't know what I was going to say. A woman answered. It was Véra Nabokov. I explained who I was and what had happened. She said, Oh no, my husband can't do an interview. He's not well. You must submit your questions in writing. I told her I had done that but there had been no response, and she repeated that he answered only in writing. I must tell you, she said, my husband does not ad-lib. Nevertheless, I asked if she would not, since I had come to Europe, be good enough to see if he wouldn't give me a few moments, merely so I had a physical impression, some description to add to the answers. She put the phone down, and I pictured her just looking out the window for a moment and then picking it up again and saying, "I'm sorry, he can't." But she surprised me by coming back and saying, My husband will meet you at five o'clock on Sunday afternoon in the Green Bar of the Montreux Palace. She repeated the date and time to be sure it was understood.

At five o'clock on Sunday, the elevator door opened, and out stepped a tall, blazered, gray-trousered man whom I instantly recognized, and a white-haired woman in a handsome Rodier suit. It was the Nabokovs. They came to the table. I was a little nervous. I was not an accomplished journalist; I knew Nabokov did not ad-lib; I was unable to bring a tape recorder because of that, and I would be unable to take notes, I knew, for the same reason. I had as my only source of strength the—I am certain—fabrication of Truman Capote that he had spent a night drinking and talking with Marlon Brando in Tokyo and the next day had written down the entire conversation exactly. It appeared in the *New Yorker*. I thought if Capote could do it for an entire night while drinking I could certainly do thirty abstemious minutes with Nabokov. I summoned all my powers and said, I'm going to concentrate on everything he says, listen, and not think of being clever or what I should say; I simply want to listen to him. It turned out to be about forty-five minutes. We were getting along quite well, and finally he said, Shall we have another julep? He was referring whimsically to scotch and soda. But I was afraid that one more drink might begin to obliterate the text. So I excused myself. I had the distinct impression we could have gone on and had dinner, but I was afraid to. I apologized for having taken up so much time and immediately went to the railroad station where I wrote down everything I remembered. It wasn't in order, of course, but it was four or five pages, and from it I constructed an interview. It was all fairly exact, I must say. I missed the train, but I cherish the memory.

INTERVIEWER: Did you interview others as part of a journalistic career?
SALTER: Well, a brief career. I interviewed Graham Greene, Antonia Fraser, Han Suyin.

INTERVIEWER: How did Greene strike you?
SALTER: I've nothing but admiration for Greene. In his case I took the trouble to read all his books since I knew very little about him, and that alone made it worth it. Afterwards he wrote me a number of letters mainly distinguished by their brevity, though they were cordial, and also by his signature, a more minuscule piece of handwriting than I have ever seen since.

It was as if they were signed by a mere horizontal line. He had asked me if I was a journalist, I'm not sure if it was curiosity or incredulity. I said that no, like him, I was a writer and I'd written some novels. He told me to send him one, and I sent *Light Years*. He wrote back and said, I found your book to be very moving, and three pages of it are absolutely masterly. He cited the pages. I went immediately to the book. I turned to those pages and, for various reasons, because of the way the lines fell, and also the flavor of the text, it turned out that all three had a faintly Graham Greeneish tone to them.

But he was kind. He wanted to know if the book had been published in England. I said that no, it had been turned down by publishers there. He said, Has it been submitted to The Bodley Head? He had a close connection to them. I believe his brother was one of the directors of the house. Yes, I said, but The Bodley had turned it down. He said, What reason did they give? I said that they felt it would not make any money if they published it. He said, That's no reason not to publish a book. Let me inquire. He arranged for them to publish it, which they did, and they had been right—but, of course, he was also.

INTERVIEWER: How do you feel about your journalistic work as a whole?
SALTER: It was a way to earn a living.

INTERVIEWER: How do you feel about your career as a screenwriter?
SALTER: In the 1950s the European directors suddenly burst onto the scene—Truffaut, Fellini, Antonioni, Godard. They seemed to cast a new light on the whole idea of movies. The New York Film Festival started sometime in the mid-sixties. All of it was seductive. It was like the band marching by, the flags, the beat of drums, and of course at that period of life I felt I could write anything—a sonnet, a libretto, a play. Someone came along and said, how would you like to write a movie? And it proceeded from there.

INTERVIEWER: Your movie *Three*, based on an Irwin Shaw short story, met with a lot of success at the Cannes Film Festival. Did that surprise you?
SALTER: It was a pleasant surprise. Finally, though, it was like everything I've done. It had its admirers, some of them ardent, but on the other hand, the public displayed complete indifference. It was described somewhere, or perhaps I described it, as being essentially a movie about meals and wine. That's perhaps not true, but I now see I was somewhat inadequate as a director. I should have spent considerably more time with the actors and the psychology of what was going on.

INTERVIEWER: Did you have strong ambitions to be an auteur?
SALTER: Yes, that's what everybody wanted to be.

INTERVIEWER: You spent about ten years in and out of the movie business, but seem to have a lot of disdain for it now.
SALTER: One earns that.

INTERVIEWER: Do you regret the time?
SALTER: Not completely. I saw the inside of a lot of places I wouldn't have otherwise.

INTERVIEWER: Was it liberating to decide that you wouldn't work with movies any longer?
SALTER: It wasn't abrupt. I just said I would like to do less of this. I would like to do much less. I would like to do none of it.

INTERVIEWER: Was journalism a better alternative?
SALTER: The wage scale is not exactly the same. Movie writers, as Lorenzo Semple and I agree, are among the most overpaid people on earth. In a certain sense you would do a movie for nothing, just for the fun of doing it. In addition to that, you are lavishly paid.

INTERVIEWER: Is it cancer-causing to write movies?
SALTER: Movies are essentially meant to be distractions. It's a very rare movie that has the power to console. Whether you get cancer or not is hard to say. There are figures like Graham Greene . . . I think the movies caused him no harm, and he worked in them extensively. There are people like John Sayles who are both novelists and full-time directors and who seem to survive it. But generally speaking, they come with the bill eventually. If you have been writing movies you have been accommodating other people.

A movie is a single performance, and it's remembered as a performance. Movies are never reperformed. They are not alive. They are sometimes remade years later, but everything in them is absolutely fixed and will always be fixed. They are not like great prose, which, as one critic pointed out, seems to catch fire first in one place and then in another. I tend to talk about them disrespectfully, but no matter what is said they have assumed the paramount position in American culture. They are unquestionably the enemy of writing, and this is something that is unresolvable. That is the way it is. I talk to writing students occasionally, and naturally that's the first thing they're interested in. I even speak to accomplished writers and writing teachers whose dream is to write a movie. We know why they have this dream. Part of it is the money, part of it is walking into a crowded restaurant with a famous actor . . . perhaps it's the same feeling one gets traveling with the president. The illusion is of some kind of authenticity. But by and large it all disappears, and the time you've spent doing that, if you are interested in writing, is wasted time.

INTERVIEWER: Is writing a memoir the sign of coming to a certain age?
SALTER: They say you should do it in your white-haired youth. I may have waited a bit long.

INTERVIEWER: Is there an impulse to rethink the experiences of the past?
SALTER: I feel the joy is in thinking about what happened and what it really meant and being able to make that come to life. There is the whole question of truth. You are perfectly entitled to invent your life and to claim that it's true. We have had the blurring of fact and fiction already. We've had writers who have explained that their books are nonfiction novels, that is to say, nonfiction fictions. I subscribe to a more classic view. I believe there is such a thing as objective truth insofar as we are given to know it. Victor Hugo's *Choses vues* is an example. No one can know God's truth, but it's not God's truth you're writing; it's truth as you know it—things that you have observed. I am fallible; we all are. There may be some errors in it, but they are not errors of omission or of carelessness. They are simply errors that crept in unknown.

INTERVIEWER: I noticed *Out of Africa* on your desk. What did you mean when you praised Isak Dinesen "for the courage she had in what she omitted" from that book?
SALTER: I take that book to be a model. As you know, she had a husband who gave her syphilis; she had a childhood, a marriage; she had a love affair; one senses—I haven't read her biography—a tremendous amount happened to her. None of it is in this story, *Out of Africa*. Her husband is briefly mentioned, so is her father. So are many other figures. One has a very strong feeling about this woman and her life. You feel you know her. And yet she was not obliged, so to speak, to lift her skirts, display the sheets. I admire that. I thought it would be interesting to write a book that tells some important things but doesn't bother to tell every detail.

INTERVIEWER: You've written that after you returned to domestic life you eventually stopped talking about your war days, but now you're writing about them.

SALTER: There was no point in talking about war days. Who was there to talk to about them? Someone at a party telling you about being over Ploesti or what he did in Vietnam usually trivializes it. You have to have the right audience. Also, when you write about it you have the opportunity to arrange it exactly the way you would like, and one presumes that the reader is going to be enthralled.

INTERVIEWER: But why a memoir?

SALTER: To restore those years when one says, All this is mine—these cities, women, houses, days.

INTERVIEWER: What do you think is the ultimate impulse to write?

SALTER: To write? Because all this is going to vanish. The only thing left will be the prose and poems, the books, what is written down. Man was very fortunate to have invented the book. Without it the past would completely vanish, and we would be left with nothing, we would be naked on earth.

Interview with James Salter

Eleanor Wachtel / 1998

First broadcast on CBC Radio's "Writers & Company" with Eleanor Wachtel and produced by Sandra Rabinovitch. November 1, 1998. Printed with permission.

The American novelist and short story writer James Salter is known for his precise and elegant style in work such as his classic erotic novel of the '60s, *A Sport and a Pastime*, and now a recollection, *Burning the Days*.

Although he's been a published writer for more than forty years, James Salter is not that widely known. But he's deeply admired by writers as wide-ranging as Susan Sontag and John Irving, Michael Ondaatje, and Reynolds Price, who described *A Sport and a Pastime* as "nearly perfect as any American fiction I know." People talk about his luminous prose, writing that is transcendent, exquisite, and lyrical while deceptively simple. When *A Sport and a Pastime* was published thirty years ago, it was considered his breakthrough novel. It recently came out in a Modern Library edition, which makes it something of a classic.

Salter is seventy-three. He was born James Horowitz, the son of an engineer turned property developer. He grew up in New York on the Upper East Side and attended the suburban Horace Mann School, where Jack Kerouac was an alumnus. Then, at seventeen, Salter followed in his father's footsteps and went to West Point. Graduating in 1945, he joined the Air Force and served for twelve years in the Pacific, the United States, Europe, and Korea, where he flew over a hundred combat missions as a fighter pilot. His first two novels, *The Hunters* and *The Arm of Flesh*, grew out of this Air Force experience. In fact, he initially took the penname Salter because military personnel had to get approval for anything they published. Also, writing was considered effete, and he didn't want his colleagues to know that side of him. But a year after the publication of his first novel he resigned. It was his birthday. Salter was thirty-two. He went on to write other novels—*Light Years*, about the dissolution of a marriage, and *Solo Faces*, about Alpine mountain climbers. And then an award-winning collection of stories, *Dusk*. Salter also worked in the film industry, writing screenplays, directing movies, and collaborating with directors such as Robert Redford and Roman Polanski. Last fall, after more than a decade in the making, James Salter produced a book of memoirs called *Burning the Days*. It captures his romantic, heroic vision of both flying and writing. James Salter spoke to me from the CBC's New York studio.

EW: You've referred to a remark by the filmmaker Jean Renoir as a source of inspiration or authentication for your work: "The only things that are important in life are the things you remember." This process of remembering, of distilling experience, of finding truth through memory, seems to interest you a lot. Why is that?
JS: I liked his remark. It's perfectly straightforward but strangely elliptical at the same time, elusive in a way. He's saying the only things that are important are the things that you remember. Well, that's self-evident, of course. If you don't remember them, in a sense they don't exist. They're not important to you. I used that remark, I referred to it in *Burning the Days* because that is a book of recollection, of memory.

EW: How has that idea—the idea that the only things that are important in life are the things you remember—how has that informed your writing?
JS: Well, your memory is your life. Imagine yourself without a memory. Each day is entirely new and then vanishes, everything that's happened to you. Let's branch off just a little bit. I'm married. One of the things I like best about being married and I like best about my wife are the things we remember. We both remember them. I can look at her and know she is remembering a certain thing. Or I say a few words, and she remembers that. Marriage is a long conversation, after all, an endless dialogue, and memory is what informs it. I suppose there is something in me that is faintly melancholic or vaguely sentimental, and likes the idea of memory. I like the word, I mean, memory, memoriam, in memorial. All these words that have to do with looking back into the past.

EW: You're also really a master of the present in the sense of a master of observation with extraordinarily precise prose. Are you conscious of filtering reality in that process in the act of writing? I just wonder how that works.
JS: You write the way you would like to read. You write things, you hope, that you would like to read. I like books that are based—and many impor-

tant ones are—based on penetrating observation, on details, really. The beauty of books, the beauty of stories, is in their details, for me, and so I think you have to observe very carefully. I like to do that. I've been told that I'm someone who has a keen eye. That is to say, someone who writes about visual things and I suppose that's true. That's part of observation. People, their motives, their behavior, your ability to write about them comes from your observation of them usually over a period of time so that eventually you're able, through experience, to re-create or to take these people that you have closely observed and perhaps—I'm now quoting Saul Bellow—give them an esprit that they didn't possess in life entirely, and so there you have a character in a book.

EW: In perhaps your best-known novel, *A Sport and a Pastime*, the narrator meditates on this theme of remembering. He says, "Certain things I remember exactly as they were. They are merely discolored a bit by time, like coins in the pocket of a forgotten suit. Most of the details, though, have long since been transformed or rearranged to bring others of them forward. Some, in fact, are obviously counterfeit; they are no less important." This is the line I'm interested in asking about: "One alters the past to form the future." How does that work?

JS: Gee, I don't even know if I understand that line. The narrator in this book—he's there to allow the book to exist. I knew what I wanted to write. I knew the story I wanted to write. It existed. It was only a question of more or less pulling it in as if it were a balloon, but I couldn't find the manner in which to write it. Finally—and I don't remember exactly how the idea came to me but it did—I thought, it should be told by someone else. It should be filtered through still another person besides me, the writer of the book, and hence that narrator came into existence. So, he often makes disclaimers, saying that this is a true story, this is exactly what happened, these are the things I saw. But, of course, he couldn't see everything. As your listeners probably know, the book is an erotic book. In fact, its eroticism is so ingrained that the erotic scenes, unlike in other books, are not arias. They are the *récitatif* of the book; they are the everything of the book. The narrator could not possibly be present or be a party to these things, so he had to invent certain things. Also, he makes this disclaimer because he is imagining some of these things—or, you are meant to think he is imagining them. That little passage that you just read is one of his various explanations of how he came to write all of this down. "One alters the past to form the future": well, I suppose if I were in class, as a student, and I had read this and I were being asked by the teacher, the professor, "Well, now, write down on your paper what exactly does that mean," I would reply that it probably means that one filters out certain memories and certain ideas to keep those that are most acceptable to you, to form the persona, the image that you believe you want to carry of yourself, and you carry that image into the future. That would be my explanation. What kind of grade would you give me?

EW: I'd give you an A or an A-, maybe.
JS: An A-? You're very tough. This is going to be a hard course.

EW: I want to ask you a little more about writing that novel, *A Sport and a Pastime*. It was published in 1967. You said that it was your ambition—this is in your recollection in *Burning the Days*—you say it was your ambition to write something *lúbrica y pura*, licentious yet pure? Why?
JS: It was just an impulse I had. It was like saying I would like to write a novel about an unhappy childhood. I didn't have one, but it just interests me. Those Spanish lines come out of Lorca. Of course, Lorca is a tremendously sensual poet, immensely, and in him—I believe he was homosexual—in him, one feels the, what can I say, the naturalness, the candor, the freshness of someone who looks at sensual and sexual things without a feeling of any embarrassment, shame, or shyness. It was that sort of book I wanted to write.

EW: You've written that sometimes you are aware when your great moments are happening, and sometimes they rise from the past. There's been no shortage, I would think, of great moments in your life and of risks taken. You describe some of these moments in your nonfiction pieces which appeared last year in your collection, or "recollection" as it's called, *Burning the Days*. Why did you want to take on the subject of your own experience?
JS: Oh, I didn't. I was occasionally writing for *Esquire*, and the editor and I had lunch one day and he said to me—he described a forthcoming issue he had in mind. There wasn't going to be a lot of text in it, maybe four or five long pieces, and the rest of it would be much shorter things, but anyway he was interested in my writing one of the pieces. He said to me, "You've been married five or six times, and we'd like you to write on love and marriage." I was staggered by this, of course. I knew that he had only been married once. I said, "No, you're wrong. I haven't been married any more than you have. Well, maybe a tiny bit more." He said, "Oh, well so . . ." A little silence fell for a while, and we cast about for some way possibly to save this idea

of my writing something. I had been thinking, vaguely—I had never done anything about it—but I had been thinking, vaguely, about writing an episode in my life years before, when in Honolulu after the War I was in the Air Force and I had fallen in love, desperately in love, with the woman who was the wife of my best friend. It was a passionate affair but unconsummated. I described this to him, briefly, and said, "Perhaps I could write not about love and marriage but about love and honor." The honor, of course, being the honoring of their marriage and our friendship. He said, "Yes, why don't you try that." I did. It was published. It was called "The Captain's Wife." It was the first piece of nonfiction, or of memoir let us say, or of recollection, that I had written that had been published. Fox read it. He said, "I like that piece very much. I'd love to see more. Why don't you do some others about various periods in your life? And perhaps we'd have a book. What do you think about that?" That's how I began to do it, urged by him. I would have never done it otherwise.

EW: In *Burning the Days*, you start, naturally enough, at the beginning. At an early age, you found an ideal to embrace in literature in Kipling, the virtue of fortitude. You say, "Fortitude, I saw, was holy." What was there in your early upbringing that made these values so attractive to you?

JS: It's difficult to know what things are out there that you respond to, perhaps because—*perhaps*, I'm just speculating now—I was an only child, I was unathletic because there were no sports around, I was not a member of a street gang or any such thing. And, consequently, I was not a tough, self-reliant kid, and perhaps for that reason the idea of courage appealed to me. I wanted to have it. I didn't know if I did have it. And, of course, Kipling is discredited now, and one mustn't read him and all that, but he's a tremendously romantic writer and one whose stories and poems are filled with life. It was to that I responded.

EW: You've written about your father and about how the Second World War ruined him. What happened to him?

JS: He joined up before the war, actually, so he was away for four or five years, and during that period of time . . . He was not exactly a real estate broker, yes he was a broker, but he was also a participant and to a certain degree in real estate, as an investor, and by the time he got back, things had changed. A new generation had started up. Men who hadn't gone away to war had made contacts and gotten ahead during that period. And then I think something else, perhaps, happened to him. He was born in 1898, so he was forty-three years old when the war started and he was forty-eight or forty-nine when he got out of the army, and perhaps he had reached another level, another plateau of life. The war was thrilling in a way, exciting, I should say, but also you paid a price for that because the war was made up of grand endeavor, tremendous in scope, I mean, and the spirit involved and the energy and the travel and the meeting of people was all something that was not going to be easy to find again, to replicate in ordinary life, in peacetime life. And so when he came back—I mean he had been a colonel, a full colonel, with whatever prestige and importance is attached to that—when he came back, all of that was taken away from him instantly, and he more or less had to start again at a much lower level. For various reasons, part of it circumstance, part of it luck, part of it his own character, part of it, as I say, what had happened to other men while he had been gone, he was never able to really reestablish himself again.

EW: How do you think his decline affected you?

JS: Well, it made me say to myself, "I hope that doesn't happen to you." Apart from that, I sympathized with him. Toward the end, then, I mean, in the 1950s, mid-'50s, he began to suffer depression and with it physical problems as well, illness, and these things are for anybody difficult to take in one's father or mother. There was that. Everybody has to face that.

EW: When you're describing your early relationship with him in *Burning the Days*, you say, "I never felt the absence of love, only of his interest."

JS: That's perfectly truthful. He was affectionate. He was admirable in every way. I looked up to him. But he was self-involved, involved in his own things. He was not what we might call a modern man, deeply involved in his child and in play and in companionship, and this is a ghastly phrase that exists, "quality time." That was not recognized between us.

EW: You ended up, at least initially, following in your father's footsteps. You found an opportunity to put some of these ideals into action when you enrolled at West Point.

JS: It was his idea, not mine. He had gone there. West Point always existed to him as a marvelous thing and part of his persona. He said to me, "Look, as a favor, I'd like you as a favor to take the exam."

EW: It was a very different world for a city child of your background and sensibility. You describe yourself as an unpromising cadet. What were some of the adjustments you had to make?

JS: [Laughs.] I had to catch up. For me, it was difficult to finally—it took months and years—to finally catch up and be able to do everything, belong, understand everything. My father, nice as he was, for some reason forbore to tell me anything about West Point and what I might expect. I mean not a word. He allowed me to go up there with a suitcase full of clothes. I don't know what I carried with me. The one thing that would have really been important, tremendously important, that we didn't have at first, was an alarm clock so that you could wake up early, before reveille and get some of the things done that you hadn't gotten done the night before. He didn't tell me about that, nor anything else. It was all absolutely a surprise to me. I had never fired—yes, I had fired a .22 in the summer at camp—but the manual of arms, I didn't have the faintest idea what that was. Every aspect of life up there was as foreign to me, as if, what can I say, as if we had moved to China.

EW: Initially, you were rebellious, resistant, a misfit at West Point, but then you changed. What happened?
JS: I resisted, of course, out of impotence, out of not being able to do it and resenting it. But finally when I began to catch up, I saw the light, so to speak. I wanted to belong.

EW: You talk about it almost as if undergoing a conversion.
JS: Yes, that's true. I did. I came in knowing nothing. I came in ignorant, not prepared to believe since I wasn't even aware of what we were supposed to believe in, and when I saw these things, when I learned them all, when I became part of it, I was converted.

EW: In a chapter in your memoir called "Icarus," you describe literary influences such as Arthur Koestler writing about an RAF flyer named Richard Hillary and also Saint-Exupéry and you say, "In such footsteps I would follow." This is in joining the Air Force as a pilot. You talk about your flying days as "the voyage, probably, of my life." What was the appeal of flying?
JS: The voyage of my life, actually, was fighting in Korea. The flying days lasted much longer than that. The appeal of flying, oh my. It's the appeal of everything in the world being given to you. These airplanes, these youths, this glamour, this victory—you see that, you want to be part of that. And the odd thing was that it was absolutely true, the appeal of it which was . . . Really you have no idea what it's going to be like when you enter, when you say, "Yes, I'd like to be a flyer," but the promise of it came true, is true. That is to say, it rewards you, it fulfills you with all that is promised, and the image of

yourself that you carry always is granted to you by that. It was a great thing. We entered it lightheartedly, but it was a great thing that happened to me.

EW: Was it an inevitable choice for you, given the values you had embraced since boyhood?

JS: Well, no. The war is what caused all this. Had there been no war, I would probably never have gone to West Point, never have been a flyer, my flying would be as a passenger on an airliner, I would be a different person entirely. It was history, it was events that formed me. I must say, to a large extent, since what you know is what you are in love with, or to put it in another way, you love your own knowledge, what you have seen, what you have experienced, the war, that second world war, is still the great metaphor of my life. That's not to say I live in the past, but those things were so urgent, so important when I was young that I remember them still and I refer to them still and certain values of them I still hold.

EW: Although you were too young to actually fight in the Second World War.

JS: Not really. I was commissioned during the war but right at the end of it, and we didn't get sent overseas in time.

EW: You make an observation that seems to underline everything that's going on there and what you're saying now, which is that it's important to fight in a war, that whatever we were we felt inauthentic, and you weren't anything unless you had fought. Being too young for the Second World War, you fought in Korea and served as an officer for twelve years and flew more than a hundred combat missions. So was it in a sense—it sounds like an inappropriate use of the word *luck*—but lucky that there was a war in Korea, lucky in the sense that it gave you a war to fight in.

JS: Remember, I was speaking as a regular officer and pilot. I was speaking as someone who had missed everything important that had been happening while I was at school and in training and emerged onto the field. Everybody around me was older, that is to say, everybody who had been in the war shone with the glamor of that experience, and, of course, we—my classmates and I—we had none of that, we were nothing. So it's from that point of view that I say you were nothing unless you had fought. Yes, the Korean War, it was lucky from a professional point of view. For a lot of people, it was not lucky. But at the time, yes, I thought it was a great opportunity.

EW: Unlike somebody like Joseph Heller in *Catch-22* and so many other writers, you don't write about the absurdity of war or the military.

JS: What they write is true. What I write is true. It just depends how you look at things. As I say, I was influenced by Hillary, by Saint-Exupéry, by people like that. I saw many of the things probably Heller saw, not the exact things, but similar things, but I was looking at the world in a different way.

EW: Do you know what made your experience of it, even in retrospect, so different, heroic and romantic?

JS: We'd have to go back to Kipling, wouldn't we? Maybe Joe hadn't read Kipling.

EW: You say that when you returned to domestic life, you kept something to yourself, as you say here, "a deep attachment—deeper than anything I had known—to all that had happened. I had come very close to achieving the self that is based on the risking of everything, going where others would not go, giving what they would not give." What is the legacy of those days for you?

JS: I had come very close. The legacy is the line you quoted a bit earlier. It was a great voyage—the voyage, probably, of my life. Those things form you and they don't go away.

EW: How does that idea of risking everything get expressed in everyday civilian life? What happens when the opportunity of that kind of risk isn't there?

JS: You change your life. Now, I'm not pretending to compare these two things. This would be perfectly ridiculous. But when you write, you approach every day as an extension of yourself and are trying to get over the hurdle, somehow, to write a clear round, to get something done, and you're not sure you can do it. There is a certain reluctance to sit down at the desk. All writers, most writers, experience this. Whenever you have to do something that is not easy to do and you say to yourself, But I'm going to do it anyway, I'm going to keep at it until it gets done, whether it be running the last half mile or whatever it may be, when you are a bit down, a bit tired, I think every time you've done it in the past makes you a bit stronger. But that is only distantly, remotely related to the idea of going out and risking your life, that is to say your existence. Of course, at that age your existence seems—you carry it more lightly than you do later on.

EW: Could you read about one of the more exciting moments when you're flying a mission?

JS: I should say that this is in Maine. I had joined a fighter group. It was the 23d Fighter Group. They had F-86s, famous at the time—jet fighters, swept wing, favorite airplane of pilots. I mean favorite because not only was it a terrific airplane but it looked the part. Here I was taking an early flight up there. I had very little time in the airplane. I had just joined. [Reads.]

EW: James Salter reading from his memoir, *Burning the Days.* Do you miss those days? When you read this now, do you miss it?

JS: Oh, I miss them sometimes. When you look up in the morning at the sky and when you see geese going over and, of course, the sound of airplanes a little bit, and sometimes I'm intoxicated sitting near the window in an airliner as we take off and humming some old drinking song to myself.

EW: You left the Air Force, and you say that there was still "the idea of being a writer and from the great heap of days making something lasting." Why did that idea start to win out then?

JS: I was getting a little older. I was thirty-two. And I had written a book, I neglected to say. In combat, I had kept a journal. I had observations again, stories about people, things that had happened, details and missions. It was a writer's journal, really, although I didn't know it at the time. There was not much confession in it as much as observation, things to be used later, although, again, perhaps I didn't know that it would ever be used. From that journal, which was written in a school notebook, handwritten, I some years later—two or three years after—decided that I would like to write a novel about that, and when that book was finished, it was immediately accepted and published. It was published under a pseudonym. That was because I did not know I was going to get out of the Air Force. I didn't want to jeopardize my career by being known as some sort of intellectual or writer, damning words, really.

This book had been published. I was over in Europe while all this was going on, and the reviews were sent to me. I read them, and they were really very good. I realized that, yes, in fact I had written a book. It had always been in me, latent, the idea of writing one day perhaps, of becoming a writer, and I decided that now was the time. If I was ever going to do it, do it now. And so I took the leap.

EW: Was it a tough decision? You describe it as an element of anguish.

JS: The most difficult decision of my life.

EW: And did you ever regret it?
JS: Well, not yet.

EW: Through your work in various fields, flying, journalism, screenwriting, you have encountered a lot of powerful personalities. You describe some of these people in your memoir, *Burning the Days*. Vladimir Nabokov, you recount that unusual experience with him. He was one of your earliest interviews in your brief journalistic career. Can you talk about what happened?
JS: Not so brief, actually, this journalistic career. I realize in the last ten days, I've written three articles for magazines. It's never really over. It's like once you get married and have children, even if you get divorced, it's never really over. So this journalism has not ended. But Nabokov was, in fact, the beginning of it. I was sent by Robert Ginna, who had been my editor at Little, Brown but was now working at *People*, he wanted me to go to Europe—well, not wanted me, he was very nice to me. I needed the money, and he helped me by arranging for me to go to Europe and do a number of interviews— with Graham Greene, with Antonia Fraser and with Vladimir Nabokov, who I revered. So, Nabokov wanted all questions—well, he liked interviews to be in writing. You sent him the questions; he would write the answers. I sent the questions, but he never responded. I had an appointment with him, however, in Montreux, where he was living then. And just before I went out to Montreux, I received word: your appointment is canceled. Nabokov can't see you. I was utterly dismayed. So I said to the stringer who gave me this information, "What would you advise doing? What should I do here?" He said, "Well, call Nabokov yourself." I said, "Call Nabokov?" He might as well have asked me to call the Pope. In any case, I called him, called the hotel in Montreux, the Montreux Palace. An operator said, "Montreux Palace Hotel." I said, "Mr. Nabokov, please." "One moment." Brrring-brrring, the telephone rang, and a woman answered. It was Véra Nabokov. "Hello," she said. I told her who I was and why I was calling. She said, "Well, my husband does not give interviews. You must write your questions." I said, "Yes, I've done that" and so forth, but I wanted to get a whiff of the master himself, to describe him a little. She warned me, she gave me a wonderful warning. She said, "I must tell you, my husband does not ad-lib," but I begged her to let me see him. She said he had been ill. I said, "Ask him anyway, would you please?" She said, "One moment." She put down the phone. I was certain that she was just going to pick it up again and say, "I am sorry . . ." But

she came back after a moment and said, "Yes, my husband will see you on Sunday at the Green Bar at the Montreux Palace Hotel." I went there and, of course, I interviewed him there. He said a lot of wonderful things. I wasn't able to write them down during the interview because he didn't want to be quoted ad-lib, as he said, and I naturally didn't have a tape recorder. He wouldn't permit that. But I had read, a couple of years before, a huge piece in the *New Yorker* written by Truman Capote following an entire night he spent drinking with Marlon Brando in Tokyo, and he had written this long, long piece and claimed he remembered it all. I thought, if that little fellow can remember all of that, then surely I can remember thirty or forty minutes of talking to Nabokov. I listened to him very carefully, and as soon as it was over, I ran outside and sat down on a bench outside and wrote down everything I remembered him saying. Of course, it wasn't all in sequence, and I did not—when I wrote the interview—I did not pretend he had said all this in sequence. I merely quoted certain things he had said, among them—he had said a wonderful thing—he said, I had asked him something about what he was doing in Montreux, was it interesting, did he find life agreeable there, and he replied, "Yes," he said, "I introduced kidding into Montreux."

EW: "Kidding"?

JS: Yes, you know, making jokes. He was very droll. He was agreeable, warm, but a bit aloof, very pleasant to talk to. His wife sat with us during the interview at the table. She was white-haired, elegant looking, wearing a blue Rodier suit. She said not a word during the entire interview, and he at one point looked at her and said, "Look at her. She never laughs. She is married to one of the great clowns of Europe, but she never laughs." And she didn't laugh at that, either. He said it fondly. It wasn't nasty. I liked him a great deal. And, of course, he's right. He shows you his dust as a writer.

EW: "Shows you his dust"?

JS: That is to say, you eat dust; he's a terrific writer.

EW: You say somewhere that *Speak, Memory*, his memoir, was a bit of an inspiration for you when you came to write *Burning the Days*.

JS: It's an exceptional book. For my own taste, I think it's his best book, but people like *Pale Fire* and *Lolita*. Both considerable, it's true. He also said, of course, he was assured by this time because he had made a fortune. He had sold *Ada* for six, seven figures, and, of course, *Lolita* had made him a huge amount of money, and I believe he wrote the script for Kubrick's *Lolita*. He was well off by that time. He was in his seventies, things had turned out all right. But he said, "I am not a famous writer. *Lolita* is a famous little girl."

EW: I'm really glad to have the chance to talk to you. Thank you very much.
JS: It was a pleasure. I feel that we've met, almost.

EW: James Salter in New York. *Burning the Days* is available in paperback from Vintage. This conversation was produced by Sandra Rabinovitch.

A Conversation with James Salter

Chris Offutt / 2004

From *Tin House* 22 (Winter 2004). © Chris Offutt. Reprinted with permission. Chris Offutt is the author of *Kentucky Straight, Out of the Woods, The Same River Twice, No Heroes, The Good Brother*, and *My Father, the Pornographer* (forthcoming). He's also written ten screenplays for Hollywood.

I met James Salter in 1989, when I was completing my MFA degree at the Iowa Writers' Workshop. He was a visiting instructor, one of the few times he has taught. It was a glorious season, the air crisp and chilly, brilliant leaves scattering along the streets, pigs browsing the harvested cornfield at the edge of town.

Jim enjoyed contact with all the students and was particularly loyal to those of us fortunate enough to be in his workshop. He joined us at the bar after class, invited us to his house for supper, and played softball and football on the weekends. Jim was like an officer who rolled his sleeves up and spent time with enlisted men. Above all, he was a terrific workshop instructor.

Jim spoke little in class, but when he did, the only sound was that of a dozen pens transcribing his words. His editorial comments burrowed into the flaws of a manuscript, revealing a way of thinking that would allow you to improve it. Jim had a knack for guiding young writers into challenging themselves.

Once during conference, he zeroed in on a line I'd written that didn't fit with the tone. "Too much Mickey Spillane," Jim said. I told him that I'd lifted the phrase straight from Faulkner, proud that I had stolen from the master, and that my teacher had somehow missed it. Salter nodded patiently, his voice calm. "Where," he said, "do you think Faulkner got it?"

Chris Offutt: I was casting around, trying to figure out how to introduce you, and I know that you hate the long-winded introductions about being a

decorated combat pilot, so I didn't want to mention that; or, how you published your first novel before I was born, but I won't mention that; or other topics you don't like to mention: the wars, living abroad for years, getting married in Paris. So I talked to people and said, "What should I bring up?" They said that I should just open with the fact that you had written the greatest anal sex scene in literature; however, I didn't want to bring that up.
James Salter: This is like a famous thing in rhetoric, where you say, "I won't speak of his deceitfulness, I won't mention his vices," and so forth. So no you haven't mentioned those things. Thank you. I was introduced once by someone who said that I was a member of a generation rapidly disappearing. I sometimes think of that; I think of myself as rapidly disappearing. Although I've been writing for a long time—my first book was published in 1957—and I've been writing more or less all that time, I don't seem to have a long list of books that have been published; but it so happens at this particular period of time, I have three coming out within twelve months.

CO: What are those books?
JS: The first is called *Gods of Tin*. It was written by me, but not assembled by me. An editor took parts of three books I had already written, sections of them that had to do with flying—I was at one time an Air Force pilot. The editor put the material from those three books together in a narrative, chronological form, to make some sense of it in that way, and added to it some material that had never been published. I was a fighter pilot in Korea, and I had kept a journal. I had never published any of it, and there are excerpts from it in the book. Then I have a book of short stories, recently written. Following that is a book that my wife and I wrote together. It's a nonfiction book, and it's like a book of hours, except it's really a book of days. There's a page for each day of the year, and on each page, there's an entry or two. The title of the book is *Life Is Meals*, and the entries all have to do with eating, drinking, food, cooking, the table, and so forth. It has some recipes in it, but it is not a book of recipes. The material is historical, anecdotal, informative, et cetera. I've read this book a couple of times, and what makes me think it's good is that every time I read it, it's as if for the first time. I can't remember having written that, and even the facts seem new and fresh to me. We wrote it in a terrific way, which is, she went off somewhere and wrote some pages. I went off in an entirely different place and wrote some pages. Then we traded them and edited them. She edited mine, and I hers. We never had a single argument. The style of the book is such as to make it relatively seamless anyway.

CO: When you first started publishing, you changed your name to a nom de plume. Why did you make that choice, and how did you come up with the name?

JS: The principal reason was I'd written a book, and I was a regular Air Force officer at the time, and regulations in those days were that anything that you sent out for publication had to be vetted, passed by some general in some office. I didn't want to do that, for a couple of reasons, the most important of which was that though I thought I'd written something wonderful, everybody feels that, and I knew that might not be true, and I didn't want to jeopardize my career. So I decided to disregard regulations and publish it under a pseudonym. I cast around for a name that was going to be completely remote from mine, that didn't use the same letters, or I was going to keep the James, I don't quite remember. I had a long list of them, just the way you name characters in fiction, and I kept crossing them out. You're a little—I don't want to say pretentious—but you're a little silly when you're young, and I had a name, Psalter, which of course is the name of a group of psalms. I liked the sound of that, and I thought it would be perfect, but somebody wisely talked me out of it and said, "You can't do that. It's too precious. People aren't going to accept it. You've got to drop the *P*." So that's what I did.

The other reason is that, after that book was published, I resigned my commission and became a writer. I was changing my life completely. Everything I had done for sixteen years I was pitching out, and I was turning into someone entirely different. I thought that it was appropriate at that time to start out completely fresh and start out with another name and another person. I didn't invent myself. I am who I am; but in a sense, I discarded the old snake skin. It was time to get rid of it and move on.

CO: You were in the military sixteen years?
JS: Yes. At first I thought it was just going to be an episode.

CO: Did you ever regret resigning the commission?
JS: No.

CO: Never?
JS: It was the most difficult act of my life, I would say, and I regretted it immensely at the time, and probably for a few years after, but you get over that. It was like a divorce, when you really have put everything into it, then you say, "It's over," and you're going to have to start again.

CO: Did they try to talk you out of it?

JS: No. I didn't confide in anybody. I wrote about this in *Burning the Days*. I went to the Pentagon to do it. I was in Washington at the time, and I went to the Pentagon, and I met a guy I knew, a colonel named Berg, who was in personnel, and I told him I was going to resign. He didn't bat an eye. There was nobody around to say, "Stop before you do something you'll regret forever."

CO: I know you went to West Point, and then you went to Korea, but before that, you'd gone to high school with another guy who went on to become a writer.

JS: Yes. Can we name him here?

CO: Yes.

JS: I was at prep school in Riverdale, and I think two classes ahead of me was John Kerouac, who was there as a ringer. They used to give an athletic scholarship for the final year of high school to gifted athletes, and he was one of them. He was a football player. I was on the literary magazine, among other things, and one day we had a submission from him. It was unheard of, really, to have one of these thugs turn in a story. We all said, "What is this? Let me see it!" It was pretty good and we published it. I don't remember what the story was, some sort of detective story. Then years later, in Pensacola, I was walking by a bookstore, and in the window, there was a book called *The Town and the City*, displayed both front and back. I recognized the name immediately, John Kerouac, and I recognized his photograph as well. I bought that book and read it, and it was pretty good. It's very Wolfeian, Thomas Wolfe. I read it with both admiration and envy, and I thought, Well, I'll be—as they say—damned. Look at this! That was in about 1950. It certainly acted as a spur for me. I thought, If he can do this, what's wrong with you?

CO: Were you writing while you were in the Air Force?

JS: No. At that time, it was before Korea. I was writing, but, nothing, just junk that you write when you're young. I was not writing stories. I was trying to write a novel, actually. I was attempting to. I had, latent within me, I suppose, some urge to do this and I was trying; but I certainly didn't have the background to do it, and I was completely on my own. I never talked to anybody about it.

CO: Your influence has been profound on me, as well as on many other writers. Who are the writers who influenced you, besides Jack Kerouac?

JS: He wasn't really an influence on me. His achievement was an influence on me. I didn't read anything more of his until *On the Road* came out, and that must have been seven or eight years later.

CO: So who did you read who had an impact?

JS: In 1948, I was in the hospital in Honolulu with blood poisoning. It was great, actually. The hospitals were not crowded then, and I knew what was wrong with me, and they were very solicitous. I sent a friend out to buy me a couple of books. I told him which ones I wanted, and they were two or three books by Thomas Wolfe: *The Web and the Rock*, *Of Time and the River*, and I've forgotten the name of the other one. I devoured them. I read all three while I was in the hospital, and they were very influential. Why do you write? Something in you makes you want to write, but also the whole, shall I say, image of it is important, and Wolfe had a very powerful, romantic image. I presume you're familiar with him, although he's not much read now. He was a big—and when I say, "big," I mean both physically, and in terms of reputation and readership—a very large figure in prewar literature. He had the most famous editor at the time, who was also a large figure, Maxwell Perkins. Wolfe was a very poetic, very lyrical, very unbridled writer . . . he's off there somewhere, just going and going. I was influenced by him. Plus, I was influenced by a lot of junk that I read, the normal, sugary diet of young people.

CO: Such as?

JS: I can remember I was tremendously influenced by a book called *My Son, My Son*. I don't remember who wrote it. It was a big bestseller at the time, a dramatic story of two families and their sons and what happens to each of the sons. Of course I still, just like your early telephone numbers, I still remember passages, or at least lines, from that book. That's one of the bad parts about not being careful about what you read when you're young. It's probably better to stick to a very healthy diet at the beginning. But there is no "way." There are ways, a lot of ways, and writers have different ways, and there are writers who've read the most horrible trash and gone right through and swept it aside, so to speak, and gone on to write wonderful things. In my case, I don't think it crippled me, but it didn't help me to read all that.

CO: Do you still read contemporary fiction?

JS: Not so much. I don't read for pleasure anymore.

CO: What do you mean? Then what do you read for?

JS: I get some pleasure incidentally. Reading is not an entertainment, or something I do to enrich myself. I read because I want to see how they did it, and to fill in certain gaps. You die with huge gaps. Even Harold Bloom is going to have a lot of gaps. So you can't really catch up completely; but there are some books and some writers that are very important to you, that become essential to you, and I often read and re-read the same writers. It's too late—well, I don't want to say it's too late—but unfortunately, I am past the point of being formed by those writers and following in their tracks. I said there is not a way, there are ways: James Jones, who wrote an exceptional book, *From Here to Eternity*, went to a writers' colony in Illinois, and the woman who ran it had a particular idea about how to teach writing. She sat every student down for two or three hours in the morning, and had them copy out, in longhand, paragraphs from her favorite three writers, who were Hemingway, Fitzgerald, and Thomas Wolfe, or maybe it was Faulkner. I laughed about that. My God, I thought, there is ignorance operating at full speed, but I'm not so sure of that now. I'm not sure that the mimetic approach to copying and copying isn't, at a certain stage in your career, something that can be beneficial. Churchill, in his autobiography, said that he was a poor pupil, that he was left behind for a couple of years. While the brighter boys were going on studying Greek and Latin, he was obliged to take English again, over and over. That way, he had fixed in his mind the exact grammatical structure, and the tone and the lyric, of an English sentence.

CO: Did you ever do that?

JS: No. I heard this much later.

CO: When you write, do you write in longhand?

JS: Yes.

CO: And then you type it?

JS: Yes.

CO: So in a way, you're transcribing your own work.

JS: It's a bit different from copying another writer.

CO: Does it change from one draft to the next?

JS: Of course. It certainly changes when you see your galleys, doesn't it? It has some authority then, and it reads differently, and you see things in it that you didn't see in the typescript. First of all, time has passed, so the fog of creation has lifted. I think it's definitely true that in each form, you see things a little differently. Here, again, I wouldn't recommend writing in longhand to anyone. I think for me it's a question of never having adopted newer methods.

CO: What do you mean?

JS: I presume that almost everybody writes on a computer now, for a lot of reasons, not the least of which is that publishers don't want a manuscript; they want your disk, so that puts you in the position of having to work on a computer.

CO: You use Wite-out. You may be one of the few people who are keeping the Wite-out manufacturers in business. I'm interested in this idea of writing it out in longhand, and then transferring it into a different form.

JS: I feel too silly talking about this. It's like saying, "Do you move the fork from your left to your right hand after you cut the meat?" I personally find it very satisfying to put a pen to a piece of paper and make marks and write. I don't know why that is. Maybe it wouldn't be satisfying for someone else, or maybe it would be if they tried it. I like it. I also like the convenience, the utter convenience of being able to write at any time; that is to say, at night, you're lying in bed, and you think, Jesus, that's an interesting name, isn't it? Or whatever comes to you, you don't have to get up, you simply scribble it on a little piece of paper, or while you're traveling, or walking, or doing one thing or another, you can't carry your laptop with you, but you can simply reach in your pocket for a piece of paper. I think convenience is an important thing. My method of writing is that I write on scraps of paper and keep accumulating things I think might be useful; then with those things, at least I go in with something. I don't have to look at a blank page. I have something in advance.

CO: Do you organize those scraps of paper, or type up the notes?

JS: I usually just organize them by marking them up in ink: A, B, C, or 1, 2, 3, or whatever. Then I make an outline, trying to find a place for them, and of course a lot of them have no place. They're wonderful; I think they're wonderful or I wouldn't have written them down, but they turn out to be not so wonderful, and after a while, you say, "Get real." But some of them are interesting, and the ones you can use, you use. Evelyn Waugh once said something like this: "People think that one writes books by standing behind a screen in a room and writing down the clever things that people say." It is true, unfortunately, at least for me, that if I don't write down something that somebody has said that's particularly right, or memorable, I'm not going to find it again. I can know what they said, but the order is lost. So I write down a lot of things as quickly as I can. Going back to Waugh, he said, "People think you stand behind a screen, but that's not it at all." What you really do—it's like working in a huge rubbish heap and you're just sifting through a lot of terrible rubbish and suddenly you come across something. Ah! There it is! It's dented, it's tarnished, but if it were polished up a bit and straightened out somehow, it might be a nice candelabra. So you are going through what amounts to a rubbish heap of your own ideas to find what works.

CO: It sounds as though the way you work is never ending. There is no break from being a writer.

JS: Well, why would you want a break?

CO: Exactly. Why would you want a break? *The Arm of Flesh* was your second book, and I don't know if it was experimental, but each chapter is from a different point of view. That book was out of print, and remained so for a while, and I assume that was your decision.

JS: Not really, but who would want to print it? The first book I wrote was a success. It sold far more than the publisher expected, which is to say, twelve thousand copies. The reviews were good, and all that business that was important to you when you're starting out. They said, "We're very eager to see another book from you," and of course, everybody has this story about the second book. So I wrote and wrote. I was under the impression at that time that if I took a book like Faulkner's *As I Lay Dying* and simply lifted the whole concept of it, nobody would notice such a thing. That's what I did, but he was a masterful, a great writer, and I simply didn't have that kind of stuff. I wrote not a very good book. My editor at Harper & Row said to me after he read it, "I don't really understand it, but it's probably good, so we'll publish it." They did, and it vanished immediately. It didn't sell at all, and got very little notice, and that was it. Decades, about forty years later, a publisher who had published a number of my things, Jack Shoemaker at North Point Press, said, "I'd love to republish *The Hunters*"—that was my first book—"and also this other book, *The Arm of Flesh*." I was not enthusiastic about either of those notions and especially about the second one. I said, "I wouldn't want to republish *The Hunters* unless I had a chance to make revisions," and he said, "Fine," and I said, "As for the other one, I don't want to republish it at all." He said, "I'd like you to think about it." After a while and the conversations and the letters, I said I would only do it if I rewrote it completely, from start to finish. He said, "That would be fine." So, not having anything else I was doing, I said I would do it. I did rewrite it, and it was republished. Is it any good? I don't know. It's better than the first one.

CO: I don't know if this is precedented in American letters: to not simply revisit, but to rewrite a previously published novel.
JS: I don't know if it's such a brilliant idea. I worked from the other book as one works from a translation. I crossed out a lot of things. I made a lot of derogatory comments in the margin and worked on it as an editor might with somebody who—I don't want to say "showed promise"—but somebody who would have to do a lot to pull this thing together.

CO: What was the biggest adjustment or biggest change from one version to another?
JS: The first thing was jettisoning the form of *As I Lay Dying*, which had been fatal. So I simply threw that away and started again as a book written in the third person. I also changed the structure somewhat, and so on and so forth.

CO: One of the stories in your other book of short stories, *Dusk*—recipient of the PEN/Faulkner Award, which is without doubt the award that has the highest esteem among the literary world—is about going to a West Point reunion. Do you still participate in those?
JS: I've been to some of them, yes. The story was inspired by one particular reunion, but a lot is made up, as you know.

CO: Do you have any relationship at all now with the Air Force?
JS: Both my roommates were killed. There were eight hundred fifty people in my class. Of those, perhaps two hundred went into the Air Force and became pilots. Of those, a lot of them got killed early on. There were a lot of accidents. Those I had as real friends, maybe a half dozen, for some reason, they're all dead.

CO: Of that generation, the ones who were your friends, isn't that the first generation that began flying space missions?
JS: Oh yes. Buzz Aldrin was in my squadron. He was a flight leader. Ed White was in the same squadron. He was one of the three astronauts killed

in the capsule fire in 1967. Virgil "Gus" Grissom, as well, was in my wing in Korea. Yes, I've been very close to greatness.

CO: If things had gone differently, you could have been an astronaut. Did you ever think that?

JS: I don't think so. Test pilots were a big romantic thing, but they were not the road to advancement. The people who went into test pilot school and became test pilots were famous, a bit, but never advanced very far. Advancement went to those on staff and in command, and when the astronaut program first came out, it was affiliated with the test pilot program, and you had to go to test pilot school to become an astronaut. Who ever thought they would go to the moon? That was just a pipe dream.

CO: You mentioned that Thomas Wolfe occupied a certain figure in the world and that you've seen the writer's position in the culture shift drastically. What is the writer's place in the world now?

JS: It's like a big bus, this culture. It's going a mile a minute. I'm on it, and I don't even know why I'm on it or where it's going. New people are getting on every minute, just raising hell, and with all kinds of baggage; a lot of them have run marathons. You say to yourself, "What's going to happen here?" I don't have the faintest idea. Is it important that a culture be elevated, or move upward, so to speak? I doubt it. I'm not persuaded that that's essential. Proceeding from that, the loss of the eminence of literature doesn't strike me as being something tragic. I feel that most people are missing a lot. They just don't know. They're not going to know. They're perfectly happy; probably happier than I am, but they just don't know. That's the way it is. I don't know what you can do about it. Every writer I've ever known who's addressed this has said the same thing. Books and reading are down a few steps. Anything except the most time-killing junk—a terrible expression, "killing time"—but that is of less interest to the country as a whole. What are you going to do? Live with it.

CO: Now you're finishing a new collection of stories?

JS: Yes, it's the most fruitful period in my life. My daughter is a publisher in France, and she had just started her own publishing house about two years ago. She asked me if she could publish something of mine to help her get started. I said yes, but I didn't have anything except some stories. She said that would be wonderful. I already had a French publisher, but we cleared it with him, and she published six of these stories in Paris. In France, for some reason, like Jerry Lewis, I'm treated differently. People often say that the French have done nothing culturally for forty years, and that it's a backwater and they're always admiring and praising the worst American writers. That's the only thing I feel a little uneasy about, but she published it there, and it did very well, so I wrote some more stories for it, and Knopf is publishing it here.

CO: The last time we talked, you hadn't completed it, and you had to write a story.
JS: I still am short one. I know exactly what it is, if I ever—I need a little quiet to sit down and focus on it.

CO: It's amazing to me that you can write stories to fulfill the book.
JS: I'm not writing them to a prescription. They're stories that I would like to write, but I never worked at this feverish pace. It used to take me a decade.

CO: Why has it changed? How did you find yourself in this fruitful period?
JS: At my back I always hear Time's wingèd chariot.

CO: You're a senior writer in this country, and you're publishing stories in *Tin House*, which some might consider a hip, young person's magazine. That has to be gratifying.
JS: There's always the chance that you're going to do something good, right? The chance may be slim, but there's always a chance. I like writing, and I like reading, and you reach a point where there wouldn't be much of a life without it. As to what's happened to me, and what I think about writing, and what I did: it's like going up and building a house somewhere, and suddenly there's a terrible cracking, and it turns out you're on an ice floe, and the thing is drifting away from the main continent, and it's melting. That's what's happened to writing—and here you have a house on the place!

Dan Pope Talks with James Salter

Dan Pope / 2004

From *The Believer Book of Writers Talking to Writers.* Edited by Vendela Vida. (Believer Books, 2005), 297–311. © Dan Pope. Reprinted with permission. Dan Pope is the author of *In the Cherry Tree* (Picador, 2003) and *Housebreaking* (Simon & Schuster, 2015).

I once heard a writer say that she plays a sort of parlor game or bibliomancy with the work of James Salter. She opens one of his books blindly, then invariably finds two of three sentences on that page that blow her mind with their lyricism, their precision, their perfection. Try it yourself. It works every time.

Salter is eighty now, and splits his time between Aspen, Colorado, and Bridgehampton, New York, where he lives with his wife and teenage son in the warmer seasons. We conducted this interview via the US postal system—I would send him questions on separate pieces of paper, and he would type the answers and send them back.

I. "Early rejections are the most painful excerpt for later ones."

Dan Pope: Can you tell a bit about your early years as a writer? The first inklings toward pen and paper? Where did it come from, that urge, do you recall?

James Salter: I began to write in prep school. A young English teacher, Richard Wooster, put his arm around my shoulder, so to speak. The impulse to write may be there, but there's the matter of encouragement. He made me feel that I had some ability. That carried me for a while.

In college—I'm calling the Military Academy college—in the bleakness of it there was a series of witty and well-written pieces in the *Pointer* written by an upperclassman named Gordon Steele. I didn't know him, but reading his mock diary called *Ducrot Pepys*—"ducrot" was a generic address for plebs—helped to keep me interested in the idea of writing. I wrote a few

89

stories during my second and third years. I had only a vague idea of how to go about it.

From the time I was twenty until I was twenty-five, I sometimes worked on a novel. I was in the Air Force and although there are examples of real writing by men under arms, they must have had a stronger spirit. I sometimes imagined myself as a writer, apart from being a regular officer, but there was no basis for it. The skimpy notebooks I kept at the time are banal. I wrote a few poems.

Finally, a year after returning from the Korean War, I completed the novel I had been carrying around so long—I had even written some pages of it during the war—and now came a significant event. I had been referred, I forgot how, to a literary agent, I think named James Oliver Brown, who in turn referred me to another one, a doughty old fellow who had been a pilot in the First World War. He took me on. Kenneth Littauer was his name. He had flown out of the same fields in France that I had. On freezing mornings they had made a big bonfire in the shape of a circle and stood inside it to get warm before taking off. "Weren't you afraid of getting burned?" his secretary asked. "No, we were going to be dead in an hour anyway, so what did it matter?" he said.

The novel was rejected, but I'd put a foot in the water. A few years later I wrote another, and it was accepted. That was *The Hunters*.

DP: And, as to those early years, what of disappointments? Were any significant? You write, for instance, in *Burning the Days*, of the dozen or more rejections of *A Sport and a Pastime*—a novel that is now part of the Modern Library—before George Plimpton took the book on.
JS: There are writers who slip through without a bruise, but the chances are greater that you'll get rejections. *Light Years* was rejected, I should say dismissed, by Robert Giroux as well as by others. It recently won the Fadiman Medal after being in print for thirty years. I had a collection of stories, *Dusk*, that won the PEN/Faulkner and nearly every story had been rejected by the *New Yorker*, by the same editor. Early rejections are the most painful except for later ones.

DP: And what of the thrills of the writing game? Do any stand out? Early breakthroughs? Certain accomplishments? The first story accepted by the *New Yorker*, perhaps? Or something less obvious?
JS: There are few thrills like the first ones, but not long ago at a party a woman I was being introduced to said simply, "Did she really just read a

magazine?" She was referring to a scene in *A Sport and a Pastime*. She assumed I would know. My God, all the things of inconsequence she might have said! I don't remember her name, but she was the unknown reader I sometimes say I imagine, the woman in her thirties or forties who perhaps lives in Buenos Aires.

When *A Sport and a Pastime* was chosen by Modern Library, my editor, Joe Fox, gave a small dinner to celebrate, or should I say, in honor of it. Alec Wilkinson, George Plimpton, and one or two others were there. I didn't tell them that as I approached the restaurant a woman's stockinged leg was extending from a limousine near the curb, and as she stepped forth I saw it was the French girl, twenty years later, whose life had been described in the book. She had gone on.

DP: Wait. You're saying it was her? The girl who was the model for Anne-Marie? She was there at the dinner? Or you just ran into her by accident? Did you say hello?
JS: It wasn't a girl. It was the woman she'd become, that Dean once knew. She wasn't living in Troyes with a French husband. She wasn't alone that night. It was sheer coincidence that she appeared at that moment. She never came into the restaurant.

DP: I've been told that the photograph of the woman on the cover of the first edition of *A Sport and a Pastime* is her. You can't see her face, of course.
JS: Yes, that's true.

II. "Once you reach a certain point, material is limitless."/a>

DP: *Burning the Days* contains poignant testaments to the writers of your generation who meant the most to you in a personal and literary sense: James Jones, Irwin Shaw. Your new collection of stories, *Last Night*, is dedicated to George Plimpton. You yourself seem as vibrant as any man your age, but does it take a toll, to write in the fall of these idols?
JS: It's not the fall of idols, it's the vanishing of a world. Everything you know, have known, becomes old, and an entirely new order of things appears.

It's like crossing a galaxy. After a while you begin to get the idea. You progress from the outside, from nowhere, towards the center or near it—stars are being born, stars are dying, and in the end you are heading for the outside once more.

DP: Whom do you miss the most, of those that are gone?

JS: Toni Ellis when she was young. Woody, who I was in Korea with, Lane Slate, Robert Phelps, and mainly for what he represented, Irwin Shaw.

DP: Of that world that has vanished, or is vanishing, what do you miss most? What has been lost? Cheever wrote of his prime that it was a time "when almost everybody wore a hat."

JS: I miss letters, ocean liners, New York when you could drive anywhere and park, and I miss the indifference that once existed toward popular culture.

DP: You came to speak at the Iowa Writers' Workshop a few times during the years I studied there. One thing you said, if I remember correctly, is "It is the writer's obligation to travel."

JS: Did I say obligation? The real obligation of a writer is to enthrall, like Scheherazade. It's not that easy.

DP: Well, then, how did your extensive travels influence your literary aesthetic, if at all?

JS: I'm not the first to feel that travel is a writer's true destiny. You don't have to go to Europe or the Far East. It can be Mexico or just a different part of the country. You see and understand things, maybe even your own life, in a new way.

DP: You also spoke about a certain sense of urgency, now, in your work. You said, if I recall correctly, "At one point it was a question of what to write about. Now, of so many stories, the difficulty is choosing which ones to tell."

JS: Once you reach a certain point, material is limitless. Perhaps that's because you come to understand what you are looking for or perhaps it's a matter of accumulation. John Cheever wrote stories in two or three days and Hemingway once wrote three, I think, in a single day. Novels have been written in six or eight weeks. For me, it always seems to take longer although I did write "Bangkok," the first version of it, in a morning. Sometimes you seem to get in a rhythm.

I also find that I am able to write more readily when freed from my usual self, as it were. It may be during a long drive or the morning after one drink too many. I'm a bit removed, looser. There is writing when you are intending to, and this other, less frequent, sometimes more beautiful writing that just comes.

DP: Regarding that sense of urgency, if you do in fact feel that now in your career, you have three books coming out in less than a year. If I'm not mistaken, you worked on *Burning the Days* for ten years or more, or at least you missed your deadline with Random House for that book by a good number of years. So, what's causing this sudden acceleration? Or have these works merely been in the pipeline for a long time?

JS: Well, I've been healthy, I suppose that's a warning. I realize it was an indulgence to spend ten years on something that could have taken far less time, but I was teaching for a living and we also had a child born to us, a son, which proved a blessing. I wrote some stories, so the collection that is coming out has been more or less in the pipeline, as you say. *Gods of Tin* was largely the work of two editors, William and Jessica Benton, although the words are mine. And the book my wife, Kay Eldredge, and I have just finished was several years in progress. I don't know where it will be in Barnes & Noble, under Food, History, Autobiography, Nonfiction, or Cooking, but I'm hoping not on the top or bottom shelf. Three books this year, none for the next five.

DP: One could say that you work slowly but surely. The books are adding up, ten of them now. Are you pleased—wholly—with your body of work, what has been published so far, or do you feel that a few pieces are missing, books perhaps you wanted or tried to write but didn't, for whatever reason?

JS: I suppose there are books I could have written. Perhaps it would have made a difference. I wrote things I was passionate about and didn't write other things. To say I am pleased or not . . . It's simply the way things turned out.

III. "There's desire, betrayal, the necessity of it."

DP: *Last Night*, your most recent collection of stories, focuses upon those pivotal moments that make up a life—missed chances, wrong paths taken, that one great opportunity, which a character perhaps did or didn't take. I'm thinking about "Comet," "Bangkok," "Palm Court," "Arlington."

JS: "Comet" doesn't have a missed chance. It's about a wife who, at a dinner, begins trashing her husband's life, his past, but in a way she can't because (*a*) it was marvelous and (*b*) it belongs to him, he lived it, it can't be touched. "Bangkok," I would say, is about a woman's attempt at revenge. "Arlington" is really just a portrait with a kind of moral.

No one I know of has been able to definitively say what a short story is or should be, what distinguishes it from an anecdote or an account—Mishima's "Patriotism" is an account but with a power that dismisses definitions—or a piece of description. I like stories that keep you reading until the line that makes it a story, as in, say, Carver's "Night School" when [the narrator's wife] says, "That's only writing. . . . Being betrayed by somebody in your own family, *there's* a real nightmare for you." Suddenly all of it, solid, with a click like steel, falls into place.

DP: Let me try again. Do you see any recurring themes in the stories in *Last Night*? Does the book function as a summing-up of sorts?

JS: Well, there's desire, betrayal, the necessity of it; these are things I keep circling around. I generally seem to be writing about men and women and what exists between them. Murder doesn't interest me, or greed, or the anatomy of family life, except in *Light Years*. But these stories don't sum anything up. They're a partial summing-up.

DP: You have a certain stature among fellow writers. Many writers, such as Richard Ford and Susan Sontag, have praised your sentence-making, your prose, your precision of language; such skill, though, is perhaps not as revered by the general reading public; does that matter?

JS: Obscurity is not so bad, especially if it is local. I can't brag that I beat Mr. Turgenev, I beat Mr. de Maupassant, and fought two draws with Mr. Stendhal. That's for fools. I didn't have the misfortune of great early success—I don't believe it would be dangerous to me now, but I don't see it coming. The bestseller list will bring you money, but it's never been much for glory. Of course, in those rare cases where it has been, that is the summit.

DP: When I read your work, when I read a story like "My Lord You" or "Comet" for the first time, there is a certain thrill. There is a first realization that "Oh well, I'll never be that good, I might as well quit." But eventually that feeling translates into a renewed vigor, which makes me, as a writer, want to get back to my desk. I feel that with your work, with Shirley Hazzard, with a few others. Were there books or writers like that for you? You mention *Under Milk Wood* in *Burning the Days* as perhaps such a book. Were there others? Are there any now?

JS: Some fade, but not many. You can't write like Robert Lowell. You can't write like Saul Bellow or Anne Carson or W. G. Sebald or Isaac Babel. They're in a different class. The coach at San Pedro used to tell his team,

"Play your position, you're not made of the stuff champions are made of."
Maybe you think you are.

IV. "When you read something wonderful there is no awkward afterwards."

DP: What's the worst part about being a writer?
JS: Having to do it. Anyone will tell you that. Or having done it and failed.

DP: The best part?
JS: The greatness of the world and feeling part of it. There is a reality in it that is greater than other realities even though it cannot replace them. When you read something wonderful there is no awkward afterwards or sense of having used something up. It's still there, it is still waiting for you, the thrill doesn't fade.

DP: Jill Krementz published that terrific book, *The Writer's Desk*. You get a peek into the writer's workroom. Saul Bellow bent over a portable type-writer. What does your desk look like? What's on the walls of your office?
JS: I don't have an office. I work on one table or another. The typewriter is thirty feet away, in another room. I don't need that until later. If I'm near my bookshelves, there are some photographs leaning in them, mostly people I knew when they were younger. The best table I ever had was in New City, New York, in our bedroom which was on the lower floor of what had been a barn. I was in my thirties; I could work late at night or start at dawn, in the quiet. My wife was sleeping, the children, the dog. The table was made of narrow strips of pale oak glued together, and it had a row of books along the far edge, the ones that I thought were important.

DP: Tell me what your day looks like, at this time of your life, when you're at home and working, whether in Aspen or on Long Island.
JS: I avoid habit. I sometimes sit down to work in the morning. After a few days, I change to the afternoon or early evening. The dog likes to walk in the fields; I begin the day with him, that's at about 8:30, and we go again at 4. I almost never go out to lunch. Through the summer and into the fall, my wife and I usually go to the beach to swim late in the day. We have an old car we keep for that. There's a tennis court in the other direction, and we sometimes go there and play.

DP: Have your work habits changed over the years? The nuts and bolts, I mean.

JS: Since they were established they've stayed pretty much the same. I write with a pen, then I type and retype, two or three times, sometimes more. Given my veteran status, publishers have let me give them typescripts. If I were to start over, I'd change things.

DP: Your books are extremely popular in France and Germany. Why do you think your work fits with a European audience?

JS: They must know something we don't.

DP: You've answered this question before in interviews but I wonder now, at this point, which of your own novels or stories stand out for you?

JS: Of the novels, I like *A Sport and a Pastime* and *Light Years* best. Of the stories, "Comet," "American Express," and the section in the bedroom of "Last Night."

DP: Do you have readers you show your work to for comments or impressions?

JS: In the beginning, of course, you want praise and only praise, but later you want firmer stuff. I have my wife and a friend, both good readers. I don't let anyone read a work in progress.

DP: How do you deal with writer's block, if that is an issue for you?

JS: I don't have that. I have inertia, lack of faith, things like that but nothing that will won't defeat.

DP: How do you know when a story, or a novel, is done?

JS: Oh, that makes itself known. When you can't do any more or any better.

DP: You once mentioned that you read a few passages from *The Book of Common Prayer* before starting your writing day. Is this something you still do? What does it do for you?

JS: *The Book of Common Prayer*, yes, it must be around somewhere though I haven't seen it for a while. If you could go to the Met in the morning and stand in front of certain pictures or sculptures, it would do the same thing, purify and more or less convince you that it can be done.

DP: What are you working on? Is it something you can talk about in any detail? Or does it harm the process for you, in some way, to discuss a work in progress?

JS: I'm writing a novel. I'd like it to be a little longer than usual. It's more or less What Mattered to Me, though *me* is not really in it—I don't like the postmodern ego. I'd like it to have a little breadth, perspective.

DP: Can you expand upon that concept for a moment, of the postmodern ego? *Burning the Days*, when it came out, seemed to confuse some readers who wanted it to be a memoir in the current vogue, that is, confessional writing. The book, of course, is not.

JS: I think of the postmodern as long-winded, clever, egocentric, and self-pitying. I like Isak Dinesen, writers like that.

V. "Writing isn't taught—it's achieved, like sin in Ireland."

DP: You went to West Point. Served as a jet fighter pilot in the Korean War in combat. Wrote and directed movies in Europe. Met or knew about every-one—Fellini, Irwin Shaw, James Jones, Kerouac, etc. Where did the writing come in? How did it fit? Was it some sort of distraction or drag? It's your life's work, of course, but you lived first and foremost, obviously.

JS: I wish I had put down what happened at West Point, but I only made a couple of pages of notes and stopped, I'm not sure why. In the Air Force I was writing undercover. It wasn't as shameful as cross-dressing, but it was an odd thing to do. You want to be a man, and that isn't part of it. I didn't write *The Hunters*, which is about flying in combat, until two or three years after the war. As I've said, flying in the war was a big thing for me, the voy-age of my life, and I wanted to somehow inscribe it. I imagined a book that would be famous although its author would be unknown, still struggling probably with the question of whether it was an acceptable thing to do.

When I resigned my commission to become a writer, it was like running away from home. I didn't know where to go or what to do. At the begin-ning, in despair, I'd gone to talk to and perhaps be consoled by my ex-wing commander, a wonderful guy, John Brooks. A couple of years ago, before he died, I went up to West Point with him and we walked through the cem-etery. His father, like mine, had gone to West Point before him; they were stationed on Corregidor before the war, in the early 1930s. He was reading the names on the gravestones, General this, Colonel that. He remembered many of them, had delivered newspapers to them as a boy, and so forth. After a while I looked and saw that tears were running down his face. The military life. He'd flown on the Ploesti raid. His father had graduated in 1912. I left all that to become a writer—what was I doing? I remember what John Brooks said when I told him I'd resigned. You idiot, he said.

So, there I was. I was free to become a writer, but it had to be built from scratch. It had to replace the other and, in a way, erase it.

DP: And life? Did it get in the way of writing? Or does writing get in the way of life? You've lived so richly, it seems there must have been a balancing.
JS: There have been a lot of things I haven't been able to do. Write enough is one of them.

DP: You come from a generation whose writing grew out of your lives and experiences, like Hemingway. I'm thinking of James Jones and Norman Mailer and the rest, even someone like Truman Capote. Today, there are the academics—writers who go directly from college to M.F.A. programs and back to college as teachers. The work, it seems, tends toward the cerebral, as opposed to the visceral. People complain about these programs, of course. You've taught at Iowa and Williams and other places. Where does this lead? How do you feel about it?
JS: I was lucky, but the same thing happens in film, directors come along whose reference comes from films rather than life. Does it make any difference? I don't know.

Writing isn't taught—it's achieved, like sin in Ireland. But there can be a favorable atmosphere and perhaps a trustworthy guide. Also, of course, you meet people headed your way.

DP: You once said that you tend to write about, or perhaps just like, dogs and woman. This is apparent in your new collection, *Last Night*. Are young women evocative because they have the power to shape a story?
JS: No, no, there are no dogs. One dog. There are women, not all of them young. You have to have women, unless you're Kafka. I don't know if they shape the story, but they're like a magnet, without them the filings just lie inert.

DP: I'm often astonished by the pacing of your short stories, the way you stay ahead of the reader, how you draw the story along through time and place. A story like "American Express," say. How do you do that? I can think of no other writer who handles time quite like you do. You invite the reader to reread, to uncover meaning on the second and third tries. It seems a story like "American Express" cannot be fully known except upon rereading, although the first reading is fully satisfying as well.

JS: I think you should get it all the first time and in a slightly different way or with different pleasure if you reread, knowing what it is. "American Express" didn't actually happen, but things like it did, and I knew the two men and two of the women in it. I thought it should gallop a little, it would read better that way. But it evolved, it didn't just set itself down. There were different versions of it and dozens of pages of notes. Maybe that helped.

DP: I'm also often amazed at the unveiling of secrets in your short stories. You pull aside the screens, one at a time, until the characters are wholly revealed, in a metaphorical sense. I'm thinking of, say, "Give" or "Last Night" or "Comet" or "Platinum" from the new collection. Is this part of your aesthetic, something you plan beforehand?

JS: Well, there's discovery in life, isn't there? You find out more about someone, they reveal more. Sometimes the reader should have that. Not every time, not as a formula—more like a painter, a sense of paintings or a phrase, then a change to something different. But the same hand paints it all, and the same sensibility.

DP: What about the phenomenon of the author tours? This is something relatively new. I've been told Jacqueline Susann invented it. Is this something you enjoy, or merely tolerate? I'm thinking more of going bookstore to bookstore, from city to city, that sort of tedium, not reading at, say, the 92nd Street Y.

JS: Readings, authors touring: that makes sense in the case of Dickens or poets going around to colleges, but it's an anachronism in the age of TV. If you're well known, it's a gesture to the public to appear in person, and if you're not well known, it won't change things. If you write something that everyone wants to read, that changes things.

DP: Last question. It seems to me there is a spine that goes through all your published work, having to do with living a certain type of life. Your characters are always seeking; they aspire toward something higher than what they have, whether it be beauty or heroism or courage or love, or even a better bottle of wine, as one of the characters says in "Last Night": "It would be nice to have always drunk it."

JS: You write about certain people and things because you know something about them and you want to tell it. Writing is the consequence of the desire to tell. I'm not one of those writers at the mercy, so to speak, of his characters in a novel. I know what happens to them and more or less how it happens, it's not a surprise.

I think the odds in life are against one, and I like people who go on despite the odds and who feel themselves held to or drawn to some standard, even if that standard doesn't really exist. Stoicism, I guess, is also involved. I don't often try to analyze it, that doesn't work for me as well as finding examples. Yes, go for the summit.

An Officer and a Gentleman

David Bowman / 2005

This article first appeared in Salon.com, at *http://www.Salon.com*. An online version remains in the Salon archives. Reprinted with permission. David Bowman is the author of the novel *Bunny Modern* and *This Must Be the Place: The Adventures of the Talking Heads in the 20th Century*.

I waited until it was dark in the Hamptons before I drove to James Salter's place intending to steal his garbage. I knew where he lived. I had interviewed the renowned novelist and short story writer that morning at his beach house. I noted the three cans standing neatly by the road. As for the contents of his rubbish, James Salter types and retypes his prose on a typewriter. What if he threw his earlier drafts away with his French newspapers and caviar tins and Tanqueray bottles?

I didn't care about that latter garbage, of course. It's Salter's prose that is priceless. What I could learn from Salter's discards, his edits! Salter is a *"frotteur"*—French for someone who "rubs words in his hand" so he can find the best phrase. In America, Salter has always been underappreciated (outside of the rarefied air of the late George Plimpton's *Paris Review*, which, despite its name, was published from uptown Manhattan). In Paris itself, Salter is considered an American treasure. French journalists assume Americans feel even stronger about the man. Salter's wife, playwright Kay Eldredge, has forbidden her husband from correcting their impression.

Salter was born in 1925 and raised in New York City; he spent World War II at West Point. He then flew fighter jets in the Korean War. Out of the service, he tried to sell swimming pools, and later worked off and on in the film industry as a writer and director. In 1967 he wrote a book called *A Sport and a Pastime*. It was and still is an erotic masterpiece about a young American Yale dropout named Dean and a French shopgirl he has a sexual tempest with. Although the summer of 1967 was the Summer of Love, the book was ignored. "Doubleday [my publisher] didn't know what to do with it," Salter remembers. "Nobody wanted to review it. It was too sexual. It had a certain language in it that is in no way obscene, but was unacceptable at the dinner table at that time. Now, in an era where even anal sex is discussed on prime-time TV, the book is completely inoffensive." He pauses. "Although the book lost that aspect of its strength, it still retains everything else. It's just as good a book as when it was written."

Eight years passed before Salter's next novel, *Light Years* (1975)—an anecdotal description of a failed bourgeois marriage set in the Hamptons before the Hamptons became *the* Hamptons. Salter's wonderfully limpid descriptions of autumnal Long Island landscapes—"The day is white as paper"; "In the morning, the light came in silence"; "The river was a brilliant gray, the sunlight looked like scales"—cause the novel to transcend its yuppie milieu. Salter knows all Chekhov's tricks.

Four years later, Salter turned an unproduced script about mountaineering into an underappreciated novel, *Solo Faces* (1979). *A Sport and a Pastime* and *Light Years* continued to sell in various paperback editions because of word of mouth. In the 1980s, a rumor took hold that Salter had written two books before *A Sport and a Pastime*. Remember, the Internet wasn't around, so such information was difficult to confirm. The story went further: Salter had hired someone to physically drive a station wagon through backwater used bookstores and buy up any copies of those early books and then burn them. Is this true? "I can't deny all these stories," Salter laughs. "I'll be left with nothing."

The truth is that Salter wrote two autobiographical novels about the Air Force in 1956 and 1961, respectively, *The Hunters* and *The Arm of Flesh*. Both were published by Harper Brothers. *The Hunters* sold quite well for a first novel, but his sophomore effort was a flop. Salter recently rewrote both for republication. He has also published a short story collection, *Dusk and Other Stories* (1998), a memoir *Burning the Days* in 1997, and now a second short story collection, *Last Night*. The new book is as elegant as anything Salter has written and his similes are to die for. In the first story alone, "Comet," a man so admires his new wife that "[h]e could have licked her palms like a calf does salt." This man is also "mannerly and elegant, his head held back a bit as he talked, as though you were a menu."

In person, Salter is also "mannerly and elegant," but he talks to you as if you were a patient whom he is coaxing to describe your symptoms. He asks as many questions about the interviewer as the interviewer asks about him. Salter himself only appears middle-aged, yet he is eighty years old. I suppose that makes him an "old man." Yet his vibe of vitality is so strong you still believe that his best work is yet to come.

Incidentally, when I drove to Salter's street my dignity kicked in. I turned around. I'd just wait for Salter's next book like everybody else.

David Bowman: Are you comfortable with your identity as a "writer's writer"?

James Salter: [Gives a dry chuckle.] Writers are the best readers. That's what that "writer's writer" means to me.

DB: One of the features of a writer's writer is that he is brilliant sentence by sentence.

JS: Sentences should not cause you to stop and admire them. They should be in the service of the page.

DB: Ah. "You have to kill your darlings."

JS: I think that was what I was trying to say—if the sentence is standing up to be admired.

DB: Have you ever abandoned a novel?

JS: Yes. I wrote a novel maybe five years ago. It was insufferable. Distance always helps. Somebody said, Mayakovsky maybe, "After you write a poem, put it in a drawer for at least a week."

DB: A good writer I know brags that he writes slowly sentence by sentence and never revises. The samurai method.

JS: William Styron says the same thing. He never goes to another page until that page is satisfactory. I don't think that works for me. If the page is not satisfactory, I just go on and come back later.

DB: What made you decide to rewrite your first two books?

JS: Jack Shoemaker, the publisher, had wanted to reprint both titles with matching spines. He finally persuaded me to revise the text. He was very persistent. Have you ever taught writing? The first book was like a student's work. I reread it and thought it was a mess. I liked it when I wrote it, but I didn't know anything back then. [Shrugs.] People get married and change their mind.

DB: It's strange to suddenly think of you as an ex-military man, a pilot.

JS: They're going to call you a pilot no matter what you do, but that had so little to do with my identity. In France—where I do all right—they keep referring to my experiences in the [Korean] war. Years from now are they still going to refer to Paris Hilton as the "former home video sex star"? I don't know.

DB: What if Paris Hilton suddenly revealed she possessed a secret intellect and began writing books with the razor-sharp prose of Joan Didion?

JS: Joan Didion! Jeez. Could she? You know, I've never even seen the celebrated Paris Hilton sex film. I don't know how to get it. I'd go into one of those video stores and they'd recognize me, and then where would I be?

DB: Your novel *Light Years* just won the Fadiman Medal (awarded by the New York Mercantile Library) fifteen years after it was written.

JS: That's gratifying. I've reread it. It's not bad. I was just thinking about the book this morning. I've only read a few books that got such overwhelmingly negative reviews as *Light Years.* Anatole Broyard, writing in the daily *New York Times*, said the book was "insulting to our patience and our expectations." Then in the *Sunday Times*, Robert Towers wrote such a well-written terrible review that even the publisher using ellipses couldn't find a few words to use. [Towers called it "an overwritten, chi-chi, and rather silly novel."] You don't just shrug reviews like those off. They are blows.

DB: How did your memoir *Burning the Days* come to be written?

JS: I wrote an autobiographical piece for *Esquire* called "The Captain's Wife." Joe Fox, my editor at Random House, read it and liked it, and urged me to write additional pieces that came from life. Gradually they assembled themselves into a book that can't be called autobiography. In fact, I didn't call it that. It's too damn incomplete—the book ended twenty years or more ago. I didn't want to call it "memoir." Even then [1997] that word had a certain pretension. So I called the book a "recollection."

DB: For the past twenty years have you felt like a short story writer?

JS: I felt like a writer. Short stories aren't very much different than other writing. They require different structure, but you still have to sit down to write them the same way. Most writers don't specialize [between novels and short stories], although they may have their forte. John Cheever, for instance, is probably more famed as a short story writer, but he wrote novels as well. Who else do we have? Hemingway, of course. It's only occasionally that you come across someone like Alice Munro or perhaps Lorrie Moore or maybe Grace Paley who seem to specialize or write only short stories. I know Shirley Hazzard, who's just won a big prize, talks about this very thing. She started writing short stories. Her first one was accepted by the *New Yorker*—by William Maxwell, famous editor and writer now gone—and the magazine accepted every story she sent in afterwards. Hers is like a fairy tale. What can I say? That's like going to paradise.

DB: Has the *New Yorker* ever turned you down?

JS: Oh, sure. Oh, certainly. As a matter of fact I take some pride in that. My previous book of short stories [*Dusk*] won the PEN/Faulkner Award. Nine of the eleven stories had been turned down by the *New Yorker*—and the two remaining stories I hadn't bothered sending to the *New Yorker* because I knew they'd turn them down.

DB: Do you get an idea for a short story on Monday and then write it on Friday? Or does it gnaw at you for a year or two?

JS: I may get it on Monday and write it on Friday, but there could be an interval of many years between that Monday and Friday. [Pause.] That's an interesting question. Short stories, sometimes you tear them out of the beak of life, so to speak. And sometimes they simply are lying there on the ground to pick up. You may have a certain idea for a story you have to tell, but the story didn't exist before because it wasn't lived by somebody else—you constructed it yourself. Some stories come completely assembled and ready to go. Otherwise it may be like one of those nightmare Christmas toys where they say "everything is included but the battery and assembly required." You may spend hours and hours feverishly trying to make something of it.

DB: Have you ever sat down and a complete story just poured out?

JS: Yes. There is one such story in this present book that was written in the morning. And that is "Bangkok." I had a start. I had two lines that someone had told me over the telephone—"Weren't you going to call me back?" "Of course not." I began with those two lines and just knew the rest of it. I knew the people. I was able to write the story.

DB: In *Burning the Days*, you mention the three essential stories of Isaac Babel to read: "Guy de Maupassant," "Dante Street," and "My First Goose." [I'd never read Babel before and the first two stories have changed my reading life!] If someone were to say, "Read these three stories of Salter's," what would they be?

JS: I can't answer that question because you mention Babel and that's completely out of my class. It's embarrassing. He is a genuinely great writer. He rewrote constantly. Revised and revised. The stories that read so effortlessly, that seem to have been written by an angel's pen, were probably struggled over for months. I'll recommend three stories in any case as long as there is no mention of Isaac Babel in the same breath. I think "American Express" in *Dusk*. In *Last Night*, I like "Comet." And I suppose, can I go back to the other book [*Dusk*]? I'd say, "Am Strande von Tanger." The title is pretentious, I know. I was in the phase where I thought, 'I'll floor them [the *New Yorker*] with this title!" It means "On the Beach in Tangier."

DB: Are there uncollected Salter short stories from some lost magazine?

JS: Not worth mentioning. They're just lying around. They refuse to come together. In short, broken pieces.

DB: Is a new novel finally in the works?

JS: I'm just starting. I don't have a purchase on it. I'm just doing preliminary stuff. If we were talking in architecture terms, I'm still excavating to lay the foundation.

DB: Don't readers complain, "Why haven't you written more books?"

JS: They mention that. But let's return to Shirley Hazzard for a moment. I notice that she hasn't written any more than I have. I think I'm being compared to too high a standard.

I flew down from Boston with John Updike yesterday. Here is a man who's written maybe fifty books—quite a few of them are really superb. I hardly know what to say. But maybe I spent a little more time kicking around than he did.

DB: Were you sitting side by side?

JS: Yes. It was wonderful. He's absolutely charming. Unpompous. I don't want to say "self-effacing," but he is an unspoiled man who knows a lot. He has a very welcoming and habitual style, which is in no way false. He's a bit shy. He doesn't begin wheeling out titles of his work or anything. You'd like him.

DB: Has Updike read you?

JS: Yes. At least one. He once wrote me a postcard.

DB: Which book did he read?
JS: *Light Years.*

DB: Was the card favorable? Wait. What a dumb question. "Dear Mr. Salter, Anatole Broyard was right. This book sucks."
JS: [Laughs.] That would be memorable too. But that's not his style.

DB: So in the end, do you feel that Hollywood ate up your life?
JS: It didn't eat up my life, but it ate up those years to a large extent. I really can't complain. I wasn't drafted. I wasn't shanghaied. I was earning a living. I enjoyed it. You always live in hope. You always say, "This fellow will be a terrific director. And this will be really a good film." And so forth. Even earlier you say, "I am going to write a wonderful script for this. It will be remembered." It's not like selling stuff on the sidewalk on 14th Street. You know John Updike just wrote an introduction to a book of Hollywood stories by Daniel Fuchs [*The Golden West: Hollywood Stories*]. Fuchs is quoted saying something to the effect of "I managed to get my name on ten films, one of which was a hit." This is in forty years. Think of this for a moment. "I managed to get my name on ten films." And it wasn't only his name. It might be Daniel Fuchs and Edward Barnett, or something. Whatever. And the film he cited is a movie you've never heard of. Even despite his optimism, it's pathetic. It's so pathetic you feel like turning away and saying, "For Christ's sake, Fuchs, get a grip."

DB: You know they say, "History is written by the victors"? Well, that's wrong. History is written by writers.
JS: And writers and former screenwriters have written most of the histories of Hollywood—thus the prejudice that writing hasn't been accorded its due of importance. [Sighs.] Writers can go on bleating and bleating, but it's not going to change things. The film belongs to the actor—the face you see on the screen. Everybody else is subordinate. There are some cases where the director's imprint is so powerful, if you happen to be educated you know something about the director, but for the hundreds of millions who delight in these movies, it's the actor they're interested in.

DB: Or George Lucas special effects. [Pause.] Here is a personal question. Your writing is constantly sexual, often directly autobiographical in your nonfiction or else sideways autobiographical in your fiction. And you've said that your wife is your first reader. It must be very difficult writing about the women you knew before you met her. Doesn't that inhibit you? "What will Kay think when she reads this?"

JS: There is a danger in that, of course. There may be some jealousy and things unexpressed, but these things still rankle her. In general, I think we can assume women do not like to hear about other previous women. I don't know what to say. If it is clearly not fiction, think it over before you write it.

Interview with James Salter

Robert Franden / 2007

From Harry Ransom Center, The University of Texas at Austin. Reprinted courtesy of Harry Ransom Center.

Ransom Center Advisory Council Member Robert Franden recently spoke with author James Salter about his archive, his writing process, and his acclaimed book *Light Years*.

Robert Franden: What do you think the significance of having your archive at some place like the Ransom Center is?
James Salter: Well, I mean, it's very flattering to me. After all, you have people like . . . Last night I was talking to Sam Radin?

RF: Right.
JS: Is that his name?

RF: Yes.
JS: He was a collector of Evelyn Waugh himself. I mean, you have Evelyn Waugh in the Ransom Center. That's an astonishing thing. A significant English writer, and here's Austin, way out of the, what can I say, great circle intellectual route. You wouldn't expect to come to Austin to find Waugh's stuff, and in addition, you have everybody else. I don't have a list in front of me, but I know you have the A-list, going right up your arm. So to be in such company, it doesn't signify anything more than that they feel that some of your manuscripts or whatever are worth preserving. It's self-evident.

RF: I was actually asking from the standpoint of thinking, is it interesting to you that people are now going to be looking at the pieces of your life very closely as to how you went about doing what you do so very well?
JS: Well, I think you're assuming there's going to be some scholarly or writ-

erly interest in it. That may happen, I really don't know. But I'm not making that assumption.

RF: [. . .] I'm aware that you've been interviewed in the past, and so much has been written about you. And people refer to you quite often as a "writer's writer," and that's a term you don't like particularly [. . .]. But I assume they're talking about the state of your craft as something that writers ought to pay attention to. What do you think about that?

JS: Well, I think that writers are fabulous readers, generally. That is to say, astute, perceptive readers. And to be a writer that such readers like to read speaks for itself. I don't dislike it because of any implication that you're only read by writers. I don't like it because it's a cliché. One person wrote it and somebody read it and said, "Ah, that's it." And they begin calling you that ever after. I suppose it's accurate, but I don't like to think it's definitive. That's all.

You know, I've never had a truly popular book. And lacking that is what makes me hesitant to say I belong there or I think I'm as good as so-and-so. I think, well, it's just something that I'm not prepared to argue. I think if I ever write one [a popular book]—seems a little late, but you never can tell. I'm working on a book. The thing about writing, of course, is—it's like Napoleon's dictum that every soldier carries a marshal's baton in his knapsack. And as a writer, you have the same possibilities. You always have the possibility until the quill falls from your fingers of writing something good. It's never the ninth inning, the end of the ninth, so to speak.

RF: Well, the archive that we have at the Ransom Center obviously we think is very important, and we do think people will come to study your craft because you are considered by many very, very thoughtful people to be a great craftsman. And I was wondering if you could talk a little bit about how you write. As you go through the archive, of course, people will see how you—the process and the many drafts and the many notes, and what have you, I wondered if you could describe that and maybe talk about, is it different for a novel, a short story, a screenplay? Or is the process pretty much the same?

JS: First of all, let me say that most writers, almost all, will give the same answer to this question. Most of them have difficulty and sometimes demoralization writing a first draft, but then having got the whole thing together, begin to work on it and make something of it. Beyond that, the mechanical things of—do you write on a yellow tablet, with a pencil the way William Styron wrote, or do you write on a computer the way Updike writes, or do you write on an IBM Selectric the way John Irving does, who happens to have three or four of them around the house so whenever he sits down, he's near one, I think these things are really of relatively little importance.

RF: I wasn't really as curious about that as I was like, for instance, the novel: Do you first outline the novel? Do you have the storyline pretty well set?

JS: Well, let me speak for myself here because here you're going to get different answers from different writers. I, in principle, try and outline the novel before I begin so I know how it's going to end and generally, what path it's going to take. But, of course, having done that, I'm at perfect liberty to deviate from it. You're not going to be judged on loyalty to the original outline, but rather what you end up with. So I do make an outline—that's for a novel, which, after all is a . . . I don't want to emphasize its size, but one can get lost. One can wander around a while as if in the woods not knowing exactly which way to go. For a short story, which is more demanding in terms of how much you can digress and also is much more . . . You're able to visualize the whole thing in your imagination. Virtually. You don't have the details, but you know what the story is. You don't really need an outline. I don't make one. What else is there? Well, for a film—well, I haven't written films for a long time, but I used to make an outline for those. Generally not scene-by-scene, just a few lines to know where you were going. A good film writer named William Goldman once defined it as saying that a film was structure and that you had to have the end scene in mind when you began because your structure was leading to that. That's not the only way of defining what a film script is, but it fits my conception of it. Generally, when I wrote the films, that was the way I did it. One difficulty with writing films is the waste. You write a lot, and only a limited amount, if you're lucky, ever reaches the stage of being filmed or on the screen itself. And sometimes your work that you think is your best work ends up unread or unused. I think that's a very high price to pay.

RF: And you no longer do screenplays, as I—
JS: I haven't done it for a long time—

RF: By choice, as I—
JS: By choice. Well, I couldn't be hired now anyway, but that has nothing to do with it. I wouldn't be if I could be. But often you'll find, I think, that movie writers become demoralized over time. Cynical. And in part, I think it's due to what I've just said. And another part, of course, is due to what they're

paid. There's a disconnect between them and other writers, except for the very top bestsellers. Most writers work for relatively little. It's not a thing you go into to make money. But there's a big disconnect—a screenwriter can do very, very well. And we're living in an age of tremendous disconnect anyway.

RF: Let's get back to how you write; you mentioned how you outline. I looked at the makeup board, if you will, for *Life Is Meals*, a large cardboard [piece] with stickies and colored dots and what have you, and it was amazingly well organized.

JS: Well, remember, that was a particular—

RF: I do understand that, but I wondered if I could extrapolate from you that you are a fairly organized person when it comes to putting your work together.

JS: In my wife's view, I am very organized. In my own, I would say there are some gaps.

RF: In the process, then, you know, you get organized and you start writing, and the question always that arises, what is the pivotal structure? Is it the sentence, the paragraph, you know, the chapter, what have you? How do you view that?

JS: Well, I try and finish chapters. You'd be a fool to be excited by a sentence, and a paragraph is really not that much better, although sometimes you feel a certain sense of warmth, having written a paragraph that seems to be close to what you had hoped.

RF: [. . .] Nabokov's *Speak, Memory*, for instance, is a book in addition to *Light Years* that I give as gifts because I can delight in a sentence in both your work and his. And I know you wrote one time that the sentence has to be in the service of the greater product, something like that. But is it not okay to delight in that sentence? And say, "Boy, that is good!"

JS: I think that's a little like looking in the mirror as you pass the entrance hall. Don't waste your time.

RF: [Laughs.] No, but I mean for the reader, is it not okay?

JS: Well, for the reader, it's okay. But remember that sentence is in the service of something larger. And so I don't count that as being a particular strength or virtue. I think it's the opposite. I had a tendency—I'm trying to work past it—I had a tendency to try and write such sentences. But I no longer want to do that. I'd rather—

RF: Is that a retreat from lyricism or something?

JS: Well, I think that's very apt. Yes, I'd like to back off from that.

RF: So, in looking back, do you consider *Light Years* too lyrical?

JS: Well, it's very lyrical. And it was damned for that when it came out. In fact, it was killed at birth for that very reason. It was said that the lyricism was unearned. I mean, you know, you really shouldn't ask me that question. But on the other hand, I've reread parts of it not long ago because Richard Ford wrote a recent introduction—not here, it's in Penguin Classics in England, and I read his introduction a couple of times, really a terrific piece of work. And then I read parts of the book and said to myself, "Yes, it's lyrical, but I love to read this." I don't know, it's too early for me to decide. I leave that up to the reader. I think it's been forgiven, in a certain sense, by people who have some critical judgment. "Forgiven" is not the right word. I think its lyricism has been accepted and understood in the context of the book. It won the Fadiman Medal about three or four years ago, which is a prize given for novels fifteen years old or more that deserve a renewed attention. And Penguin Classics, which rarely, only in a couple of cases, publishes the works of living writers, took it as one of theirs just a month ago or two months ago. So, I'd say that's been a very contentious . . . a point that has been criticized and unaccepted by certain readers. On the other hand, I know there are a number who feel that that's the glory of the book.

RF: Well, that leads then to another question that I wanted to ask you. How does one handle criticism? Like you indicated, there were a couple of writers, I know, when *Light Years* first came out, that did not review it well. And then also the concomitance of that perhaps might be the rejection, when you get rejected. How do you handle those? How does that affect James Salter?

JS: Well, just the way you would feel getting your nose bloodied in court. I mean, it's certainly not pleasant. And you say, "Does this mean that I'm no good really?" or "Is it just one of those things that happens?"

RF: The reason I ask that—

JS: The writer is as human as anybody else. And probably a little more sensitive because he or she has spent so long preparing this and hoping that it's going to be good. And then to have somebody slap you in the face is, you know, not pleasant.

RF: Well, I had something else I was curious about. After, you know, the product is completed and what have you, and you now have put the final period there, how involved do you become in the stylization of what you're doing: the print, the size of the book—
JS: You're speaking of the book itself.

RF: Yeah, the dust jacket. I mean, how—
JS: Well, it depends on your editor, your relationship with the editor, your importance as a writer, and a number of other things. I've had a variety of experiences, depending on the book and the publisher. Sometimes if the publisher is particularly cordial and likes you, Jack Shoemaker, for instance, who ran North Point Press for about ten years, it was probably the most eminent of the small, independent houses. Apart from New Directions. And Jack would say, "What do you think? How should we do this?" or "What should be on the jacket?" You don't do the design of the book, of course. It would be a rare writer who had the know-how to say, "This is how many pieces of lead should be between the lines—"

RF: No, no, no.
JS: —but when they show you a sample page or two, which they may, depending on your relationship, you may say, "The margin at the bottom, it runs too close to the bottom." Or, "These lines seem to be a little close together. They make it difficult to read." But I don't know. If you're a publisher, this is going to be a pain in the ass, isn't it? "You mean we have to talk to that person? About what the book's going to look like? Forget it." So, one of my closest friends was Joe Fox, who was an editor at Random House, the editor of *Light Years*, as a matter of fact. Fox would not dream of wasting his time consulting with you about these things. He'd say, "It'll look great. Don't worry about it."

RF: Speaking of *Light Years*, would you talk about *Light Years* a little bit? Tell me how the idea for *Light Years* came about.
JS: I don't recall exactly. There was a period in my life when we lived on the Hudson River, or close to it, upriver from New York City. About half an hour up. And we had certain friends, and it was the first civilian period of my life. I'd gotten out of the service, and it was like, I don't know, your first

years when you're out of college, or something. It was all new. The people were different. Life was different. And we had one particular couple that we were very close to who were essentially the model for the couple in the book. And of course when I say "model," you understand that you take liberties. You make an effort to make these people a little more—what can I say?—a little more exalted. A little more interesting than perhaps they were in life. However, I was thinking of them one day, I suppose it'd been in my mind for a while, and suddenly it began to take form. I do remember this: I sat down and started writing. I remember I thought, "I'd like to write a book, but not a Tolstoyan book about the backgrounds of people and how it all came about and what happened to them." In short, not a carefully plotted social novel of the late nineteenth century and the first half of the twentieth, of which I had read many examples and was brought up on. I thought I'd like to do something a little different. I'd like to write a book that was only the things you remember from all that, that stand out from it all, that life is really composed of. Things that people said, certain moments. You don't remember all the stuff in between. That has to be invented or reconstructed anyway. And starting from that premise, which I later saw reiterated in something that Jean Renoir said, that the only things in life that matter are the things you remember. That's self-evident in a way. If you've forgotten them, they can't be very important. Unless you forgot them on purpose. You remember the things that are important. I thought I'd like to write a book with that as the pattern of it and leave out all the rest. I thought, "Now that's an original idea." It may not be. I really don't know. But I was pleased with the idea, and I sat down one day, I remember, and wrote down what I thought those things should be. There were, I don't know, about thirty-five or forty-five of them, and those essentially became the chapters of the book and then the book itself.

RF: In that book, I think it's Viri who says, "There are really two kinds of life. There is . . . the one people believe you are living, and there is the other. It is this other which causes the trouble . . ."
JS: Yes.

RF: And then, at the very end of the book, he's standing there at the shore of the river, and he says, "I am ready" and what have you.
JS: Yes.

RF: And I've often wondered if that "Now I am ready," "Am I ready now to"—

to try, to take away that distance between the is and the are, in other words, the life that people see me living and the life that I am living. I mean, it—
JS: Well, I don't object to that, but that's not what I had in mind.

RF: I'm sure I—
JS: I mean, what the author has in mind, in a sense, can be irrelevant because the book is what it is. And things people think about books later—books worthy of talking about, often things people ascribe to them were not intended at all. Or the author was unaware of what he or she was writing. No, I didn't mean it that way. I meant it, you know, I wish we had the book here, I'd like to just scan the last pages quickly, but I believe what happens is his marriage had broken up, his children are grown, I think his wife has died—his ex-wife—by this time, he's gone abroad, he married another woman—a woman devoted to him, but very ordinary in many ways compared to the glories of this difficult woman he had—difficult, but rather marvelous, the woman he had been married to. And now he returns to the old house, for no particular reason. He's not restoring it or anything. He happens to be wandering there. And I think he sees a turtle on the shell of which they had scratched their names years before, and here's this tortoise. I mean, it was twenty years before, making its way through the leaves. Have you ever seen that? I'm sure you have, the way they move along, and his life has moved along, and there's the river. People have said to me, "Did he kill himself?" Well, that's the farthest thing from my mind. I mean, I don't think that's implied or signified. I think he's saying in a metaphysical way, that he's ready to face and to acknowledge the whole thing. To be part of it, even in this third act, a part of it. "I've always been ready, but I am really ready," is what I think he's saying. But as I've just said, you don't have to find that. And maybe it's not there for some readers. You know, it's a poetic book, it's a lyrical book, there's a poetic line at the end. If you get it the way it was intended, fine. If you don't, well . . .

RF: Well, the way you stated it is the way it actually reads. "I have always been ready. I am ready now—"
JS: I am ready at last.

RF: Yeah, "ready at last." Once you read things several times, you say, "Gee, I wonder if I have that right." So that's why I wanted to ask you.
JS: On the other hand, I really shouldn't have gone this far into it because when you start doing it, certain lines don't bear that kind of inspection and

examination. You have to take them whole, so to speak and accept them. Otherwise, it's like the English class where they're saying, "What are the motives behind Hardy's repetition?" Then you know, you're saying, "Let me out of this class."

RF: Well, we take it whole and accept it, and by that I mean your archive, we're thrilled to have it.
JS: Thank you.

RF: We're certainly thrilled to have you numbered among our authors. Thanks very much for your time this afternoon.
JS: It's a pleasure. Thank you.

An Interview with James Salter

Kevin Rabalais / 2010

From *Brick* 87 (Summer 2011), 79–87. © Kevin Rabalais. Reprinted with permission.

Kevin Rabalais interviewed James Salter in New Orleans on November 9, 2010.

KR: In *Burning the Days*, you write about beginning your literary life while still in the Air Force: "I had three lives," you write, "one during the day, one at night, and the last in a drawer in my room in a small book of notes." What did you hope to achieve with *The Hunters*?

JS: I hoped that it would be published. And I hoped it would be well known but that the writer of it would be unknown. I had some idea of anonymity at the time. Beyond that, I knew the novel was accurate and I knew there was nothing written quite like it.

KR: What were you learning about craft, about the novel as a form during the writing of that first novel?

JS: The book speaks for itself. I hadn't written a novel before that. You know, looking back it seems that it was easy to write because there it is, all on the page. People talk. Events and situations are described. But if you've never written before, you simply don't know how to go about it. When you sit down as a young person or an untried person and you think, "Here's the paper. Now begin," then what happens? It's more complicated than you would think. I can't reconstruct it for you because now I know how to go about it, and it's hard to find again that ignorance, that innocence, that heightened state of being confounded. You would say, probably, that sounds a little disingenuous, because, after all, when you read a book, there it is. Once you know how to put it together, the puzzle loses its power. You've already taken it apart. You know how to put it back together again. It may take you a little more time to do it, but you know it can be done.

KR: How did having written *The Hunters* prepare you for writing your second novel, *The Arm of Flesh*?
JS: It didn't prepare me.

KR: How so?
JS: I had written *The Hunters* with parental pride, and also it was praised by critics and the publisher was very pleased. It sold copies. Then the publisher said, "Now let's have another one." And I had no idea what to do. I was very impressed with *As I Lay Dying*, and I had the idea that if I wrote a book like that nobody would notice that it was really modeled on Faulkner's novel. The difference, of course, is that Faulkner's novel is fabulous, and I wasn't able to ever get mine to really do its job. I think it's a poor book. It's self-involved, self-indulgent. In the end, I didn't like it, and I didn't want to have it reprinted later on. So I rewrote it to try to correct it, and maybe that did some good.

KR: What was that process like—rewriting *The Arm of Flesh* as *Cassada*?
JS: It was like getting a novel from a writing student. You can see immediately that there was a lot wrong with it, and you're just making red marks on the paper.

KR: What wasn't working?
JS: There were too many characters. They were not well defined. The impudence of thinking that you could merely write in technical terms, that is to say about flying, and people would understand it or be fascinated enough to attempt to understand it: that was something that was ill thought out. Also, things had to be added to make the characters more interesting. They were simply too briefly and too lightly sketched.

KR: You also revised *The Hunters* around a similar time.
JS: I only fiddled with it.

KR: Between those first books and your third, *A Sport and a Pastime*, there is a huge shift in voice and subject matter. What kind of risk was *A Sport and a Pastime* for you?
JS: This is about four or five years after I had written a first book. By this time, I had been reading a little, and I had grown up a little, you might say. I didn't think of it as a risk. I thought that finally I was doing the right thing. You're attempting to find, in some way at the beginning, an unmediated

voice, to be able to write down what you really want to write down. Somehow with that novel, I had crossed that line, I think, and was able to write in that way. Also, I had a subject that was compelling for me. It was about France. I had been there before. I always liked it, and this time I spent about ten or eleven months there. It was in Chaumont, in small-town France, and I had an opportunity to really observe and to see the detail of life, which is what makes the book. Well, a number of things make the book. It's sexual, but it's also a series of poems to provincial France. I had read Henry Miller by then. It's hard to remember that his books had to be smuggled into the United States. *Tropic of Cancer* was a legendary book, but you couldn't get it. College girls used to pack it in their underwear to bring it through customs. I am nothing like Henry Miller either as a person or a writer, but I admired very much his really fabulous freedom and iconoclasm, his poetic sense. I took a cue from that. I listened to that note and said, "I could probably sing in that key if I tried." And I had the subject for it. That was really the story of the book. For myself, I feel that's the first real book I wrote.

KR: Do you remember the initial spark for *A Sport and a Pastime*?
JS: Of course. It's patterned after real people and, naturally, a girl I knew. I had a lot of notes that I liked to read. That was the spark of it. I thought I would like them probably even more if they were given their full shape, and that's what happened. There is a certain amount of calculation in writing a book, maybe not if you're an impassioned, wild person, but otherwise there's construction in it. The book is a contraption, and you're making it work.

KR: Did *A Sport and a Pastime* begin with the character, with Anne-Marie?
JS: Yes, of course. That was central to the book. When they talk about *A Sport and a Pastime*, they're always talking about the narrator and the unreliable narrator, the curiosity of this person. As is often the case, what you intended, what you thought you were doing, is not what you have at the end. When I started thinking about writing it, I made some preliminary attempts. I wrote some pages, and they seemed offensive to me. I didn't like the tone. It seemed smutty. I thought, This is not going to work, and for some reason, I can remember when it happened, I hit on this idea for the narrator. I was with a friend, and I said to him, "What would you think of a book where the story is described by a narrator who is not off-handed about it, but he stands back from the story in a way and says that he's really making it all up and not to believe all of it?" The friend showed very little interest in the idea, but

that didn't bother me. I then tried writing from the point of view of someone in the book—not me, not the writer—but someone who disclaims complete truthfulness so as to put the whole story one step removed from realism. And I wrote some of that and said, "Yes. I think that's it."

KR: What technical problems did *A Sport and a Pastime* present that you hadn't encountered in the previous novels?
JS: I think the quality of the writing, if you can call that a technical problem. I wanted to be able to write more admirably than I had before.

KR: The voice of *A Sport and a Pastime* is markedly different from your first two novels. How did you hit on that voice?
JS: It was a question of getting rid of the mediation, of throwing off any inhibition of writing.

KR: Is there anything typical about the way your books or stories begin?
JS: They tend to begin in different ways. I don't have a formula. If I did, I would have written many more books.

KR: When you were writing *Solo Faces*, you wrote a letter to Robert Phelps, published in *Memorable Days*, noting there would be "No Fine Writing."
JS: There was a book before that, a book called *Light Years* that, when it came out, was damned for a lot of fine writing, meaning unmerited poetic writing. It was absolutely savaged. I said, "Well, I don't want to do that again. Let's move away from that." And the subject matter of *Solo Faces* called for something else, called for a more—for want of a better word—*masculine* tone. You will probably find more in the letters than what I'm giving you now. The letters were written at the time and to someone I was completely open with. I naturally wanted Phelps to admire me. I don't mean in a false way. I wanted his respect. I told him the absolute truth.

KR: *Light Years* begins in the first-person plural and then makes the transition to a more traditional third-person narrative. What brought about that point-of-view shift?
JS: It's hard to write the beginning of anything. Sometimes you have to write for a while, and then you find the beginning. In this case, I thought, I'm going to write about the river—most of the novel takes place in a house near the Hudson. You don't want to be constrained by the idea of "Their house was near the river" or "The river was wide and glistening." The third person

seemed pedestrian to me. So I thought, Let's get out there and kick it a little and see what happens.

KR: Was that a case where your first drafts of the beginning became the opening chapter of the published novel? Has that happened with other books?

JS: Usually I'm able to find the beginning. I wasn't able to find the beginning in *A Sport and a Pastime*. A lot of times I wrote without ever finding anything that was in the least interesting to me. You want to in some way to approve of what you have written. You yourself want to approve of it. In the early stages of *A Sport and a Pastime*, I was unable to do that. Finally, we got on the train. I don't remember how that happened, but that's the way it happened.

KR: In another letter to Phelps, you write, "You must write as if it were a letter to someone you love. . . . You must write without an audience, without thought of being read."

JS: Oh, that's some young guy going on. You have to somehow get it down *truly*, to use Hemingway's word. That's the same thing. You want it to ring true in a way that is peculiar to you. Nobody is going to quite write the way you do. I was reading Trollope the other day. We're still reading him. He wrote dozens of novels. He wrote them three or four pages a day, in longhand, and when you read them, you think, There's nobody who writes quite like that. What is it? Well, it's his voice. It's what he chooses to describe and how. You're not going to be Trollope. You can't be. He's already done that. And you're not going to be him even if you try. But you're trying to be whoever you are. . . . I think this is veering off into the self-indulgent. Sometimes you're able to get it and sometimes not. Saul Bellow's letters were reviewed in the *New York Times* today. I knew Bellow very well. He was a friend. I have some of his letters, and I read that book of letters in galley. The letters go on about what a novel should do and what was wrong with American novels and what he felt the American novel should be. That's all very well and good, but in the long run, I think you read Bellow for the same reason that you read anybody. You read him because of the life in his books, and the way he sees that life and describes it in a manner that nobody else can really do, and his voice just comes through. There's such a huge chorus out there—all these books written in the past and being written now and those that will arrive in another month or year. There are fifteen thousand voices out there all going at once, but Bellow's is special for some reason. Ah! You listen. You hear it clearly. Popularity is no accident.

KR: You've talked about voice being what we're attracted to in a writer. If you're browsing in a bookstore, say, and you're reading the beginning passages of novels, what draws you in?

JS: I think that's indescribable. I would say it's like judging anything else, judging singers or dancers or horses, for that matter. After a time, you know something about it and you have a certain sense of discrimination. You can judge it and say, "That's pretty good" or "No, no. Next."

KR: Back to your own work: *Solo Faces* has a different biography from your other novels in that it began as a screenplay. Then, at your editor's suggestion, you turned the screenplay into a novel. What did that process entail?

JS: After I stopped writing films or having anything to do with them, I rejected them. I'm over that now, but I had contempt for screenwriters—that's probably self-contempt, among other things—and thought if anybody knew that I had written this as a script and turned it into a novel, then they would look at it with scorn and without really attaching any possibility to it. I didn't want to make it known or have it appear that it had anything to do with the movies. Now I know differently. Having lived another decade or two, I recognize that you're really the handmaiden of movies and screenwriting. I wouldn't have that problem now.

KR: What do you mean by that?

JS: I would say that movies are in a higher cultural position than literature, which was formerly not the case.

KR: What has the influence of cinema been on your writing?

JS: It's hard for me to say. I think in a way it's been a liberating influence.

KR: What do you think your work as a screenwriter and filmmaker taught you about writing fiction?

JS: They're entirely different things. A script is a structure, really. It has very little description. It's almost all dialogue and description of action. Those are its obligations, unless you're dealing with really arty stuff by auteur directors who are willing to make beautiful films that critics talk about but that nobody ever sees and that certainly don't make any money. Those scripts would be something different. I wrote a couple of those, but they were never made. The usual thing is you have to write a script that *grabs* people, which is something that is usually a little foreign to my impulses.

KR: You've said that you make outlines for your novels. Despite having an idea of where the story is heading, what surprises have the novels brought? With *Light Years*, for instance, did you know the beginning, middle, and end before you started writing?

JS: The book is divided into two-thirds and one-third. Two-thirds of it is when Nedra and Viri are together, and maybe one-third of it afterwards. I had more specific ideas about the first two-thirds than I did about the final third. As I remember, I discovered what the final third should be from what preceded it. But I may have had an outline for the whole thing, I don't remember. I was writing this book about the time my own marriage really was irretrievable. I just quickly wrote down on some scrap paper about twenty or thirty situations or events or people that I thought stood out in one's memory of married life. I jotted down all of those things as if you were forced to abandon your home. You were fleeing from it in the face of some calamity—flood, enemy fire, I don't know. There were a few things you could throw into a suitcase and take with you. Those were more or less the things I was thinking illuminated a marriage, what you remembered, and that's the way the book was constructed.

KR: Unlike your novels, you don't make outlines for your short stories. What are some of the other differences between writing stories and novels?

JS: With a short story, of course, you can more or less keep the outline in your head. You can only keep the general flow of the novel in your head. You can't keep all the details. So, it's easier to approach a short story. My wife was asking me this morning about this. She's writing short stories. What makes them good? First of all, the definition of the short story is difficult. Rust Hills used to say that a short story is a story in which something happens to someone. That's probably as good as any of them. You have to have someone, and I suppose that can be not-someone, it can be an insect, as in Lafcadio Hearn, or it might even be something inanimate, like a rock, but something has to happen. There has to be some point to you hearing this. Mere description really doesn't qualify as a short story. You might admire it. You might even remember it, but it's not going to move you very much. Something has to happen. Beyond that, there's no formula. It's like searching amid the rubble for diamonds. Most of what you find will turn out to be clay or imperfect. Even the masters, even someone like Babel had tons of drafts of stories, notebooks, copies of this and that. They weren't finished yet. He wasn't satisfied with them. They didn't work out. Most people have the same human problems you do. I think it's rare to find somebody who can actually sit down and write a short story and then for an editor to say, "We have to have two by tomorrow," and for the writer to be able to produce them. That would be difficult. We're talking about good ones. You more or less have to stumble across them.

KR: Can you talk about one of your stories, such as "American Express" or "Platinum," as an example? How many drafts did those stories go through? How long do you work on a story?

JS: Some of them come out more quickly, more readily than others. "American Express," well, I don't remember how many drafts, but that's a long story. It has a number of details in it that had to be—for want of a better word—gathered, laid out to see if they fit in the story. I knew what the story was, but I didn't know how to present it. So I probably wrote sections of it a number of times. The other story, "Platinum," there I knew the same thing, too. I had difficulty in figuring out how the girlfriend would get the earrings. The rest of the story seemed to me to be imaginable. Maybe a mystery writer could do it more easily.

KR: The girlfriend—the mistress—sees the earrings, which belong to her lover's wife, on the marital dresser and asks if she can borrow them. Do you remember how you reached that point?

JS: Brooding about it during the washing of dishes.

KR: Your two most recent works of fiction—*Dusk* and *Last Night*—are works of short fiction. What attracts you to that form?

JS: I didn't have a larger idea.

KR: You've written that Babel had what you consider the three essentials of greatness: style, structure, and authority.

JS: Style is voice, essentially. Authority is partly voice. And without those things, no writer can make a claim to being alive to me.

KR: Near the end of *Burning the Days*, you write, "Art, in a sense, is life brought to a standstill, rescued from time. The secret of making it is simple: discard everything that is good enough." What is your editing process?

JS: Be strict with yourself.

KR: What are you still learning about writing?

JS: I don't think much. In the end, it becomes a matter of energy and, of course, in time you develop a certain cynicism. That's probably not appealing. It's more a question of those things than it is of discovering any technique, any new method or approach. After a while, you know most of those things. You know that dialogue is a good way to get out of a ditch. Or that a troublesome section might best be approached by not describing everything but maybe focusing on the light, on color like Matisse, on sounds, on something else. These are all merely the use of techniques. They don't mean that much. You're trying to write down what you really in your heart meant to write.

In the Light Where Art and Longing Meet: My Day with James Salter

Sonya Chung / 2010

From *Tin House* 50 (Winter 2011). © Sonya Chung. Reprinted with permission. Sonya Chung is the author of the novel *Long for This World*.

I disembark the train at Bridgehampton on the coldest morning yet this winter. As I make my way down the platform, tote bags full of his books, I spot him, standing at the top of the stairs, hands in pockets, shoulders squared, wearing dark sunglasses. I wave a hand, but he remains still. Embarrassed, I fix my eyes on the concrete, hurrying toward him. When I come within a few feet, I see that he's relaxed his posture, and we each reach out a gloved hand. "Well," he says, doing a kind of mock grouchy-old-man, "it must be you."

A year after my first correspondence with James Salter, we are finally meeting. Later that night, when I return to New York City for a faculty holiday party, my colleagues and I will laugh as a few share crushing stories of encounters with elder writers whom they'd admired: venerable poet X grumble-coughing at one young poet after he'd expressed affection for a particular poem; novelist Y drunkenly scolding a (now Pulitzer Prize-winning) essayist for interrupting his intermission at the ballet.

But James Salter is nothing but polite, if a bit subdued, as he drives me the quarter mile from the station to his Hamptons home. Behind the wheel of an old compact Benz that seems as fitting to his person as his wool pants and navy blue parka, he asks me about the train ride and comments on the weather. It occurs to me only later, on the dark ride back to the city, that he may have been as nervous as I was.

The house is a simple, light-drenched cottage that he and his wife, Kay, built in 1985, after renting a few different houses in the area. (These were the early years of his second life, with a second wife twenty-some years his junior.) It is a house in which I feel immediately comfortable—spacious but thoughtfully proportioned, tidy but not immaculate. The walls are lined with bookshelves, but not all of them, and not in the imperious way I've seen in other writers' homes, as if the books preside over the people.

Kay Salter appears, fresh and brisk, and welcomes me with a smile and handshake. She is a warm host, taking my coat, offering tea, asking me about my novel and my teaching. A journalist and playwright, Kay tells me that she is working on her first novel and that she commutes to the city often, as she will this morning, making use of a pied-à-terre as a writing office. "So he can have the solitude here," she says, and I remember something from an interview about his preferring a completely empty house.

> *Thanks very much for your essay, which I just read, a bit late—apparently we're deeper in the woods here than I thought . . .*
>
> *I agree with the comments about Hemingway always writing about sex, or something to that effect, meaning it was a subtext. He wrote a startlingly sensual English, very male and very sensual, alive to the senses, and sex, as we like to call it, is sensationally alive, both in the flesh and/or in the mind. I don't like Hemingway, in part because he looms and also I don't like the man. He's a type you run into.*
>
> *Women have more or less tipped the cart over—you probably don't realize that because you're, I assume, just a kid—and some confusion is the result. I don't mean that it shouldn't have been tipped, there is no should or shouldn't. I always liked Robert Phelps's citation—he must have been quoting someone—first the flesh, then the spirit.*
>
> *Again, with thanks. JS*

We sit down to tea and talk for a while without pencil or paper, the digital recorder I've borrowed switched to the off position and nestled in a fold of the tablecloth between us. "Oh let's not start that," he'd said, "we're just getting warmed up, we're going to talk about you for a bit." He asks about my book, how is it going with sales and so forth. I demur, not wanting to bore him with debut-novelist drama, though he nods gravely, knowing better than I the frustrations of literary publishing—having bounced from publisher to publisher over the years and bearing the "writers' writer" label that must over time start to feel like a branding of one's hide. The subject moves to teaching, which he did in spurts in the '80s at Iowa, Williams, and Alabama. "It can be enjoyable, but it was a lot of work; you earn your money. I don't want to discourage you, I mean, it was glorious—the students were interesting, I met many writers, [Frank] Conroy brought everyone [to Iowa]. But your own writing? There was precious little writing going on. And that, in the end, is what you're graded on."

I notice a few books stacked at the end of the table and ask how he decides what to read these days. "These days? Well, let's see . . . these days." He says this in a way that makes clear his age—eighty-five years, with attendant fatigue—is central to "these days." We talk briefly about Ivana Lowell's memoir ("This is a good book"); essays by M. F. K. Fisher ("Not as good as I remember them"); and a library copy of Junot Diaz's *The Brief Wondrous Life of Oscar Wao*. I ask him what he thinks of Diaz's novel, and he says, "We were at the Institute Alliance Française for a panel on Jean Genet, and across the street there was a line all the way around the block. We asked the people—mostly young people—what they were waiting for, and they said Junot Diaz was speaking. That was impressive."

> *It's awfully kind of you to write. I am thirty-seven years old, so am not sure if that qualifies as a kid these days. I teach a fiction workshop . . . and I notice that a certain phobia of physical-sensual writing has crept in for literary women—a bubble-wrapping of their intellectually perceptive, emotionally remote female protagonists from sex, really anything sensual; as if the full-force entry of women into intellectual life has come at the expense of bodies. I like Tan Dun's words: "If you are too sophisticated, you lose courage."*
>
> *Re: Hemingway, and in general, I am interested in how or whether you think the quality of the man and the quality of the work are related. And what "very male" means in writing, or "very female" for that matter. I've been thinking about this a lot.*

The essay was called "Sex, Seriously: James Salter Trumps the Great Male Novelists." Published in the online magazine *The Millions*, it was, ostensibly, my response to a *New York Times Sunday Book Review* essay by Katie Roiphe, "The Naked and the Conflicted," in which she asserts that our twenty-first-century young literary men have lost their sense of sexual potency; that is, their belief in the power of sexuality to ignite, and to immortalize. "[I]nnocence is more fashionable than virility, the cuddle preferable to sex," Roiphe wrote. "Rather than an interest in conquest or consummation, there is an obsessive fascination with trepidation, and with a convoluted, postfeminist second-guessing." Her observations resonated, and I argued in my response that we should look not to Roth/Bellow/Mailer/Updike (Roiphe's touchstones) for this lost potency, but rather to Salter.

The book—*A Sport and a Pastime*—appeared in our apartment about five years ago. My partner, J., reported that a friend of his, a frustrated corporate writer, had given him two of Salter's books (the other was *Light Years*), saying, This is the kind of writer I want to be, and endowing them with a kind of tragic longing. J. seemed to avoid the books as if they were contagious; I decided I had to read them.

It's been said of John Cheever that, as a teacher, he had one of two words for you when he read your work: Yes or No. With *Sport*, for me, there wasn't much else to say but Yes. Even more striking was the sense while I read that I should be repulsed, that it was a book I should find objectionable. As a woman. This is pornographic. This is misogynistic. But I did not. Oh, no. Not at all.

One legacy of the novel may be that it features, as Chris Offutt wrote in a 2004 interview with Salter in these pages, "the greatest anal sex scene in literature." I prefer a different assessment, from the 1967 *New York Times* review:

> Arching gracefully, like a glorious 4th of July rocket, [*Sport*] illuminates the dark sky of sex. It's a tour de force in erotic realism . . . a continuous journey of the soul via the flesh . . . This is a direct novel, not a grimy one. Salter celebrates the rites of erotic innovation and understands their literary uses. He creates a small, flaming world of sensualism . . . We enter it. We feel it. It has the force of a hundred repressed fantasies. And it carries purpose: Salter details lust in search of its passage into love.

But really I prefer, simply, Yes.

Salter's short stories are perhaps his most masterful work. In *Dusk and Other Stories* the prose is superfine, more demanding; Europeanist, in both subject matter and sensibility. The stories in *Dusk* (written between 1967 and 1987) are populated by peripheral artists, or otherwise not-quites, compelled to wander Europe, longing for greatness and purity, the romantic and the brutal. ("Europe gave me my manhood or at least the image of it," Salter once wrote.) Many of the stories were written while Salter lived in Aspen, in the midst of a divorce and building a new life, his own wandering days behind him; yet there is a rawness in the stories, the same sensual force of *Sport*. The protagonists of *Dusk* may be lost and longing, but the pulse of desire throbs—inexorably, consolingly.

A second collection, *Last Night*, was published in 2005. In these chilling stories, the lush eros of *Sport* and *Dusk* and of his 1975 novel, *Light Years*, is displaced by the starker truths of life lived. Whatever had compelled the sexes to erotic celebration and tenderness, quests for greatness and purity, is now submerged; foregrounded is the tragedy of isolation, male from female, self from self. What persists is the compulsion of desire—desire as all we have and all we are. The prose leans toward severe, and yet every word seems to burn and glow, an argument for beauty as bare essence. As a rendering of post-romantic adulthood, *Last Night* is a lamentation. There is brutality in these stories, both quiet and feral, but we feel it ultimately as loss—for all of us, male and female, anyone who has known or longed for sensual abandon, anyone who has loved to love.

As to the quality of the man and the quality of the work, there must be a connection, though perhaps not of the obvious kind. Men with what might be thought of as faults or vices can be wonderful writers. Alcoholics aplenty, thieves, murderers, slave owners are among them. Philanderers too numerous to count. So it is not the virtue of Sunday school or even the Ten Commandments, although I myself admire the cardinal virtues—prudence, fortitude, justice, and mercy.

As to "very male," I think male characteristics are too well known to discuss. I was looking for a wonderful sentence from Isak Dinesen that succinctly describes it, as I recall, but couldn't find it. [He later e-mailed it to me: "The love of woman and womanliness is a masculine characteristic, and the love of man and manliness a feminine characteristic."]

Are there great women writers? Are they different than men? Oh, yes.

"Well, then," he says. "I suppose we should get to it. What do you have on your agenda?"

Despite the eight typed pages of questions, follow-up questions, and page references with which I've armed myself—and despite the hospitable kindness of my hosts thus far—I grow nervous and begin to wish Kay (who's now en route to the city) were still in the house. I'd watched recent interviews in which Salter seemed irritated by his interviewers' lines of questioning, and, with the recorder now on, I watch him lean back in his chair, and I perceive a kind of armor flip into place like a welder's mask. Acutely aware of my inexperience as an interviewer (Remember, it's an interview, not a conversation, a journalist friend warned; just think of it as a conversation, advised another), I proceed cautiously—perhaps too cautiously.

Half an hour in, I feel him begin to stonewall. Precision is all for James Salter, and if the semantics are mushy, if the question fails to get at something true, it is simply not to be answered. This morning he is prone to silent staring—a look somewhere between doubt and weariness—rubbing his hands over his face, cutting himself off in midsentence with "Let's just leave it at that," and responding curtly to my questions with "That depends" or "Possibly."

By noon, I'm not sure what we've covered, if anything. There is too much to read and not enough time, on this we agree. He has been working on a new novel for almost ten years; he struggles with energy and productivity. He invokes Roth's hyperproductive daily regimen, the one Roth (eight years Salter's junior) himself has described. "Can this be so?" Salter asks, shaking his head. "I don't know." The tone of the conversation slips intermittently into futility; the specters of resignation and mortality hover. I've asked him about the "manhood" he found in Europe ("Ah, but I'm a romantic writer, remember—I don't really know what that means"); about this word pure, which infuses all of his work (he laughs off the question, referencing Chekhov's protestation that asking, What is life? is like asking, What is a carrot?). I've come here to talk about these things—about romanticism, about manhood (and womanhood), about purity—but how? How to talk about them?

Oh, God, I think. I am Richard Yates's Frank Wheeler, talking talking talking the hell out of that which is better left unspoken, better lived and experienced than discussed.

I take a breath. The jig may be up. Really, I am no interviewer. Okay, well: what, then, is something true?

The truth . . . is that I have been watching an awful lot of *Mad Men* and this notion that we—the Gen X literary set—watch it to celebrate how far we've come, how progressive our gender identities, is, I feel, hogwash. Salter is an octogenarian white male, a former fighter pilot who flew in Korea; who wrote an erotic tale, a hundred repressed fantasies, of rich boy and poor girl; whose descriptions of women almost invariably offer legs, breasts, hair, shoulders, skin to evoke character essence. There is nothing "right" about my looking to him (or to Don Draper, for that matter, who would be just Salter's age if he were both real and alive today) for insights into sexual essence. At the same time his stories and novels move me—as a woman—in ways I have struggled to understand.

He is also—I remind myself now—a man who has deeply, expressively loved another man and shared that love, in the form of their unedited letters, with the world.

> *Dear J Salter:*
> *I received* Memorable Days, *which I've finished and have been rereading in sections over the past weeks. Thank you for sending it. I read it hungrily, and*

with envy . . . the notion of a "pure voice" in one's life moved me . . . It's a rare and beautiful thing. Thank you for sharing it with us.

His correspondence with the writer and critic Robert Phelps began in 1969. "[T]hese are love letters," writes Michael Dirda in the foreword to *Memorable Days* (2010), a collection of some two hundred letters over twenty years; and indeed they are. Phelps dwelt in literature, and in the wonder and heartbreak of a writer's life. "I saw in him the angelic and also something, call it dedication, for which I yearned," Salter wrote in his memoir, *Burning the Days* (1997). "I longed to know him . . . I have never passed [the Chelsea Hotel] without remembering [our first meeting] in the manner of a love affair." Upon Phelps's death in 1989, Salter wrote to his widow, Rosemarie Beck, "I loved Robert. I love him still and always. He was an anchor to seaward for me and one of the few pure voices of my life." To Phelps himself he wrote: "You are my beacon, my idea of life," and "Your life is the correct life."

The bulk of the letters is literary talk—books, plays, screenplays, stories, films, travel plans (and fantasies), personalities, and gossip; to read them is to take a whirlwind tour through a pantheon of the great uncanonized—Colette, Glenway Wescott, Cyril Connolly, Marcel Jouhandeau, Gabriele d'Annunzio, Brigid Brophy, Violette Leduc, Cesare Pavese, Paul Léautaud. Phelps introduces to Salter, the late-blooming autodidact, "some of the marvels of my life," and Salter is for Phelps (a literary Europhile) the American romantic he's been missing. "[T]he most romantic writer we have," Phelps wrote. "You restore a sacredness to profaned aspects and relations. . . . you are tender, and unperverse." A free-flowing passion infuses these exchanges, an amorous purity, to use Salter's word. I miss you. I am lonely. I love you. The light is where you are, Robert. "From the first moment I recognized him for what he was," Salter wrote in *Burning the Days*, which was to say, bisexual, and living a painful double life. (While Phelps never detailed these struggles explicitly, according to Salter, they were "not difficult to perceive.") But the love between the two men in these letters is not in the sexual realm; it is somewhere else—somewhere in the light where art and longing meet.

I begin again. "When we first corresponded . . . "

"Yes."

I remind him of the Roiphe essay. Yes, yes, he remembers. What, I ask, does he truly perceive in all this evolution of the sexes?

He takes a moment, genuinely ponderous, to consider, then speaks slowly, deliberatively. "It's very hard to look at culture qualitatively—this is better, this is not better. The culture is what exists. You say take it or leave it. This is it. The same thing applies to these questions about masculine, feminine. Sex. Homosexuality. I mean all of this has evolved. Is it good? I don't think the question fits the situation."

"Okay, forget good or bad," I say. I think now about what brought me here—lamentation, the compulsion of desire, lust in search of its passage into love. "What about . . . real? What about . . . loss?" I swallow a ridiculous lump in my throat. Is my voice shaking? What is it in his work that does this to me, and why is it so difficult to speak of?

"I think your young men have made a real attempt to accommodate themselves to . . . women's freshened ideas of themselves. Is this a permanent situation? I don't know."

I don't either. "Is anything a permanent situation?"

"Well. That's a good question. Is anything permanent." But he says it like a statement, followed by a thick pause. Then a burst of energy, somehow fierce and reluctant at once. "Yes, yes, sure. I believe . . . the sexes are permanent.

"Now, you're going to say, Oh, for Christ's sake, this guy is stuck with archaic ideas. But I believe . . . maleness and femaleness are qualities, there is something unalterable . . . there is something that cannot be . . . something immutable at the center of them. And I think this is so obvious.

"But, I understand this attitude isn't acceptable, and I don't express it. Is it in things I write? Well, I suppose so, inevitably, since it's what I feel. You can't write . . . you can't be false to your own feelings. Are these ideas crude and . . . no. No, I believe . . ."

He detours now into praise of a female writer—Nora Ephron—whose pluck and wit he finds appealing ("She has unclouded vision"), particularly regarding the sexes. This lightens the mood, but not much.

How strange, I think, how remarkable: the difficulties, all the shadows, in affirming an unqualified heterosexuality.

"You know, I think I've already belabored this. I don't think it merits that much." Let's be careful now, he seems to be saying. Let's be truthful. Okay, I think; let's. It merits something. We both believe it does.

If it is possible to be exhausted and energized at once—well, of course it is—here is where we've arrived. It's after 1 p.m. The orange recorder light blinks.

"Well, then," he says. "Shall we go have some lunch?"

The day has brightened and warmed. Before lunch, we'll tour the Hamptons in the Benz. "Since you've hardly been here," he says. "I'll show you around a little."

Driving through a tony section of East Hampton, our next subject seems inevitable. "I want to ask you about something you might find . . . disagreeable," I say.

He nods, pulls down the sun visor.

"I want to ask you about money."

"Ah, but why are you considering this disagreeable?"

Something opens up now, a looser, easier feeling. Maybe it's the sun, the feeling of motion and speed. I'd hesitated to ask, but on some level I sensed we have in common this relationship to privilege—close up but never fully inside.

As we drive, he speaks at length, goes into a kind of storytelling mode:

"Money. Well. At the military academy, the big figures were not the ones who had money. There was no money; it's like the priesthood. Those were formative years for me. The heroes at West Point were the athletes. That was influential, unquestionably, to me, because I wasn't a football player, or a boxing champion, and I wanted that feeling of manhood. That was why I became a fighter pilot, you know.

"And in the Air Force there was also no money. So that lasted a long time in my life. I was thirty-two when I left the military. Now, when I got out, this was a different world. Suddenly money was important. It's the trump card in a lot of ways. But I never quite accommodated myself to that, I suppose. Because all of that time, the twig was bent a different way.

"Now, intellectually, I understand all this, but I still have trouble with it. So I've never been tremendously comfortable with rich people. Why is that? I don't know. Some of my good friends have been rich, but that aspect of it is difficult for me. It represents a certain kind of achievement and position that is inaccessible to me. And whatever achievement I have is invisible to them."

"And yet you've managed to live a very rich life," I say. "You have three homes [in Aspen, Bridgehampton, and Manhattan]. You've traveled the world; you've lived in Europe. You've enjoyed fine things. Somehow you've disentangled 'riches' from 'wealth' in your life."

He laughs. "Well, wouldn't it be nice if you could do that." I sense that he enjoys my comment, even as he begs off. "I wasted a lot of time, making money." He is referring to the fifteen years he spent writing screenplays (including the acclaimed *Downhill Racer*, starring Robert Redford), the majority of which were never produced. "And I mean, we don't drink great wines; we don't travel first class. I remember Joan Didion said in an interview, 'I would love to go off and go to the Bristol Hotel.' Well, see, that's another life."

We drive down a wide street lined with English-style hedges and, behind these, mansions, one after the other. "They call this Gin Lane; you can imagine why. The parties."

"And you are invited to these parties?"

"Oh, no. I must be giving you a wrong impression. This isn't our world at all."

It's an odd statement, given that he's just pointed out the former homes of John Irving (a friend) and George Plimpton (who first published *Sport*), along with the house of Jean Kennedy Smith (also a friend). "You said you considered Robert Phelps's life to be glamorous . . ."

"Well, I was intrigued by how well he was connected to a lot of things that seemed galaxies away from me—*Vogue, Harper's Bazaar*, the *New York Times*. That was rather glamorous, I thought; and doubly glamorous because he was threadbare, he was simple, himself. He had certain elegant tastes—he had velvet trousers, he liked Tanqueray, he knew something about the forks on the table; but as he admitted readily, he came from, wherever it was, a small town in Ohio."

"But didn't you ever consider your own life glamorous? You were also having dinner with Saul Bellow and Edna O'Brien. Susan Sontag was an admirer. You were hanging around with Robert Redford."

We come to a stop at an intersection, and he turns to me, looks down over the rims of his sunglasses. "Ah yes, but I knew those people, you see."

Lunch at 75 Main in Southampton. We talk of food, travel in France, holiday plans. I muse inwardly at the fact that he has ordered a burger and fries, and I am picking at an elaborate salad. He returns to the subject of what he is reading, specifically the memoir by Ivana Lowell, the adopted daughter of Robert Lowell and biological daughter of Guinness heiress Lady Caroline Blackwood. Lowell, he tells me, described being sexually abused by her nanny's husband when she was six years old, not primarily as trauma, but rather as an episode of empowerment over an adult male. "I found that very interesting," he says.

We revert to talk about teaching, his concern about the quality of what young writers are required to read, and about other writers of "my generation." He asks about the Brooklyn literati, and I tell him that I am not much a part of that—that, like him, I am a literary late bloomer, and essentially an autodidact.

"Autodidacts, in my experience, tend to be unreliable," he says. He looks away, tracing back some line of memory. He tells me that he never shows his drafts to anyone. "Too embarrassing."

We pass on dessert but linger over coffee, and suddenly it's two and a half hours later and near time for my return train. He pays the check, ushers me to the car, stepping aside to open doors, and we rush off. Back at the house, it becomes clear I won't make the train, so we plan for the next bus, which leaves in twenty-five minutes.

"How are we doing then?" He gestures to my pile of questions, tea-stained pages scattered on one side of the table.

We sit again, still wearing our coats, and I flip through the pages. I realize we haven't focused as much on *Memorable Days* as we'd planned when we initially arranged the interview, and I want to hear more about this love, this passion, between him and Robert Phelps.

"There is a lack of an appropriate word in English. The word love may be too suggestive of something I don't think we're referring to here. There is no component of sexual attraction in what I am expressing. Robert Phelps I can't speak for, though I can say that I never felt I was desired. At the time I didn't reflect about it. The letters are extemporaneous. It seems to me evident in the letters themselves that they have no self-consciousness. It's what's great when you first fall in love—you're not thinking about it.

"His importance to me was his feeling about what writing meant, and what certain writers and books meant. There was no one like him in my life. I was by myself, in a figurative sense, and it was important to me to write to him. You write your best letters to people you feel will understand them. Just as in talk. He understood every word, and more."

He has described Phelps as an angel, and as a saint. Perhaps James Salter himself is no saint in life—I suppose I know too much of his personal history to go in for that—but on the page, on Salter's page, the mark of the autodidact seems to me that of a kind of chasteness. A solitary boy (only child), man (fifteen fish-out-of-water years in the military), and artist ("I was by myself; there was no one like him in my life") cultivates a priestly reverence for words as both truth and consolation; he understands his vocation as beholding, apprehending, rendering—the holiness of a pure soul, the ecstasy of the flesh, and the desolation of estrangement from these.

A final question.

"Now, you're going to say none of this is conscious, you can't make any claims," I say, sparring gloves up a little, mimicking his previous anticipation of my counterresponses. My question comes out long and winding; he is patient and even helps me along. We both toss out and trip over words like evolved, sensitive, advanced. The essence of my question is: Where does it come from?—this finely tuned knowledge of the way in which the sexes are, must be, cannot be, so deeply desire to be. His higher-profile peers—Mailer,

Roth, Updike, Bellow—have a way of notoriously alienating the female reader, sexually and psychically, with male protagonists of the piteous, wretched variety. Salter, not so. How? Why?

"Well, that covers a lot of ground, many years. As a boy, you are superior to and afraid of girls at the same time. Then, I suppose, you continue that way for quite a while. Then there comes a point in life when the superiority fades. Because you see and understand more. I think there's always a little bit of fear. I mean you are simply not of the same stuff. You are a man. And she is a woman. Yes, a great deal is the same. But you can't be made the same. There are fundamental, unalterable things that stand between you; I don't mean things to be overcome, but that were placed there to make your . . . your absolute adoration of each other greater than anything . . . it just doesn't go in a straight line. I mean, you're afraid. Here, again, the word is not quite adequate—but you feel a trembling, and it's not mere passion that makes you tremble.

"In the writing, it comes down to, Will it be embodied somehow in what you're writing? All writing is, in a sense, an approximation—that's why I sometimes go to other books, Gogol, or Dostoevsky. You say to yourself, Ah, of course, it's so simple. Just tell . . . the . . . truth. Can you do that? Try.

"But I don't think I know more than anybody knows, really. In fact, there's only a certain amount you can know, and I don't know any more. If I did, it would be truly remarkable. I can't believe that I know something that other people don't know."

I beg to differ, but not out loud. I think through my bookshelves: Rilke. Sherwood Anderson. Jack Gilbert. Cavafy. The romantic writers are fading into the past. And echt romantic—tremblingly sensual, direct, not grimy—truly rare.

The bus leaves in nine minutes and counting. As we gather papers and bags and keys, I ask—because I just have to ask—how it was meeting Matthew Weiner (the creator of *Mad Men*), who introduced Salter for the PEN Center USA Lifetime Achievement Award he received just a few weeks before.

"Well, he was as nice as could be. Open, intelligent."

"I'm sure he's read your books."

"Well, no, he hadn't. Or, he said his father had *A Sport and a Pastime* on a shelf where the children couldn't reach it."

Later, I watch a video clip of the introduction, which Salter himself didn't see or hear, as he was backstage. Weiner confesses that, in preparation for the awards, he "placed [him]self in a Salter immersion program."

"The one thing that I've learned about James Salter over the last few weeks is that he is interested in the truth," Weiner says. "His investigation of the desire or the ambition to be better, to be honest, to find love, to kill one's enemies, to not be alone, is unflinching and brave."

"Have you seen his show?" I ask. Salter lowers his chin, shakes his head gravely. I tell him that he might be hard-pressed to find a literary writer under the age of forty who doesn't watch it.

His eyes open wide in mock, and to some degree genuine, fascination. "Please, more." In the car, we decide together that the appeal may be nostalgia for an apparent (glamorized) simplicity—each sex tightly and explicitly packaged. "Of course that had its own problems, you understand. It wasn't Arcadia. And neither is this now. It's just a different part of the thing. It may have an appeal because it looks simpler, because it's past."

In the dark, in the cold, on the shoulder of the Montauk Highway, we shake hands—"Well, the day went quickly," he says, "It was a pleasure"—and I hurry onto the bus seconds before it pulls away. I scribble notes all the way back—notes of a most memorable day. The three hours flash by like no time at all.

The next morning, I receive an e-mail:

Dear Sonya, It was a long day for you. I hope the trip back was okay. Perhaps I was too dismissive of the idea that I know more than others about women, men, and their deep feelings regarding each other. It's the "knowing" I have trouble with. I've jotted down a lot on the subject. I think I understand a lot of it. And, of course, I'm always drawn to it. I know I have a man's point of view, but not exclusively. À bientôt. —Jim

Life Passes into Pages:
A Conversation with James Salter

Tim Sohn / 2011

Edited from an interview conducted on April 5, 2011, over lunch. A condensed version of this interview appeared in the July 2011 issue of *Outside* magazine. Printed with permission.

It's a tricky thing, having lunch with a legend, especially one as variously accomplished as James Salter. He is many things: West Point grad and Korean War fighter pilot; skier, climber, traveler, and raconteur; playwright, screenwriter, and novelist; New Yorker, Aspenite, and expat. His writing, like his life, covers a lot of ground, but his work about young men in the mountains first seduced me. In particular, it was his 1979 novel, *Solo Faces*, which follows climbing purist Vernon Rand as his ambition propels him from California to Chamonix, and his script for the 1969 film *Downhill Racer*, in which Robert Redford plays a similarly driven member of the US Ski Team. Although those sports have evolved almost beyond recognition in the decades since, Salter's insights into those places where manliness, risk, adrenaline, and the natural world intersect remain acute, timeless.

Salter seemed timeless as he arrived for our lunch, settled into a corner table, and ordered a glass of cabernet sauvignon. We were at Eleven Madison Park, one of New York's finest restaurants—I'd aimed to impress—and Salter, age eighty-six at the time, had just returned from a winter in Aspen. He cataloged the surroundings as he contemplated his appetite. Piercing eyes, alert, set in an expressive, energetic face lined from long years outdoors. He rubbed his forehead with his right hand as he formulated his thoughts. When they came, his voice was soft and a bit raspy, still lightly accented by his New York youth, weathered, but, like the face, in a way that suggested seasoning more than age. He was incisive, precise, occasionally backtracking to fine-tune a phrase, editing as he went. His conversational style resembled his writing: crisp and with a calm sparseness that belied the often revelatory nature of what he was saying. He also proved a gracious but critical listener, pulling on loose conversational threads, interrogating claims, working toward clarity.

TS: It's rare I get to come to a place like this, so thanks for the opportunity.
JS: It's rare for me as well. This is a top deal here [laughs]. We're starting off great.

TS: It's certainly a city pleasure—something to welcome you back from the West. That contrast, city and country, seems to be a recurring theme in your work. Is there a tension between the two sides for you?
JS: I don't think so. It's not that complicated. I mean, the country is more or less serene and you have some solitude and silence there that you don't normally have in the city. In the city if you're in solitude and silence, you usually feel you're missing something, and in the country, you don't care about that. Things look different out there, even the sunlight. It simplifies your life. And you think different thoughts out there. Having access to both is great, but it's not easy to arrange. For a long time I was stuck in the country, and it seemed everything was happening in the city, so you want to be in the city as much as you can. Then later, a lot of things are happening still, but you're not so interested in them. I wouldn't go to a lot of places I went thirty years ago [laughs], even though the same thing is going on. You know, you lose interest. And of course friends vanish. So, the city, really, for me, I don't want to say it's a museum, but it's not the same place that I lived in some years ago.

TS: I'm also thinking of a character like Rand in *Solo Faces*, whose city interludes soften him a bit.
JS: Well, there's that too, but he's a hard case. He's not a city boy. I was thinking of *Solo Faces* the other day. I saw a thing on YouTube, the guy [Swiss climber Ueli Steck] who soloed the Eiger in two hours and forty-seven minutes. Have you seen it? It makes that whole book seem like the day of sail. It made it almost irrelevant, I thought.

TS: I don't know that it made it irrelevant. Don't you think there's continuity in the kinds of characters who are attracted to climbing? I think that one of the reasons why *Solo Faces* and *Downhill Racer* still speak to people is that there are the same challenges, motivations, maybe an essential character type.
JS: Well, I grant that. But climbing is different now, there's more rock and

roll, I think—new generations have come through and changes in music and behavior and what's cool, what grown-up means, all that stuff. That dates it [the book] in a way. Although, as you say, the nature of certain characters hasn't changed.

TS: Did you get any skiing in this winter?

JS: I didn't ski this year because I have a bad leg, but if it heals up, I'll go next year. It was hard, because of course when you look up at the mountain from town, you see Corkscrew, you see the bottom of Little Nell, and that calls to you.

TS: And your house is still in the west end of Aspen?

JS: Yes. It's quiet there. I can work there. I worked all the time I was there this year.

TS: I remember something in your essay on Tyrol about how the crowds have ruined it. Have the crowds ruined Aspen? Do they come knocking on your door?

JS: No, nobody bothers us. They sometimes ask you to put on your hat and pose by your house.

TS: Do you oblige?

JS: It depends if they're nice. They want to see authentic old-timers. But it's not the crowds that have changed it. It's a different town. It used to be remote, it was a partly ruined town. A different sort of people were there, people who had more or less discovered it. Back then, even just to come for a week of skiing was difficult. Eventually it began to be a moneymaking thing. Before that it was a ski town.

TS: For you, for the things you enjoy there, are there still glimpses of the old Aspen?

JS: Well, its natural aspects haven't been changed, can't be changed.

TS: Skiing's changed a bit. Have you seen the X Games?

JS: Oh my God. I mean, I don't go to them, but there's a brilliant blue light reflected in the heavens that comes from those games when they're in town. Well, you can't explain them to me. It's a modern outbreak. Unbelievable what they do. They're skiing in these steep barrel-shapes on skis that are rounded front and back, and they're sixteen years old. Phenomenal, but the connection with what used to be skiing and the life of skiing is tenuous. They have the snow in common, and the skis or snowboard, but it's not quite the same thing.

TS: It's always an open question, the idea of third acts, of the sunsets of those sorts of lives, of what they do after the glory. It's implied at the end of *Downhill Racer* certainly, with the young guy coming up, and the end of *Solo Faces*, the Florida coda, and there's an element of it as well in *The Hunters*, but this idea of a burning ambition and whether if it's not realized it's a tragedy and if it is, it's a different sort of tragedy?
JS: It's not necessarily a tragedy. And of course it's not a tragedy not to achieve it either. They might say, It isn't any good, this book, but it took courage to attempt to write such a thing. That's meant as a compliment, and it is a compliment in a way.

TS: That sounds like something a critic would say. One thing I loved about your letters with Robert Phelps [published as *Memorable Days*] was that you were something of an outsider, and he was this consummate literary world insider who would challenge you and recommend different things for you to read. I have a few friends like that and their suggestions open new windows for me. It's nice. Sometimes.
JS: I like that and I hate it at the same time. They're really overturning your world. You've already made up your mind, although you can never make up your mind about writing in the end. Something to change it always comes along. Also, you're constantly forgetting what you read, not immediately, but it does tend to become more distant and diluted and then you have to go back and look at it again or reread it. Well, there's no answer to that.

TS: This is a gross over-simplification, but there is, for me, a line from Cleve [in *The Hunters*] to Chappellet [*Downhill Racer*] to Rand [*Solo Faces*]. It's not necessarily a personality type, but there is a tension in all of them about how to deal with ambition, about solitary struggle . . .
JS: Rand is definitely a loner. First ascent implies loneliness, doesn't it? I mean, nobody has done it before. You're alone in that distinction. I'm drawn to a certain kind of person, people who are not completely reliable or let's say predictable. And in serious climbing you are dealing with a specialized life, a life that's unpredictable. I'm writing now about the exact opposite, a book editor—a novel [*All That Is*]. So it's not the hero striving to do something alone.

TS: How far along is that?

JS: Two-thirds of the way. I've been working on it for a while.

TS: My apologies for creating another distraction. And you have the *Paris Review* Revel coming up as well, where I understand you'll be introduced by Redford. Have you kept in touch with him?

JS: I saw him not long ago. He's a remarkable guy. Even if he weren't an actor and an idol, Sundance would be a great achievement.

TS: I've heard some great anecdotal stories of when the two of you went to Europe, to the 1968 Olympics in Grenoble, to do research for *Downhill Racer*. I've heard it was kind of improvisational.

JS: Exactly. We weren't invited. We went over there to be with the ski team, and as I recall there was some additional business—I believe the Olympic organizers had sold the film rights to somebody else (Claude Lelouch), so I think Redford was trying to bootleg some footage of the Olympic races for the film. I wasn't involved.

TS: Of course not. Did you two get along immediately?

JS: We'd met in New York before that. He was on the stage, in *Barefoot in the Park*, and I had written him a film script. It was never produced, but he read it and liked it and wanted to meet and have lunch and that's how it all began. We stayed in touch and later he asked me to write that and then for a while we were a bit closer because we were talking about doing a subsequent movie, a climbing movie.

TS: Which was *Solo Faces*.

JS: Yes. The book started as research for a film script I wrote for him. He finally didn't like it. Probably for a good reason: I don't think I'm very good at writing movies, so I think he saw that. I mean, he's nice, he's never said get outta here.

TS: Why do you think you're not good at writing movies?

JS: I think you have to have a broader thumb.

TS: I think *Downhill Racer* is a remarkable script, but that "broader thumb" seems everywhere these days. I'm curious if, as skiing and climbing, and Aspen and Bridgehampton, have gotten more popular, more mainstream, whether something has gone out of the experience of those places for you.

JS: I think it happens everywhere. It's even happened in New York City. It's not only in the natural world. When I was a boy there were 130 million people in America. That's the figure we learned in grade school. There are 330 now, 200 million more people. The city is very changed. There's no point in becoming sentimental about it. Things change except that if you're born now, everything seems perfectly normal to you. But it used to be that you'd walk out on the beach in the middle of August and there might be forty people. It's now many more than that. When you're on the beach in a little shack before all the condominiums were built, it's a different world.

TS: But some human monuments to an older Aspen held on, at least until recently—Hunter Thompson, for example.
JS: Hunter led a very—can I call it Aspen life? He was there for a long time. Tourists didn't mean anything to him, but now tourists go to the Jerome bar because Hunter Thompson used to sit there. But the bar is not the same, that bar is gone, really. And then Klaus Obermeyer—you know Obermeyer ski clothes—just broke his leg in Aspen. He's ninety-one and I saw him on the street the day before I left, two weeks after the break, and he was walking in half crutches and looking forward to getting back on the mountain. He's an old-timer: he fought in the Second World War and he's been in Aspen since 1950 or thereabout.

TS: Are there any other illustrious Aspen characters still there?
JS: Almost all have died. But you know, when the Paepckes first came, they didn't come there and buy up a lot of land, that wasn't their idea at all, though their idea has dwindled away. There is still an Aspen Institute, bigger and better than ever. Walter Paepcke organized that originally. But I don't know if he thought of it as being an influence on government, a forum for ideas and action. It was, to begin with, mainly a cultural idea. They would give businessmen who hadn't read a book of any importance since college two weeks to come and read and talk about fundamental ideas and viewpoints in this remote, beautiful place. If it were up to me I would go back to what it was.

TS: Back to the dirt roads.
JS: Well, it was muddy, it was hard on the floors in the spring but otherwise terrific, a cut-your-own-firewood place.

TS: That's a recurring motif: cutting wood.

JS: Well, it's a saintly act. It's a sacred act, I should say.

TS: I look at a place like Snowmass [near Aspen]. I first went there when I was five, and it's now completely changed.
JS: Well, they've torn up Snowmass since you've been there. They said, Let's have a new one. That's a peculiar American idea. The European ski towns, the old ones are not like that. Have you ever skied at Wengen? You literally ski down through the town itself, through people's back yards, down little streets, through the kitchen so to speak. It's a different style of things. Or Chamonix: I was there a couple of years ago. It's changed a little, but it's an old French town. You feel it is an old place. They didn't throw it together just now for you. And of course when you go there, you know—we were talking a little earlier about *Solo Faces*—that it is outdated, but is somebody going to ski down the Eiger now? Of course they're not going to, it's vertical rock, long rock sections and one outcrop or another but they'll figure some way. They'll get wings or something and then get on the skis again.

TS: I know some guys who have parachuted off of it.
JS: They jump away and then open the chute? Well, I mean, I said that jokingly but who knows. And then it won't amount to anything, will it? Except when you go there, even though you know some fool was smart enough to do that, the mountains are still overwhelming.

TS: Smart fools. In *There and Then*, you mention that the kinds of people you like being around are ones who can name the parts of a motor, people who can do things, fix things.
JS: Did I say that?

TS: I think so.
JS: Well I must like them, then.

TS: Practical people, let's say. Competent.
JS: There's something appealing about that. My father-in-law has an old Volvo and there's a mechanic in Denver, Tim, who does nothing but work on Volvos. You have to like this guy. He knows right away this is the something bulb, you need this particular one, it's on the '68 model and one other, and he doesn't charge you a lot of money, he's just earning . . . it's what they used to call an honest living. You say to yourself, "Ah, that's very Norman Rockwell." Nobody is interested in that [kind of life anymore], but it's good when

you see it. It's like a dog walking alone along the side of the highway. You say, "Look at that, that's a brave dog. I wonder what's going to happen to him."

Don't Save Anything:
A Conversation with James Salter

Dexter Cirillo / 2013

From *Aspen Sojourner* (Summer 2013). Reprinted with permission.

Shortly after my husband and I moved from New York City to Aspen in 1993, we were invited to a small dinner party to meet Jim and Kay Salter. "He's a writer's writer, you know," the hostess informed me. In fact, I didn't. So I quickly ran out to buy *A Sport and a Pastime*, my friend's favorite of Salter's works. Worried that I might face the hardline questions hurled at me during my doctoral exams years earlier, I practically memorized the novel and even went back to reread Camus, since Salter clearly loved France. Instead, on the appointed night, I met a charming, inquisitive, and slightly diffident man, who effortlessly deflected every question that came his way in favor of the stories others had to tell. That first dinner would be one of many the Cirillos and the Salters would share.

I would learn Salter's own stories through his literature. Of mountain climbing and the real meaning of heroism in *Solo Faces.* Of the breadth of his life in *Burning the Days.* Of passion in *A Sport and a Pastime.* Of the joys of the table in *Life Is Meals.* Like the dinners and conversation he so clearly relishes, Salter's writing is to be savored one sentence at a time. Or, as Susan Sontag put it: "Salter is a writer who particularly rewards those for whom reading is an intense pleasure." In the April 2013 issue of *Harper's*, the author Jonathan Dee wrote, "*A Sport and a Pastime,* in particular, is more eminently than ever one of the best, most sophisticated and moving American novels of its generation."

Over the years of my friendship with Jim, my Salter library has grown steadily with each new publication, as has my appreciation for his stunning prose. Before the release of *All That Is*, I had a chance to sit down and talk with Jim Salter about his extraordinary career.

Dexter Cirillo: This is an auspicious year for you. You have just won one of the largest literary prizes in the world, and Knopf is publishing your seventh novel, *All That Is*, in April. Have you reached the pinnacle of your career?

James Salter: Well, I believe I've passed the pinnacle. It's been a jammed-up year for me, beginning on December 12, 2012, with winning the PEN/Malamud Award. Then, at the beginning of March, the phone rang in Aspen at 7 a.m. Someone calling from the Beinecke Library at Yale asked, "Am I speaking to James Salter?" "Yes." "I'm calling to inform you that you have won the first Windham Campbell Prize in literature," he said. "Yes," I said. "And it comes with a cash award of $150,000." "Who *is* this?" I said.

Cirillo: Did you know you were being considered for the award?

Salter: No. The whole process took place without any knowledge on my part at all. As it turns out, any writer in the world who writes in English, regardless of nationality, is eligible. I later found out that there are twenty-nine judges worldwide who make the nominations. The nominations then go to two juries. Their list goes to a third jury, and the final selections are made. You cannot apply for the prize.

Cirillo: *All That Is* is a sweeping title for a book. Can you give us a sneak preview of the novel?

Salter: The book is really about a journey through life, in this case, of an editor. It's also a story of what we now regard as a golden age in publishing, from 1920 to 1980, when there were legendary editors like Maxwell Perkins, Thomas Wolfe's editor, and publishing houses like Scribner's, where publishing was more familial than it is today. I didn't have a title when I began. Toward the end of the novel, "All That Is" appeared on a list—stood out on it—and became the one.

Cirillo: It has been more than thirty years since you published your last novel. In the interim, you have published short story collections, poetry, memoirs, travel writing, and a book on food. Why did you return to the novel?

Salter: I didn't make what might be called a decision to return to it. I was simply writing something that was too long to be a story. A book was its natural length. Also, I wanted to write one more book.

Cirillo: Knowing that there is the possibility *All That Is* may be your last book, did that change your approach in any way?

Salter: It didn't make me become solemn. And it didn't tempt me to sum up anything. I did want to write in a somewhat leaner, less showy language. As always, you try to put everything you have in a book. That is, don't save anything for the next one.

Cirillo: Let's go back to the beginning of your career. You graduated from West Point in 1945 and were a commissioned officer in the Air Force. You served for twelve years and flew as a fighter pilot in the Korean War. You left a promising military career to become a full-time writer in 1957 after you published your first novel, *The Hunters*, which became a movie starring Robert Mitchum in 1958. How did your military experience influence your writing?

Salter: Powerfully. My first book was about pilots in the war. I went on writing about pilots in a second one.

Cirillo: Did you study writing at West Point?

Salter: No, the only writing we did was demerits and laundry lists. I was lucky because I'd gone to Horace Mann, a good preparatory school in New York, where English was intensive.

Cirillo: You were born James Arnold Horowitz in 1925. When you published *The Hunters*, you changed your name to James Salter to separate your literary and military worlds. In 1962, you then legally changed your name to Salter. How did you pick Salter?

Salter: Well, I made a mistake obviously—it's much too colorless. When I wrote *The Hunters*, I was in the Air Force and hadn't made the decision to give up my commission or career. And I didn't want myself stained by being literary. That wasn't an asset, especially at that time. The service may have changed. I tried to pick a name as far from my own as possible to be anonymous. The novel was serialized by *Collier's*, and pilots read it. I was asked if I had. Who do you suppose wrote it? The pilots knew it was accurate. They found it interesting. Nobody identified the book with me, to my knowledge.

Cirillo: In 1967, you published *A Sport and a Pastime*. That put you on the literary map. It also forever identified you with France. When did your love affair with France begin?

Salter: It began before I ever went to France. You fall in love because of what has been written about a place. Hemingway, who I read as a boy, had written about France—I read *The Sun Also Rises* and said, "I want to go there." The

Normandie, the most luxurious liner ever built, burned down at the French Line pier in New York in 1942 when I was a boy. You could see it burning from all over the city. Everything was written about France in those days. French restaurants were the height of dining. French women were considered the most sophisticated, the most chic. However, when I first went to France in 1950, Paris was in terrible shape. It was not that long after the war. It was in the winter. The buildings were freezing. Everything was threadbare. Even so, as we drove down the avenues, there was the grandeur, Notre Dame, the great hotels, the buildings along the river. I said to myself, "Yes, this is it."

Cirillo: In 1969, you wrote the screenplay for *Downhill Racer*, starring Robert Redford. How did that come about, and how did you prepare for it?
Salter: Originally, I had been asked to write a film for Roman Polanski. He was replaced, and Redford was cast and took over the film's life. In 1968, we went to the Grenoble Olympics for two weeks to be with the US Ski Team and to absorb real detail. Bob Beattie was the coach then. He still lives in Aspen. The star of the team was Billy Kidd, who had a somewhat withheld personality. A blond kid on the team, famous for having broken his leg three or four times, was from California and was named Spider Sabich, and Redford immediately recognized him as the ski racer he related to. I thought he was superficial but later found out I was completely wrong. When Sabich lived in Aspen afterwards, I knew him and admired him tremendously.

Cirillo: Your 1979 novel *Solo Faces* is a compelling story about the terror and exultation of mountain climbing. It started as a screenplay and then morphed into a novel. Did you do a fair amount of climbing yourself to prepare for the novel?
Salter: Yes. I was still working with Redford, whose favorite climbing story was "one man falls, the other can't pull him up and must make the decision to cut the rope and let him go." Well, it doesn't exactly work like that. I contacted Royal Robbins, who was the moral spirit and soul of American climbing, as well as the preeminent climber. Without much enthusiasm, he agreed to talk to me. He and Gary Hemming had made the first ascent of the American Direct route on the Aiguille du Dru in Chamonix in 1962. I wanted to see that route and asked Robbins if he would go with me to Europe. I paid for his ticket and his wife's. Of course, I didn't climb the Dru, but I did climb, some of it with him and Tom Frost for a year, including routes around here: Monitor Rock, the Grotto Wall, the east face of Longs Peak.

Cirillo: In 1981, you wrote an essay for the *New York Times* about Aspen, remembering your first trip here in 1959, when the Jerome Hotel had the only switchboard in town. If there was a fire, the fire truck went to the Jerome and waited for the deaf bellboy to bring out a note from the operator telling the firemen where the fire was.

Salter: That has to be an apocryphal story. We'll have to check with the fire department. What I do know is we always gathered at the end of the day in the bar at the Jerome Hotel. That hasn't changed. But the hotel has.

Cirillo: When did you move to Aspen, and what prompted the move?

Salter: In New York, I happened to meet someone who was working as a bellboy at the Jerome, a skier and ice skater named Lefty Brinkman, who had been a 1948 Olympic silver medalist in ice skating and was a director of the Aspen Ski School. This was in 1959. He said, "You have to come out to Aspen to ski." I did, and in 1968 I stayed.

Cirillo: You divide your time between Aspen and Bridgehampton on Long Island. Where do you do most of your writing, and what is your process of writing?

Salter: I write in both places. I usually try to write something else before I get really started for the day. I might write a letter or some notes for myself so as not to have blank-page fright. Sometimes, I read a paragraph or two to remind me of the level, usually of a writer I have no possible connection with—*The Book of Common Prayer* or Chaucer or something like that to clear my mind.

Cirillo: You and Kay have become famous in Aspen for your intimate dinner parties with many of your literary friends—John Irving, Peter Matthiessen, Toby Wolff, Jorie Graham, to name just a few. In 2006, the two of you published *Life Is Meals: A Food Lover's Book of Days*, which grew out of more than one thousand dinner parties you have given together. What is the importance of the dinners to you?

Salter: Well, first of all, the meal is the central act of civilization. I think I said something a bit lofty on the jacket of the book about this, "What would one know of life as it should be lived or nights as they should be spent apart from meals." The most important thing to begin with is the company. Sometimes the guest list can be very offhanded, but you try to invite people who are entertaining. It's useless if people have nothing in common. Hunter Thompson came to dinner several times, but he wasn't a wonderful conversationalist. He was a show.

Cirillo: Peter Matthiessen has said, "There is scarcely a writer alive who could not learn from [Salter's] passion and precision of language." You have been praised in the *Washington Post Book World* as "the contemporary writer most admired and envied by other writers." You also have frequently been called a "writer's writer." How do you respond to that?

Salter: Well, I appreciate Peter's comment, but "writer's writer" is just a cliché picked up by second-rate critics and passed along. I think it started with a piece in *Esquire* a long time ago in which the author described me as "the best little-known writer." It's now become a pejorative term, somehow suggesting only another writer would read my work. It's like saying he's a winemaker's winemaker.

It doesn't mean anything. In my experience, writers are generally very parsimonious in their praise for other contemporary writers.

Cirillo: How would you describe your work?

Salter: I don't know. I try to write things that are better than I am able to write. I also try to write things that I would very much want to read. I write about a certain terrain, a certain portion of humanity and life—everyone does. You have your own ideas and obsessions that you circle around in every book. For me, it's the emotional, the physical, and the sexual life—generally between a man and a woman.

Cirillo: You may be the last writer on the planet who still writes in longhand.

Salter: I don't think so. I like the physical connection with a pen and paper. I used to have good handwriting, and the efficiency of it cannot be matched. You don't need a device of any kind to sit down and make a note, write a thought. Writing is tactile. That's one of the joys.

Cirillo: Who are the writers you have most admired? And who are the writers you feel have influenced you?

Salter: When I was young, I was influenced by the American writers of the time, especially Thomas Wolfe. I've gone back and read him, even though he hasn't remained popular. He also influenced Jack Kerouac [who went to Horace Mann ahead of Salter]. The world really was enlarged for me in my forties when I met Robert Phelps, who was a writer and critic with a particular level of taste. He introduced me to Colette and Isaac Babel. He brought to maturity my interest in reading.

Cirillo: As you approach your eighty-eighth birthday, what do you think your place in American letters will be?

Salter: Well, I imagine I'll be listed as a novelist and short story writer of the twentieth to twenty-first centuries. Of what importance, I'm obviously unable to say. Maybe a book or two of mine will make it through. All writers hope that.

James Salter

Thad Ziolkowski / 2013

Originally published in *Interview* magazine (April 2013). Courtesy BMP Media Holdings, LLC. Reprinted with permission. Thad Ziolkowski is director of the Writing Program at New York's Pratt Institute and the author of *Wichita*, a novel.

Picking my way through the snow and slush of James Salter's driveway in Aspen this past February, I was both excited and apprehensive. A legendary, if relatively little-known, writer, Salter is the author of the 1967 erotic masterpiece *A Sport and a Pastime*, about a Yale dropout's love affair in France; the virtually perfect novels *Light Years*, a portrait of a family's dissolution, and *Solo Faces*, about mountain climbing; as well as some of the finest short stories of the last century. Yet his literary persona is rather magisterial, characterized by a fine, somewhat chilly polish. He's too often been accorded the dubious distinction of a "writer's writer." In truth, he's the great American writer that most of America doesn't know it has produced.

I was in Aspen to talk with Salter about his sixth and most recent novel, *All That Is*. There was much to discuss in Salter's A-frame mountain retreat before my return flight back to New York later that afternoon. There are very few writers I would fly across the country to meet. Above them all is Salter. There is something about his prose, which blends lushness and classical restraint in the service of a wise, epicurean view of life, that calls me back to it. I have reread Salter more often than any other living author and have memorized lines and passages by dint of sheer repetition. Also, in an era characterized by sex writing that defaults to irony and comic dysfunction, Salter restores that erotic experience to a kind of exalted, tantric level throughout his books (including this new one) that is simply hot.

When Salter opened the front door and welcomed me into a cozy, book-lined living room, I found the author less bearish than photos lead one to expect. At eighty-seven, he is trim and has close-cropped curly white hair and a lively, handsome face. He offered me a drink and mentioned that his wife, the playwright Kay Eldredge, was away for the day. Behind him on the shelves, I noticed volumes of early-twentieth-century Russian writer Isaac Babel, one of Salter's favorites and, like him, a soldier-writer. Salter proved warm and solicitous. At dusk, he threw on a stylish down coat and showed me around the mountainous area he has lived in for part of the year since 1959, when the streets were unpaved and he bought his house for a song. Now the shops that once sold climbing gear have Fendi bags in the windows. Salter pointed out a bar that, during the town's heyday in the '70s, would be packed with upward of one hundred skiers who had glided from the slopes right up to the bar door. "There were five gorgeous women who were always there back then," he says wistfully, "real standouts."

Thad Ziolkowski: First of all, congratulations on the publication of *All That Is.*
James Salter: Thank you, thank you.

Ziolkowski: What do you think is the relationship of this new novel to your other books?
Salter: I'd say the biggest relationship is the repetition of certain themes. I don't want to say "topics," but certain points of interest.

Ziolkowski: Well, the protagonist, Philip Bowman, was born the same year as you were, 1925, and, like you, in New Jersey.
Salter: He was born in 1925?

Ziolkowski: Yes.
Salter: Ah . . . Well, this will certainly lead people to think it's autobiographical.

Ziolkowski: Then there's the military experience. One of the remarkable things about your life is the long period up until you were in your early thirties when you were an officer in the Air Force. Before that you were a cadet at West Point, where you were miserable for much of the time due to the hazing and general harshness of the regimentation. Why did you stay the course there when you could have gone on to Stanford—or was it MIT? I've heard you considered both.
Salter: I'd been admitted to Stanford, but my father was not a literary man or a man with aesthetic tastes to any degree. And he'd gone to MIT as a postgraduate, and he said, "That's a wonderful school. You should go up

there." I'd never even been to Boston. So I did go up there, and you know the way kids choose schools: by the smell of it, so to speak, and by somebody they happen to see on the campus. I said, "Okay, that seems fine, but I'd like to go to Stanford." So I applied for it. In those days, from an Eastern prep school—Horace Mann was a good school—you could get into these colleges without much difficulty. I didn't have a precise idea of my path, but I'd say if anything, it was toward more of a literary or liberal arts education.

Ziolkowski: But then you ended up at an improbable third alternative, West Point, and you had this utterly rude awakening there. Having discovered how brutal it was, what kept you from dropping out?
Salter: I didn't have the nerve. My father was not tyrannical, but it would've been a huge disappointment to him. He had gone there, as you know, and he had a reputation. And I just felt I couldn't.

Ziolkowski: You did manage to graduate just as World War II was ending.
Salter: Well, I got with the program. And having had such a poor first year, and having rebelled against it so much, naturally when I turned, I turned completely the other way.

Ziolkowski: Do you have regrets about getting a military education?
Salter: Yes, I regret it. Yes.

Ziolkowski: The narrowness of it.
Salter: Its narrowness, exactly, and various other aspects that you cannot rid yourself of, really.

Ziolkowski: For instance?
Salter: Oh, moral notions—notions of honor. Things that may even be out of step with contemporary life.

Ziolkowski: A kind of puritanism?
Salter: West Pointers tend to be rigorously honest—more than necessary, in my view. Habits that you form there, that you're made to form there, are very difficult to get rid of. I hate a messy room, for instance. And I like things to be in twos—I mean, where's the other sock? I'm unwilling, in small things, to just say, "Oh, to hell with it!" I think that comes from those years and the insistence to "do it right, make it right."

Ziolkowski: Was it the love of flying that kept you in the military as a career officer in the Air Force?

Salter: I can't really answer that specifically, because I don't know what I would have done. I was into flying before I graduated. So I graduated as a flyer.

Ziolkowski: You were waging warfare as a pilot. You went out looking for the enemy over Korea. That habit of seeking out the danger, of seeking out the enemy—what happened to that when you were no longer a fighter pilot?

Salter: I was still a fighter pilot. You consider yourself one for a long time. But fighter pilots don't necessarily have to be aggressive personalities: cocky and daredevil, there are those kinds too. The best ones, in fact, are somewhat measured, often quiet and very capable. Aggressive, yes, but not in personality. Aggressive in spirit, not in act.

Ziolkowski: Not brawlers in a bar.

Salter: No, nothing like that.

Ziolkowski: Some of the most breathtaking passages in your work concern aerial battle. I often put them on the board for my students and we pore over them in amazement. One of my favorites from your memoir, *Burning the Days*, is the description of a plane you shot down. The pilot has ejected, and you watch as "the MIG, now a funeral craft that bore nothing, was falling from thirty thousand feet, spinning leisurely in its descent until its shadow unexpectedly appeared on the hills and slowly moved to join it in a burst of flame." But some of the beauty in your war writing has to do with the fragility of memory and the way the faces of your comrades are as in a dream, and they're fading. Yet, I know from having written a memoir myself that people from the past tend to get in touch with you. I was wondering whether any of those aces from your squadron actually said, "You know, I read your book. I'm still alive and well. How are you? Let's get together."

Salter: If they read it.

Ziolkowski: Did you hear from any of them?

Salter: Oh, some of them, of course. Somebody called me this morning, as a matter of fact.

Ziolkowski: Having read *Burning the Days*?

Salter: He wasn't in the squadron with me, but an Air Force classmate of mine, with whom I've never been in touch . . . I mean, I knew who he was, but he called out of the blue.

Ziolkowski: What did he have to say?
Salter: He said, "I loved your book. I've read it three times and I just wanted to call you and tell you that."

Ziolkowski: That's gratifying.
Salter: He's a rare one, believe me. [Laughs.] I don't want to malign them. They're all literate, completely literate, but generally speaking, I'd say that they read a different kind of book—biographies, histories.

Ziolkowski: When you were flying those missions, did you ever take notes and think, I'm going to write about this? Or were you utterly in the moment and consumed by it?
Salter: No. I thought, I'm probably not gonna get through this! [Ziolkowski laughs.] But I was keeping a very rudimentary journal. I wanted to keep track of the missions, and generally of what I felt and saw, and what other people did. I knew I was going to forget all that. I mean, sometimes you flew two, occasionally three missions in a day. By the time you're flying the third one, details of the first have already been mixed in. So I did keep a journal. And I thought, "Well, if anything happens to me, somebody will take that notebook. They'll send it home."

Ziolkowski: Do you keep a journal now?
Salter: I used to, but I've become a bum.

Ziolkowski: There's that great line in *Burning the Days* about a fellow West Pointer who died in World War II: "His death was one of many and sped away quickly, like an oar swirl." In your work, a death can happen suddenly and be dispatched with, which gives it a paradoxical kind of poignancy.
Salter: I don't fear death. I'm not obsessed with it the way everybody else seems to be. It's wrong to say "everybody," but in literature I see it all the time—preoccupation with it, philosophical preoccupation, in fact. That's a principle element of literature and philosophy, often cited as the main element, the only real element. I say give it up.

Ziolkowski: Another theme that recurs in your work is that of what you call "the upper world." It often has a European context—the traditional aristocracy of England or the continent.
Salter: In the Air Force, I was stationed in Europe for four years, and that was an awakening.

Ziolkowski: You were in Germany and France?
Salter: Yes. I didn't know about Henry Miller then. His books weren't even available in the States. But I was eager to see Paris—and France, for that matter. And, of course, we'd been fighting Germany for three years. So to go over there was immediately to see these places in reality. It made a big impression. And one thing you see very quickly, in France particularly, but in Germany as well, everywhere you go, is the waterline of culture. The culture and the aesthetic seem to be higher—you notice that immediately. Then as I got to know the life a little bit, I found it even more attractive. Not to the extent of wanting to live in Europe, but of wanting to eat it. I wanted to take a big bite out of it.

Ziolkowski: You depict the world of the aristocracy, loosely defined, as desirable and admirable. I'm thinking of *Burning the Days*, but there's a tendency in all your books to ground the narrative in elites of one sort or another—elite fighter pilots, American blue bloods in *A Sport and a Pastime*, the semi-bohemian lifestyle elites in *Light Years*. For me, as an American reader, with an American's traditional hostility to the notion of an aristocracy, I'm always a bit conflicted by this in your work, as well as seduced by the way you present the whole thing, the appeal of the sumptuous, the richness, and a kind of structure of sexual secrecy—their great privacy. As if those great estates were made, above all, for pleasure and for doing as one likes. In *All That Is*, London is "the hidden luxury from imperial days with its guardians in the form of silver-trimmed doormen at the great hotels."
Salter: Sumptuous and rich implies a certain leisure and perhaps laxity. I don't mean that—I meant the rigor of the culture. All the bridges, the roads, the buildings, the attention to details in daily life that I suppose you could find if you went to Milwaukee, to German families, or to wherever the French are in America—maybe Louisiana . . . But in general, American life is more easy-going than that. And civic pride, national pride in a cultural sense, isn't as great in America. I think what they esteem in America is character and energy, and being different and superior to other peoples. Of course, every nation feels itself to be superior, but in America it's a jaunty feeling, and in some cases a rather ominous one among the super-patriots.

Ziolkowski: In your new novel, that superiority and style comes up first in the form of the Virginian elite, which is the world the first wife of Philip Bowman comes from. It's a world of foxhunts and drinking and horses, and the marriage doesn't last long, but Bowman is fascinated by their self-assurance and insularity.

Salter: I like aristocracy. I like the beauty of aristocracy. I like the hierarchical feeling. You could, if you want to be mean about it, claim that it's due to my military experience. But it came before that. I love their freedom of behavior. They're not constrained by these penal attitudes, these puritanical attitudes about behavior, both socially and morally. I don't mean they're immoral, but they have a freedom that I admire. An unquestioned freedom. And odious things happen, which they admit to openly—I envy that.

Ziolkowski: The epigraph to *All That Is* is "There comes a time when you realize that everything is a dream, and only those things preserved in writing have any possibility of being real." Which brings to mind the long years you spent as a screenplay writer in the film world. Did you hold the same conviction about the superiority of the written word when you were involved in the making of films?

Salter: Oh, yeah. I've believed that from the beginning but was not able to express it, I suppose.

Ziolkowski: When you fell in love with film in the early '60s, it was the New Wave moment. In *Burning the Days*, you remember Lincoln Center and its huge screen and the feeling of being in the presence of art.

Salter: I wrote a script in New York because I was asked to do it. I'd never written one before. Was that after I'd seen the New York Film Festival in 1963? I don't remember precisely. It's about the same time. It's a time when you're going to the movies frequently, when you're talking to people about them, when you're talking about films that not everybody has seen, perhaps, so there's a certain, I don't want to say superiority, but you're somewhat elevated in your feelings about them. And, of course, they're glamorous. You must remember also, I was trying to earn a living. I thought, This is a possibility. So I wrote that first script; that was the one that Redford happened to read.

Ziolkowski: *Goodbye, Bear*. Redford was a stage actor at that point.

Salter: Right, he was in the play *Barefoot in the Park*. Perhaps Jane Fonda was in it with him? Or maybe she was in the movie.

Ziolkowski: In the memoir, you describe yourself and Redford as "two naïfs in the sunlit city."
Salter: Oh, I was naive. Well, he was naive, definitely.

Ziolkowski: With regard to the film world?
Salter: And a lot of other things, I might add. But I felt he was more naive than I was. I've since changed my mind.

Ziolkowski: You wrote the screenplay that became *Solo Faces* in 1977, at Robert Redford's request, but it never got made. Redford felt it wasn't quite right for him.
Salter: Well, lots of scripts are written and not made, even scripts that people want to make. In this case, I think Redford felt it didn't exactly strike the right tone. He likes to play loners, outdoor figures, figures with their own moral standards. And in *Solo Faces*, the main character, Rand, has all of these, but it didn't quite click. For him. But a good friend of mine had become editor in chief of Little, Brown, and he said, "This would make a wonderful novel. Will you consider doing that?" And eventually I did.

Ziolkowski: *Solo Faces* is a great novel. I hear it has a cult following among climbers.
Salter: [British author] A. Alvarez, who's a genuine climber, said that it's the first novel, or the only novel, he's read that has the genuine feel of climbing in it.

Ziolkowski: And that's because you had done some [climbing] yourself. You took up climbing in your early fifties. What was that like?
Salter: Jesus. I don't know how I did it. I was climbing with Royal Robbins—he was then the soul, the spirit of American climbing. He was a record-setting climber. And we were climbing not far from here, up the Roaring Fork, a big granite face. We were having dinner that night and I said, "You know, Royal, when we were doing a certain part of the climb, I was just dying. I was in terrible anguish because I knew I couldn't do it; I just knew I couldn't do it and I had to do it anyway. Do you ever have a feeling of anguish?" And he said, "All the time."

Ziolkowski: Your prose can have a cinematic quality. Do you think you developed a certain style from those years when you were writing screenplays?
Salter: Not consciously. But I think everybody's been influenced by the cinematic, the cutting, also long passages followed by silence.

Ziolkowski: That's an interesting category, silence in writing.
Salter: Yeah. Well, I'm sensitive about this—that I don't write enough dialogue, that I'm not gratifying the desire for just listening to people talking. I'm inclined to write dialogue that I think needs to be there, rather than just spending time talking about this or that.

Ziolkowski: Maybe descriptive writing is the closest thing to silence in a novel.
Salter: I've never thought of it that way.

Ziolkowski: For instance, in *Burning the Days*, there's a description of your father's breakdown toward the end of his life: "He was just lying down for half an hour, he said. We sat in the living room, my mother and I, crushed by finality while he lay in bed in the city he had meant to triumph in, in the afternoon, traffic blaring in the street, the tall buildings shining their dead windows, gulls sitting on the water." That's an example of how you deploy this technique of showing individuals surrounded by an indifferent, multi-dimensional world. These other microcosms don't care about the human, but they lend the human dimension and pathos; they create a richer, more complex reality.
Salter: Yes.

Ziolkowski: I love in your work how a few phrases create the effect of the Bruegel painting of Icarus. He's falling, but the peasants are going along. It's not always so poignant, but it's an effect that is close to silence for me.
Salter: Yeah.

Ziolkowski: A lot of *All That Is* takes place in New York City, where you were raised from the age of two. Your relationship to New York as a native son is complex. On the one hand, you write in your memoir that you were "born to the city and thus free not to love it." On the other hand, you have an authority about New York that non-native writers lack.
Salter: I never left it. I mean, it's always your city. And it seems completely familiar to me, even the newness of it, wherever it is. And of course the geography, the emotional geography of my life is all right there in New York. You pass certain buildings, certain corners, certain streets, and parts of your life are illuminated for a moment again. It's like the smell of the earth to people who come from the country.

Ziolkowski: I was reading *Charlotte's Web* to my son recently, and in the introduction, E. B. White is quoted as saying that the main thing he wants to convey with his writing is that he loved the world. I think of that as something that comes through in your work also. At the heart of it is a celebration of experience—as if to argue that the world and what happens in it is enough. That's how the title *All That Is* strikes me, as a kind of summational claim for the adequacy or the fullness of life as it's lived, as opposed to another world or some metaphysical longing or longing for elsewhere.

Salter: I think it's an astute description of a lot of what I'm doing. I mean, it's tremendous: this world, this life. Take it while you have it.

Ziolkowski: So what's next for you? What are you working on now?

Salter: Are you kidding? You think there's going to be a next? My dear fellow, let's have lunch!

Master of the Slow Reveal

Kevin Rabalais / 2013

Edited from *Sydney Morning Herald* (April 27, 2013), 26–27. © Kevin Rabalais. Reprinted with permission.

In the driver's seat of his well-worn Volvo, James Salter spreads a map of Long Island across his knees. His voice fragile but deliberate, he offers tales of the region's natives and of European settlement, also of the artists who lived and worked nearby, among them Willem de Kooning and Jackson Pollock. "Walt Whitman called it by its Native American name," Salter says. "Paumanok: 'the island that pays tribute.'" Then, pointing to the map's eastern edge, his fingers fan out. "See how it fishtails."

It's an observation of someone who is used to looking down on things. Salter flew F-86 Sabre jets in the Korean War, an experience he chronicles in *The Hunters*. That debut novel, published in 1956, reads like *Top Gun* written by a fighter pilot with the soul of a poet. Now, on the day of the American publication of *All That Is*, his first novel in thirty-four years, Salter, aged eighty-seven, moves with cool confidence.

He is unrushed, his words measured. Here is someone who has survived dogfights with Russian MIGs. In another life he worked on film projects with Roman Polanski, Sidney Lumet, and Robert Redford. He's also one of the most revered American writers of his generation, author of eight works of fiction, including *A Sport and a Pastime* and *Light Years*, novels long considered contemporary classics.

For the past thirty-five years Salter and his wife, Kay, have divided their time between Bridgehampton, Long Island (population 1756), and Aspen, Colorado. Evidence of their Rocky Mountain life, from which they returned last week, greets you at the door in the form of Salter's vintage hiking boots. They're a reminder that this is the man who decided in his fifties to become a proficient alpinist in order to write *Solo Faces*, a novel many critics and climbers cite as the best written on the subject. Around 1979, the year *Solo*

Faces appeared in bookstores, Salter began making notes for a new novel. His readers have been waiting ever since.

An unfortunate trend in the media has been to claim *All That Is* as Salter's first book in thirty-four years. Since *Solo Faces*, however, he has published two story collections, one—*Dusk*—the recipient of a PEN/Faulkner Award. Other recent publications include a book of travel essays, the unforgettable letters collected in *Memorable Days*, and the memoirs *Gods of Tin* and *Burning the Days*, the latter as generous in its offerings as any novelist's autobiographical writings. The gap between novels and the cultish allegiance of Salter's readers—some of whom cling to the work as though it constitutes a secret order—have made *All That Is* one of the most highly anticipated books of the decade.

"I was making notes for a book like this thirty-five years ago," says Salter, dressed in jeans and a sweater and now seated at his book-strewn dining room table. "This," he leans in to whisper, "is one of the hazards of being an author." Those notes have long since disappeared.

"I remembered what they were like in a ghost-story sense," Salter says. "They were like that line that you write down once and you can't remember and that cannot be paraphrased. This novel is what resulted because of that loss. But the book is not a substitution for something lost. That's just how it came about. I didn't postpone it. I didn't say, 'I'm going to start writing novels again.' It was something I had been thinking of and was delayed."

As Salter writes in the epigraph of *All That Is*, "There comes a time when you realize that everything is a dream, and only those things preserved in writing have any possibility of being real." It's the sentiment of a man who, after publishing *The Hunters*, left a venerable military career in order to assume the uncertain existence of a novelist. They are also the words of someone with firm convictions about the role of literature.

It's unsurprising Salter's home is filled with books and other objects of the literary life. More surprising, yet entirely appropriate, are the dozens of die-cast airplane models, positioned on a low shelf as though on the flight line. ("That's from my son," Salter says. "I thought they were yours," Kay says.) In the next room, near the dining table, hangs a black-and-white photograph of the Soviet writer Isaac Babel and his young daughter, Nathalie.

"Babel was always my favorite," Salter says. "There are books that are different kinds of books. Like things that are done by hand, they have another quality to them. This is a quality difficult to describe exactly, but any reader, anybody who likes books and reading, recognizes the difference. It's handmade. It's created rather than just written down."

Salter could be referring to his own work. Long praised by fellow writers and critics, mass readership has eluded him. That deserves to change with *All That Is*. An ambitious, page-turning novel, it follows the life of Philip Bowman, a naval officer-turned-book editor, and progresses with vigor and intensity through the final days of World War II and into the postwar era. It's at once classic Salter and an unexpected addition, in both style and content, to his esteemed body of work.

"I suspected that my age was going to be a factor in people's learning about the book." Salter says. "I didn't want to be doddering along and sentimentally and nostalgically petering out, so the idea of pace was on my mind when I was writing."

He has also grown tired of the "writer's writer" label. "I wanted to write in a somewhat leaner style than I had in, for instance, *Light Years*, which is abundant in its metaphors and its recognition of the beauty or the singularity of certain things," he says. "With this new book, I wanted to let the story and the instances give you the sense that it's moving along."

All That Is stems from Salter's long fascination with the lives of editors. "I thought it was a rather perfect life," he says. "Editors are involved in reading, in books, and doing something that might have some real importance. The editors that I knew had friends in other countries who were also editors. It was a kind of family, a possibility of friendships that were long-lasting and put you in contact with other cultures, other countries. The editors I came to know were all mature men. I didn't know them before I had written a few books. Only then did I come to know them both professionally but also socially, personally. That's how the book came about."

There were three editors in particular whom Salter admired. "And there were two other men who impressed me and who I wanted to write about," he says. "So I took a shot at doing a cubistic kind of method of putting them together."

About Philip Bowman, the character amalgamated from these lives, Salter writes, "What the joys of music were to others, words on a page were to him."

An alert sounds, signaling a new message on Salter's computer and he excuses himself, saying, "That may be from my publisher." Seated at his living room desk, he breaks into laughter. Richard Ford has written to discuss the pair's upcoming on-stage event at the 92nd Street Y in Manhattan. "He doesn't want introductions," Salter says. "He just wants the two of us to go out and do it." Returning through the kitchen, Salter passes two boxes filled with the Knopf hardcovers of *All That Is*. He holds up a copy, proud to show it off. "Suddenly what you have written has an authority that it didn't have before," he says.

Back inside the car, Salter turns right out of the driveway and almost immediately pulls over to examine a mansion under construction with an attached guesthouse. "These are Wall Street executives," he says, going on to talk about the many changes Bridgehampton has undergone since he moved here. The conversation returns to literature, with the appropriately timed detail: "Here is Peter Matthiessen's house," he says. "You can't see it from the road, but trust me. It's back there."

At Bobby Van's, a restaurant on Bridgehampton's picturesque shop-front block, Salter says, "I want to show you something."

Perhaps the lunchtime patrons recognize him as the greatest American prose stylist of his generation, but it's unlikely that this detail makes them turn to watch Salter pass. Handsome and elegant, he moves with gravitas and grace down the long bar and stops beneath a black-and-white photograph of four men standing outside the restaurant, circa 1975.

"That's James Jones, Capote, Willie Morris, and John Knowles," he says. In one photograph, a generation of elite American writers, Salter's age or younger, each long dead. He pauses, as though offering respect, and it's easy to imagine that Salter's ambitions have changed little since his school years when the idea, as he writes in *Burning the Days*, had been inside him "like a pathogen—the idea of being a writer and from the great heap of days making something lasting."

James Salter—en intervju [an interview]

Hans Ingvar Roth / 2013

Published in Swedish translation at www.dixikon.se (October 19, 2013). Original English transcript (with assistance from Patrik Ekström) printed with permission. Hans Ingvar Roth is professor of human rights at Stockholm University and a literary critic for the daily newspaper *Svenska Dagbladet* in Sweden.

In April 2013, at the age of eighty-seven, James Salter published *All That Is*, his first novel in more than thirty years. In May, Salter also made his first visit in many years to Ireland and the United Kingdom, where he filled great lecture halls. British literary critics asked themselves why his international breakthrough did not come sooner, considering the literary quality of his works, especially the novels *A Sport and a Pastime* and *Light Years*, as well as the memoir *Burning the Days*.

Before James Salter set out on his lecture tour, I had the opportunity to conduct an extended interview with him on April 3, 2013, in the restaurant Gramercy Tavern in Manhattan, the same neighborhood in which some of the events in the novel take place. It has been thirteen years since we first met at the publishing house Wahlström and Widstrand in Stockholm. Salter still makes the same energetic impression, and I can tell that he is proud of his latest novel, which may also be his last. Salter talks about the characters in his new novel as if they were people living close to him, which is not strange considering most of them were inspired by his own encounters and experiences. His eyes become focused and attentive when I try to interpret and evaluate certain actions and characteristics of the main characters.

Hans Ingvar Roth: Why did it take so long for *All That Is* to come out?
James Salter: Before *All That Is*, I tried to write a completely different novel—a project that I eventually abandoned because I could not quite get into the main character, who appeared too subtle and elusive. Over the past two decades, I have also focused on writing short stories. The main character of

All That Is—Philip Bowman—was in many ways inspired by people I have met in the publishing world over half a century, a world that truly deserves being written about. In my life as an author, I have had the privilege of meeting famous publishers such as Joe Fox, Robert Ginna, Roger Straus, Michael Holmes, George Plimpton, Richard Weaver, George Weidenfeld, and Olivier Cohen. To me, all these people represented a civilized and cultivated world, and their lives overlapped in intriguing ways. Similarly, my novel revolves around the network of Bowman and his friends in the publishing business. Some of the publishers I mentioned also became close friends of mine.

Books and novels carry civilization on their backs, for reading books is one of the best ways to gain a greater understanding of the complexity of life. Reading also makes us more human. Furthermore, writing has a special place in human existence: it provides meaningful contexts to other art forms, which enable us to understand and engage in them more deeply. For example, after reading an art critic's views on the current Edvard Munch exhibition at the Museum of Modern Art, I will have a much different understanding of Munch's paintings than if I go to the exhibition with a completely open mind or without any pre-understanding of who Munch was. In this sense, writing is perhaps the most important foundation of all other art forms. Language is the key to human existence, and without it we can never truly experience the beauty, complexity, and richness of life.

I find writing to be a very disciplined and time-consuming activity. I jot down the outline of the story on a large sheet of paper on the wall, and then the story develops on the basis of my notes in several notebooks. The words are rubbed and polished until they feel adequate. That certain words or a certain sentence ends up in the book is motivated by the fact that they feel appropriate based on multiple senses, such as hearing and sight. While spoken language is like breathing—easy and spontaneous—written language is hard-won. Once the latter has been conquered, endless worlds and possibilities open to an author.

Roth: What is your view on the future of the printed book and the publishing world?

Salter: The readers of my book will probably realize that it is marked by a certain sense of nostalgia. I have written about a publishing world that no longer exists. Today, it is more or less all about money. Admittedly, publishers and authors used to be business colleagues with financial motives in the past, as well—the publishers had rents and salaries to pay, and the authors had to be able to survive—but there was something more to it. In some cases, they became close friends, and their relationships were imbued with the notion that they, together, were protecting the book's status as the pillar of civilization.

Another disturbing development is the closure of reputable bookstores around the country. In New York, there are almost no quality bookstores left since the closure of such stores as the Gotham Book Mart and Books and Co. When such bookstores disappear, the public loses important education centers and "people's universities." Qualified literary criticism has also been weakened, and now we have a cacophony of more or less unqualified opinions on the Internet. Indeed, cultures and information flows change all the time and I do not know what will happen to the novel and the printed book in the future. For the first time in its five-hundred-year history, the status of the printed book is being threatened. However, I still believe that it will ultimately survive, even if its status has weakened considerably in our civic culture.

What gives me hope for the future of the printed book is that electronic editions cannot fully replace a physical book. Think of all the things that you can do with the book that you have with you. You can make notes in the margin, underline, tear out a page, and quickly flip back and forth through the pages in a completely different way than in the electronic edition. The physical book also has such qualities as a clear beginning and an end. It is not like the genie in the bottle that vanishes into cyberspace. In addition, the books have protective covers with illustrations that often constitute works of art that reflect the zeitgeist. Even if you were to meet someone who told you that he or she could create an electronic equivalent to all this, it would still not be the same. It is similar to saying that, in the future, we will be able to create a robot that can do everything a person or a human being can do; in the end, it is still not the same thing. Humanity is the benchmark and will always go above and beyond any attempts to create artificial counterparts. One might say the same about the physical book: the electronic editions strive to match and surpass the printed book, but ultimately, the latter is the primary benchmark.

Roth: Tell me something about the title of your novel and the cover of the American edition.

Salter: The cover depicts a man moving through the water. There is a scene in the novel where Bowman jumps into the high waves to impress his girl-friend, Christine, who then follows him into the water. After a few minutes they find themselves in a dangerous situation, and Bowman is not sure if they will survive and make it back to the beach. They do survive, however, and after this shocking experience they make love to each other. To Bowman, this event has profound meaning, but to his girlfriend, Christine, it is just a brief dramatic sequence in a relationship that she probably never really took seriously.

I have an epigraph in the novel that many readers have embraced: "There comes a time when you realize that everything is a dream, and only those things preserved in writing have any possibility of being real." The title of the novel does not refer to this epigraph, however, even though it expresses something important. The title *All That Is* is deliberately ambiguous. It might represent everything related to human life—birth, love, loss, aging, and maturing as a person—but it might also represent all that exists in the world.

Roth: Does your new novel have any particular message or underlying pattern?

Salter: No. My novel does not have any particular message or underlying pattern. Nor is there a breaking point or any specific event that can open the book like a key. Rather, *All That Is* presents a tapestry of personal fates that are intertwined with each other in more or less obvious ways. The novel is like an open life, and every reader can relate to its events in their own personal way. What I am trying to say here is that my novel should not primarily be seen as a document to be analyzed in a literary seminar. When dealing with strong emotions and dramatic events in people's lives, which are frequent in this story, one does not have to dig very deep to understand their meaning. The novel describes a person's life journey with all that it implies in terms of aspirations, risks, and aging.

The fact that the novel includes several themes from my previous books, such as military life and privileged artistic communities, was not a conscious choice on my part, either. In other words, I did not set out to create some kind of synthesis of my previous work. However, the book does convey the insight that no human life—no matter how privileged it may appear to be—can avoid disasters such as accidents, illness, betrayal, and crime. This vulnerability is something that all of us must learn to live with. In fact, we can only be truly safe for the present moment. Once we have had the opportunity to experience the ultimate happiness, such as great love or becoming a parent, we become the most vulnerable. Losing somebody close to you, such as your own child, is something so terrible that it is beyond the realm of understanding.

Roth: Which authors and books have been important to you over the years?
Salter: Isaac Babel might be one of the authors I admire the most. His short stories are so intense, and each phrase carries a loaded meaning. This intensity and tightness is very difficult to transfer to the longer format of the novel, however. It would simply be too much.

I keep returning to Isak Dinesen's *Out of Africa*. This is perfect in terms of both language and content, and I can read it over and over again. Dinesen herself was an extraordinary person who demonstrated courage, forgiveness, and reconciliation in spite of all the difficulties she had to go through in life, not least because of her husband, Bror Blixen. I am often struck by Isak Dinesen's capacity for forgiveness and reconciliation—for example, that she was able to speak well of Bror Blixen in spite of everything he put her through.

I also admire Southern authors like Tennessee Williams—possibly one of America's greatest playwrights—and Eudora Welty, Peter Taylor, and Flannery O'Connor. The conflict-ridden areas that these Southern authors lived in helped to add a certain luster and drama to their work. I greatly admire all these authors, although I have not consciously tried to emulate them. To me, writing has always required a focus that involves excluding the work of other authors. One might also say that most authors are jealous of certain other authors in some sense. While you are not jealous of the person, you are jealous of the work that you would have liked to write yourself.

Roth: Something that many authors today envy you is your novel *A Sport and a Pastime*. Can you tell me how it was received when it first came out and how it came to gain cult and classic status?
Salter: When the book came out in the 1960s, thanks to publisher George Plimpton, its primary theme—sexual love—was not particularly controversial, and erotic classics by D. H. Lawrence and Henry Miller were already available. However, the American company Doubleday, which my publisher—Plimpton—worked for, was a conservative publishing house that did not want to promote the book in any active way, although the company at least kept its promise to publish the novel. In the few ads that did surface, it was written that this is not a book about baseball! In other words, the novel soon fell into oblivion, and it would take several years before it attracted any interest. The increasing attention was probably due to word of mouth, because the novel has never been used in schools or in higher education—probably due to its loaded erotic depictions.

Sexual love is probably one of the hardest things for a novelist to write about. It is all very personal and difficult to express with words. At the same time, sexuality is one of the key dimensions or axes of life. Our experiences of sexual love are also what we really remember through life. Over the years I have received many requests to make a movie of the novel—I have had five proposals in the past year alone. I have always declined, however, and I probably always will. The risk of it turning into a pornographic film is far too great.

Roth: You worked in Hollywood for many years as a screenwriter and director. Why did you leave that world?

Salter: I eventually realized that it was not my home. I did not have much success either as a screenwriter or a director. The first movie that I was involved in was a war movie based on my novel *The Hunters*—a partly autobiographical novel in that it portrays my time as a fighter pilot in the 1950s. The movie was a disaster; it did not even have the right aircraft! On the upside, it enabled me to support myself as a writer for many years. Writing literature also suits me much better than working on screenplays. In the movie business you are constantly circumvented and have to compromise on the content that you have created. One of my most famous novels, *Light Years*, is also very difficult to imagine as a conventional movie due to its chain of events and its metaphorical content.

However, I think that some of my novels could be successfully made into movies—*Cassada*, for example, which is based on my experiences as an officer in West Germany during the Cold War. My novel about mountaineering, *Solo Faces*, was based on a script for a movie in which Robert Redford was meant to play the leading role. He did not like the script, however, and I later turned it into a novel. The novel is likely to be adapted into a movie soon, which I am happy about, although the mountaineering world depicted in the novel is long gone. Today, mountaineering is an entire industry; very different from the mountain climbing I was involved in in the 1970s.

Roth: Will there be another novel after *All That Is*?

Salter: There is a person at the end of *All That Is*, Ann, whom Philip Bowman meets in his old age. He falls in love with her, and it seems as if he has finally found a life partner. She is a very interesting person whose life I would like to return to. In what form remains to be seen, however.

Another Kind of Life: Jonathan Lee Interviews James Salter

Jonathan Lee / 2013

From *Guernica* (May 1, 2013). © Jonathan Lee. Reprinted with permission. Jonathan Lee is a British writer and the author of the novels *Who Is Mr Satoshi?* (2010) and *Joy* (2012). www .jonathan-lee.net

I have a confession to make to the proprietors of the Brasserie Cognac in midtown Manhattan: I stole a menu. The menu bears the words "*Le thé n'est qu'une excuse*" ("The tea is just an excuse") and the accompanying picture is of an elegant continental blonde feeding confectionary into the mouth of a man in a turtleneck sweater. France. Romance. Food and drink as tools of flirtation. It all seemed so one hundred percent James Salter and, since James Salter was the man I was waiting to meet, I claimed it as a memento.

Would Salter have disapproved of my theft? It's hard to know. He's an intriguing combination of solemnity and playfulness, candor and manners. He entered the restaurant briskly, smart and only slightly stooped, a handsome, white-haired eighty-seven-year-old man. There are lines written on his forehead and papery crinkles in the corners of his eyes, but he's still thick-shouldered, powerful-looking, a former military man with a firm grip on my hand. Along with a handful of others, he has a good claim to being the greatest living American novelist.

When the waitress arrived at our table, Salter's eyes, custom-built to twinkle mischievously, twinkled mischievously. He asked her for some "tiny sandwiches," and five minutes later some tiny sandwiches arrived. Macaroons, too. Miniature cakes. He doesn't laugh easily (not at my jokes, anyway), but his lips always seem to be resisting a grin. He looks like a man struggling to contain some great indescribable amusement with the world. You sense a desire to make a pleasing impression, but also a resignation to the fact his statements may well be misunderstood. If you stumble upon a decent question, he is nodding well before you've finished asking it. Pick a more predictable topic and his eyes politely die as he reaches for more food.

All That Is, Salter's new novel, is big in its ambitions, episodic in its structure, and written in prose which he told me is deliberately lacking in "ecstatic lines," "showy" sentences, anything which "could be accused of being chi-chi and silly." It's a sad, hopeful work that beautifully evokes the pleasures and disappointments of a life lived in books, relationships, America. The prose may glitter less than in his previous novels, but you still know from the first pages that Salter is the author. "Vicky Hollins in her silk dress, the glances clinging to her as she passed." Who else writes lines like that?

We talked about Zadie Smith (he liked her recent *New Yorker* story, "The Embassy of Cambodia") and then we talked about Sarah Hall (he admires *The Beautiful Indifference*, and wrote her a letter to tell her so). When I switched on my recorder, he leaned forward a little in his chair. Halfway through the interview I heard a man at a nearby table whisper "Who is that guy?," but Salter, if he heard this, ignored it.

Guernica: How did *All That Is* start its life?

James Salter: I think I probably began several other books first. I don't mean that I started book after book in succession, but I toyed with—considered—various novels I thought I might write. And I finally saw that what I was really trying to write was a book about the life of book editors, of publishing. It's a subject I've been interested in for a long time. I've been an observer of the business for years—more than that, of course, since I've known editors not merely as editors but as good friends. So *All That Is* began with that impulse, the impulse to write about a life in books. And at some point I realized I wanted to make it broader than that. I didn't know exactly how. I spent a couple of years just filling notebooks.

Guernica: You said in a *Paris Review* interview in the early '90s that you like to go into a new novel "with a lot of ammunition."

James Salter: Yes, in an echo of my supposedly colorful past . . . I still like to make a lot of notes. During the couple of years I was filling out notebooks for *All That Is*, I had nothing definite except a one-page outline of a life. That life changed slightly. At one stage he was married. He had a couple of children. He was a slightly different figure in a slightly different life. When I'm filling notebooks, I'm trying to pin down what I'm really interested in and to find those details that are so hard to come by, details that I can look at and believe are right on the mark. Things which bring a novel to life. They can take a while to come. [Smiles.] Unfortunately a big point has been made that this is my first novel in thirty-some years, so that's been everyone else's first question: why did it take you so long to write this? Why did you wait thirty-four years? And those really aren't the right questions. I know they make sense, but I can't give a really satisfactory answer when I'm asked. I get asked those questions much more often than I get asked about the title, for example.

Guernica: What does the title mean to you?

James Salter: Well, you're a writer, so I'm sure you know that these things—while interesting—can be difficult to explain. But let me try to answer my own question. There are at least two ways of looking at the title *All That Is*. One of them is that for Bowman, the pages are "all that is"—all that is his life. And in another way, it's not his life, but all that there is in life generally, in any of our lives: a series of moments, of relationships. Neither interpretation is exclusively right, but I suppose together they explain why I felt it was the right title for the novel.

Guernica: There's a moment in the book when Bowman, after a failed relationship, talks about what's "judged inessential" in a life. That line had a resonance for me because this felt, at times, like a novel which sets out to rescue everyday "inessential" things from being forgotten—giving fragile, daily moments a beauty, a place on the page. That says: these things are essential, they're all there is.

James Salter: Yes, can I see your copy? [Reads the relevant paragraph.] That was meant purely in terms of the relationship—he cannot understand how something that mattered hugely to him could turn out not to have mattered equally or at all to her. Something tremendously important to him has been judged inessential by her. That was all I meant, but I see that it does have a wider resonance. All the moments that would be lost if they weren't set down. It's not something I had in mind when I wrote it, but I see that it stands well for certain elements in the book.

Guernica: The first book of yours I read was *Light Years*, which also concerns this idea of what's remembered and what's lost. The language of that novel is quite different to the language of *All That Is*. It feels like in this new novel you've taken a conscious decision to—I'll use a bad metaphor—dim the wattage a little bit. The prose is less dazzling, and I wondered if that was a deliberate decision. A different lighting which brings out different elements of character and story rather than individual sentences, rhythms.

James Salter: Yes, it was a deliberate thing.

Guernica: Can I ask why?

James Salter: I suppose the truth is I became a little self-conscious about people telling me how much they loved my sentences. They'd come up and say, "You know what, I've memorized lines from *Light Years*." At book signings you'd see them with the corners of pages turned down, particular pages they'd loved and sentences they'd underlined. It's flattering, but it seemed to me that this love of sentences was in some sense getting in the way of the book itself. And perhaps I also had in my head the fact that the first critic who wrote a big review of *Light Years* said it was "chi-chi," a "silly" book, words to that affect.

Guernica: This was [Robert Towers in] the *New York Times*.

James Salter: Yes, the *New York Times*. At the time, that review was wounding. I thought, "It wasn't written to be chi-chi, or silly, so this must mean that I am essentially chi-chi and silly, and that I am a writer of chi-chi, silly books." Anyway, I was sensitive to that thereafter. I don't mean morbidly sensitive but, you know, it was on my mind. After a year or two you move on and say, "All right, that's happened." But the criticism remained in my consciousness and I didn't want to write a book that could be thought of as being chi-chi and silly again.

Guernica: I loved *Light Years*. It has its die-hard devotees, many of them other writers. It's surprising to me that a review—however wounding—could affect how you felt about your prose style. In the UK the book is now a Penguin Modern Classic, a rare thing for a living novelist, and is published with an admiring introduction by Richard Ford.

James Salter: [Smiles.] That introduction is better than the book. But no, with *All That Is* I decided to modify myself a little bit. I don't mean changing my writing in a serious way, but I was crossing out some of those sentences that stood out, that were more showy. I crossed out some of the things which seemed to me excessive. I didn't want to write ecstatic lines that were going to get in the way or annoy—consciously or not—the kind of reader I wanted to attract.

Guernica: What kind of reader do you want to attract?

James Salter: Sometimes I write with a particular person in mind. I think it's fair to say that I write for a perceptive reader. You have to get it. If you don't get it the first time, you may not understand. If you like repetition, analysis, explanation, you probably won't like my books.

A writer writes a book. People read it. You don't know what they're reading, really. You read a review and think, "That is so inaccurate. You can't have been reading my book at all. You can't have been reading it with any kind of attention, because that is all wrong, that's even the wrong name you're including there." But, you know, these reviewers, generally speaking, have been diminished in importance, the work is so little respected. If you're reviewed by a real critic, by James Wood or Louis Menand, then you get something that is informed, interesting, and highly articulate. But the average review doesn't have that kind of depth anymore.

Guernica: You mentioned relying on readers to draw inferences from a single line or paragraph of your prose. Do you think there's a trend in American fiction towards novels which go the other way, working by accumulation and repetition? The layering of detail upon detail over the course of five hundred or six hundred pages to achieve psychological realism. A reader is told a lot more about a Jonathan Franzen character than he is about a Salter character.

James Salter: Amplitude is a powerful quality in fiction. It results in involvement, in sympathy with the characters. After a while, a reader can't avoid being involved with a book, caring about it, even if it's not a particularly good book. You're in it, and you're committed to it.

Guernica: Could you say a few words about the epigraph to *All That Is*? "There comes a time when you realize that everything is a dream, and only those things preserved in writing have any possibility of being real."

James Salter: This refers to the summation of life, in the same way that the title does. In the end, it finally all seems to have been a dream. Only the things written down have any gravity to them. The other things are ready to disappear.

Guernica: Late in the novel Bowman thinks of himself as "not related to other people—his life was another kind of life. He had invented it. He had dreamt himself up . . ."

James Salter: I think what he meant by that is that he was inventing, and was aware of it, his ultimately false, glorious life with this woman. It did not really exist, he discovers. Not as he pictured it. But there's the paradox. How does one explain it? Can a relationship be nonexistent after his having lived it, believed in it, for several years? Does it cease to be real simply because it fell apart? No. But it's still been proved false, in one sense.

I've written about this before in a story called "Comet." In that story a woman complains that she's discovered her husband has been having an affair for the last seven years. She's going to have to rethink those years, she says. But how can you rethink them? How can you rethink whole years of your life? You've lived them. And as much as you may come to think you were living false years, they were perfectly true to you at the time.

Guernica: Bowman is born in 1925, in New Jersey, and has a military background. He has these things in common with you. Is it helpful, when building up characters, to take some of the basic architecture of your own life, or of the lives of other people you know, and to start from there? Does it free you up to then invent the details which you mention are essential to your fiction, the ones which add that special ingredient which Saul Bellow called "esprit"?

James Salter: That was a great phrase of Bellow's. It explains it all, really. But as for whether it's a helpful thing for me to take elements from my own life, you could make a case for it, but I don't think you could prove it. I was born in New Jersey, but I left when I was a year old and the state has not meant much to me in my life since then. I picked New Jersey for the character of Bowman because a friend of mine who was an editor and writer came from Summit, New Jersey. I'd never been in Summit, and didn't even know where it was. But the name was intriguing to me, and I thought, "Why not?" I appropriated it for the novel. Of course, I then had to go to Summit. I got to know it very well.

Guernica: It makes for a good chapter heading at one stage in the book. The word "Summit" surrounded by white space.

James Salter: Yes it does. And there's an actual diner in Summit, New Jersey, which people think Hemingway wrote about in one of his stories ["The Killers"]. But it turns out that he wasn't writing about a diner in Summit, New Jersey. He was writing about a diner in a different town: Summit, Illinois. But Bowman doesn't know that—his youthful literary ignorance is illustrated in a number of ways at the beginning of the book. He's naive.

As for having Bowman be in the war, I felt I had to do that, and it comes down to something Christopher Hitchens said. He made a remark once that struck me. He said that no life is really complete that hasn't seen love, poverty, and war. I thought, "That's very succinct." So the war and the love part I could relate to, and I kept it in mind. I wasn't in the Navy, as Bowman was; I was in the Air Force. My personal experiences were nothing like Bowman's.

Guernica: You mention Bowman's naivety. Was it important to you that he should lose that over the course of the book, that the novel should trace that process?

James Salter: I think he loses his naivety, yes. Midway through the book, he's got to a point where he's able to handle himself very well in company with writers, with women, with friends. He ceases to be naive. But I don't believe he ever becomes more than an intelligent, relatively stable man satisfied with his work and with his life. I don't believe he's seeking himself, or any such thing. If you haven't found yourself by the time you're forty . . . Well, actually, I guess a lot of people haven't. Bowman is intelligent and mature, but not cunning, not shrewd, not aggressive. You'd like to know him. In fact, I did know him.

Guernica: You knew him?

James Salter: Not a specific individual, really. I simply meant he's modeled after people I've known.

Guernica: The novel starts at war, in battle, and from there moves toward more intimate, private moments in Bowman's life. You give a sense in these pages of the publishing industry back then as a somewhat quiet, genteel, intimate profession.

James Salter: It did interest me that publishing was a genteel profession back then. Perhaps not quite as genteel as we think it was, but probably more so than it is today. The book doesn't really go into this point, but many of the publishing houses then were privately owned, a single publisher or a publisher and a few associates who were responsible for everything. They could take whatever risks they wanted, could essentially publish what they liked according to their taste. Publishers today are working for big corporations. They have different pressures. I don't think they can make decisions quite as independently as they used to be able to. They have more corporate and financial responsibilities weighing on them. They're not free to go broke or go to jail.

Guernica: Maybe we can talk a little about *A Sport and a Pastime*. It's another novel that deals with the intersection between reality and the imagination; the narrator drops hints that his own account is at least partly fictitious. It was your third novel, but you've said before that it was the first "real book" you wrote. Why so?

James Salter: Well, it seemed to me that *A Sport and a Pastime* was the first novel I wrote that didn't have amateur touches. Touches that are purely technical: how to use conversation, how to attribute conversation. How to interweave thought, supposition, actuality—to put them together at the same time. I felt I was able to do that really for the first time in *A Sport and a Pastime*, or at least for the first time with any authority. To do them and make them invisible, unknown to the reader. I think that's what changed with *A Sport and a Pastime*. I became better at making my technique invisible. I felt I was writing well.

Guernica: Was there anything about the reception of *A Sport and a Pastime* that surprised you? Perhaps the level of eroticism people seemed to find in it?

James Salter: It's still an erotic book, even in these advanced times. There's nothing in that novel that high school students aren't texting to one another. And there's no shocking language in it, not any longer. There might be the word "fucking" once.

Guernica: Just once?

James Salter: I think so. I can't recall. And—yes—there's the word "prick" and "cunt." But these only appear when they're meant to have an effect. I think *A Sport and a Pastime* has a purity to it, its tone. It's a book deep in that time of life when nothing but love seems to be of importance to you. Most people go through that period at some point. That's really what the book is. It's an act of reverence. It doesn't mean to be any more than that. It should make you a little envious, perhaps, but that's all.

Guernica: In the *Paris Review* book *Object Lessons*, Dave Eggers calls your story "Bangkok": "a nine-page master class in dialogue." The power of that story and some of your others comes almost entirely from speech.

James Salter: Generally speaking, I tend to like dialogue that has some reason for being there, that tells you something. In a lot of books people talk and they're not interesting, merely talking about things that are inconsequential. Personally, I prefer dialogue that tends to have a reason for being there.

Dialogue's a method of revelation, of course. A few words of dialogue can reveal worlds about a character. I thought Dave Eggers was very perceptive about "Bangkok." I thought he picked out essential things. For example, somewhere about a third of the way into the story the woman says to the man, "Tell me something, Chris." And as Eggers points out, it's a rather soft, civilized name compared to Hollis, the man's surname, which he's been called by until that point. And we suddenly have a different notion of who the character is, and who she is, and of what has passed between them.

Guernica: Has any of your work writing for films been enjoyable, or helped to inform your fiction?

James Salter: I don't know. I always say "no" because of my lack of any real success in films. I had films made, but they weren't as good as I anticipated. But of course films are dialogue, so you're writing dialogue continually. I suppose you learn something by writing it over and over.

Kathy [Zuckerman, Deputy Director of Publicity at Knopf] was talking to me today about the new Julian Barnes book, in which he writes about being up in a hot air balloon. I haven't read the book, but when I was asking Kathy what the relevance of the air ballooning was in a book which I'm told is about grief, she indicated that the reader comes to realize he was inferring, with that image of being up in the balloon, a broader point of view. A sense of perspective. Seeing the earth in a different way. Usually when I'm asked if being a flyer has influenced my writing, I say "not much." But listening to Kathy today I thought maybe I'm not giving flying its due. You become accustomed to a very different scale of things, up there. You pay attention to things you don't normally pay attention to. Perhaps flying did have an impact on my writing. I don't really know.

Guernica: Were there times, after you left the Air Force, when you regretted having done so?

James Salter: Yes. Every day. For a long time, every day. I wasn't really a writer yet. And I didn't know how to become one. Just writing things down on a page didn't make me feel like a writer in the way I'd felt like a pilot. And meanwhile everyone was going on with life, especially the people I knew and had served with. I felt very powerless and lost in those years. Futile is the word. Complete futility. You go from being a kind of aristocrat in the Air Force to being, as I said in the *New Yorker*, a nobody on a bus. If I wanted to be somebody, I had to start my life again. Being somebody: it's one of the ideas in life, no? That's what my father made clear to me. The importance of being somebody. He wanted to be somebody. And he underlined to me the fate of trying to be somebody and not quite managing to do it.

Guernica: Your writing offers perspectives on second-rateness, on the idea of striving for recognition and success and those things, often, remaining just out of reach. It's something discussed by Vernon Rand in *Solo Faces*, and also Viri in *Light Years*. Then there's a moving moment in *Burning the Days* where you describe your father lying "in bed in the city he was meant to triumph in."

James Salter: Well, it seems to be recurrent with me. In climbing, being first-rate is part of the whole enterprise. The important climbers want to be the first man up the mountain, the one who put up the first route. You're usually only remembered if you put up the first route on a very important climb. The route might even be named after you. That's a kind of glory.

Guernica: Do you write for glory?

James Salter: We all do. You write for glory. You play for glory. There's an ambition to excel, isn't there, to be a star? To score more, to do more, even when it's a team sport. So I think striving for glory is a natural subject for a writer. Seeking fame. I think Viri puts it well when he says in *Light Years* that there's no greatness without fame. Writers want to be read. They want to be admired. And they want to be known, I would say.

Guernica: Immortality?

James Salter: You would have to be very optimistic to think that any of your books will be among the books that survive in the very long run. I think if a writer is lucky enough to still have a few books around after he's gone, a few that are still being read, then he's accomplished quite a lot.

Guernica: "Write or perish." That's something you've often been quoted as saying.

James Salter: Oh, that was a stupid thing to say.

Guernica: Was it?

James Salter: [Laughs.] Oh, God yes. The really stupid thing was the "perish." I'd given up everything to be a writer, and if I didn't then go on to do that—to write—then I didn't know what would happen to me. That's all I really meant to say, but I got carried away by some kind of poetic impulse.

Guernica: Without spoiling the ending, do you think Bowman has, by the last pages of *All That Is*, come to terms with the sweep of his life? That it wasn't, perhaps, all he at first imagined for it?

James Salter: I think he's content. He's with a woman, and he talks about whether they can have a life like the lives in art, by which he means the lives of painters and sculptors, lives on a different level from yours or mine. In place of getting married, that is, which he feels he is too old, too used-up for, perhaps. But meaning to stay together always. And he says that he wishes he could introduce her to his past, have her somehow able to share in the past, things that have happened to him, and they are going to go on together, in immediate terms to Venice as they've talked about but only vaguely. I think he's bound for a long happiness, but naturally some reviewers and readers will decide otherwise.

Guernica: And what about the lives of books? There's a line towards the end of *All That Is* where you write that "The power of the novel in the nation's culture had weakened," but that, nonetheless, "fresh faces kept appearing, wanting to be part of it." Your character thinks publishing has "retained a suggestion of elegance, like a pair of beautiful, bone-shined shoes owned by a bankrupt man."

James Salter: It seems to me that literature is giving way a little bit to the immediacy of other diversions, other forms of entertainment. What will it be in fifty years? I don't know. Will there be printed books? Probably, but I'm not sure. There's always going to be literature, though. I believe that. I think literature has a way of getting deep into people and being essential. Literature has its own powers.

Salter on Salter: An Interview

Kay Eldredge Salter / 2013

From *Narrative Magazine* (Spring 2013). © Kay Eldredge Salter. Reprinted with permission.

It's a major event in the world of letters each time James Salter completes a new work. Anticipating the publication of Salter's seventh novel, *All That Is*, a dazzlingly adult, sexy, and heartbreaking book that captures what passes between men and women over a lifetime, we asked the woman who knows him best—Salter's wife of thirty-seven years, Kay Eldredge, a playwright and novelist herself—to share with us Salter's views on life, love, work, and how writing is the most demanding and satisfying of all mistresses.
—The Editors, *Narrative Magazine.*

James Salter has done all the interviews he's prepared to do for the moment. As his wife, I probably know him as well as he knows himself, so I'm conducting an insider's interview and taking the liberty, with his approval, of both asking and answering these questions.
—Kay Eldredge

KAY ELDREDGE: Where do you like to write?
JAMES SALTER: Usually someplace other than where I am. I'm always longing to write if circumstances mean that I can't actually do it—when taking a long drive, for instance.

I like to write in an empty house, when I have either the whole house to myself or at least a part of it where I won't be disturbed.

ELDREDGE: At your desk?
SALTER: I have more than one and like to move around. I have a big table upstairs with my typewriter, a table in the bedroom, a desk in the living room, and the dining table. In the summer, there's also the table on our porch. All are full of books and papers. Anyone who comes to clean the

house likes to tidy everything, which is a disaster. In the clutter, I know where things are, more or less, but if it's all been put in neat piles, I can't find anything.

There are cycles to some of this, of course. When friends are coming to dinner, I clear the dining table or the one on the porch, temporarily.

ELDREDGE: Your typewriter isn't very portable.

SALTER: It usually stays in one place. I use an old IBM Selectric. It's getting harder to find the ribbons, not to mention a repairman. When I need one, I have to take it into Manhattan. And it's so heavy, I bought a small moving cart to transport it.

I'm pretty fast, even though I use only two fingers. People ask if it doesn't drive me crazy to have to retype pages rather than just insert changes the way you can with a Word program. But I like the process. Every time I retype, I rewrite, even things I wasn't planning to change. Editing is everything, and that forces me to look a number of times at what I've written. Computers make it too easy for too many writers to just spew it out endlessly.

I like computers, but I don't trust them. I'm afraid they'll eat what I write and then refuse to ever regurgitate it. You can never write the same thing again.

ELDREDGE: At what point do you show someone something you've written?

SALTER: When I think it's finished. I think you can undermine what you're trying to write if you show it or talk about it too soon.

ELDREDGE: Many writers show their work as they write it. Some even read it aloud to friends or family.

SALTER: I've done that sometimes. I tend to be secretive, though. I don't like to reveal personal things. Even close friends say so. I like to ask them questions about their lives, but I don't want to have to answer theirs. And it doesn't have to be about anything that particularly matters, though sometimes it is.

ELDREDGE: Are there exceptions?

SALTER: My wife knows me very well. But I can still surprise her even after thirty-seven years. As she can me. Not all the time, but now and then. That's a very good thing. It would be tedious to know everything about the person you're closest to. On the other hand, what counts between two people in the long run is pleasure in conversation with each other. I don't mean discussing the basics of domestic life, but talking about people, books, the garden, except we don't have a garden. You have to do the other too, but I try to minimize it.

ELDREDGE: You make domestic life sound negative.
SALTER: It can be, if you let it take over. I do like a certain domestic routine, especially in the morning and evening. Tea and talk at breakfast. And later, as the light fails, ending the workday by putting on music, drawing the curtains, having a drink and conversation before dinner, which shouldn't just be something thrown together at the last minute. I like to read in the evenings. I don't go to movies and rarely to restaurants. We have friends to dinner sometimes or go to them. We used to do one or the other three or four times a week, but I've reached the point where I appreciate an evening at home.

ELDREDGE: How would you describe yourself?
SALTER: Contrary, sometimes even just for the sake of it. Argument, even if fierce, can be irresistible.

In private life, though, I hate argument and confrontation. I suppose part of that is that I want things—important things between people—to be understood, not discussed. Maybe that means there are sometimes things that need to be talked about but aren't. That's fine with me.

I'm hard to satisfy. I like things done the way I like them done. I think of it as having standards. Others tend to think of it as being critical. But then, I'm rarely satisfied with myself, either.

I like the Oscar Wilde quote "Only a fool does not judge by appearances." I'm sensitive to aesthetics, whether of a room or a person's clothing or a road leading someplace or the food on a plate.

My wife says I'm able to change, though most people find that a difficult thing to do, especially after a certain age. I don't do it on request, but I recognize it when something needs to change or be reconsidered or when it's important that I behave differently—I'm really talking about things between myself and other people, not the way I shave or chop vegetables. But maybe the vegetables.

ELDREDGE: What comforts you?
SALTER: Nature, in almost all its forms. Weather. The difficulties of others. Going in the ocean on late summer afternoons. A martini in the evening, or an Old Fashioned. Telling a favorite story. Anchovy paste.

ELDREDGE: And writing itself?

SALTER: It's almost impossible to feel content at the end of a day of writing. But I know that and don't expect anything different.

I keep journals and draw on them. There's a lot about people. Fiction doesn't mean "made up."

I try never to save anything for a later work. If it's right, I use it. On the other hand, once I write about someone, in a way I'm more or less finished with them, so there can be repercussions.

I like the idea of writing for a certain number of hours at a certain time of day, but that doesn't work for me. The time of day I like to work varies. The number of hours is sometimes at the mercy of life itself. I worked longer and harder finishing this novel than I have in years. I had certain things in mind about how I wanted to write it—looser and more flowing and less refined. I think I've achieved that. It's a book I like very much.

You Are Writing What You Are, All the Time: A Conversation with James Salter

Dan DeWeese / 2013

James Salter interview by Dan DeWeese. Copyright © 2013 by James Salter, originally appeared in *Propeller*, Fall 2013. Reprinted with permission. Dan DeWeese is the author of the novel *You Don't Love This Man* and the story collection *Disorder*.

James Salter's first novel, *The Hunters*, was published in 1956, when he was a fighter pilot serving in the Korean War. Over the course of the ensuing decades he has published five more novels, two story collections, the memoir *Burning the Days*, and *Life Is Meals*, a "bedside book" coauthored with his wife, journalist and playwright Kay Eldredge Salter, that includes recipes and culinary hints, observations, and anecdotes. His work has been recognized with the PEN/Faulkner Award (for *Dusk and Other Stories*), the 2012 PEN/Malamud Award, and the inaugural Windham-Campbell Prize, among many other laurels and notes of admiration. Salter's latest novel, *All That Is*, was published in April.

We had planned to meet at a restaurant in Manhattan, but Salter had broken his leg a couple days before the interview, so Kay Salter kindly showed staff writer Rachel Greben and me to the Salters' small sublet apartment near the United Nations building. Despite his injury, Salter was generous and uncomplaining throughout an hour and a half of questions over coffee and croissants. The interview was conducted on October 4, 2013.

Dan DeWeese: Did you know from the beginning that you wanted *All That Is* to have the kind of scope it has, or did this project change over the time you worked on it?

James Salter: I don't think the scope, that is to say the arc of the book, changed. But the way it proceeded changed a little bit, with events and people mostly moving in and out, well defined but perhaps not reappearing. I didn't plan it that way. It just started to happen, so I kept doing it; it seemed that might be interesting. And that eventually became the general—I don't want to say "structure," but maybe "architecture" is a better word—the general tone of the book. But I knew it was going to take up the same span of my own life. I wanted it to start with the end of the second war and go up to, I don't know, somewhere around now—nothing precise. And the events were all along that chronological line. But there were many things that I thought that would be in the book that I didn't put in, and vice versa.

DeWeese: When I'm reading it, you seem very free, in a good way, about a willingness to have episodes in the book that are well drawn . . . I'm just thinking about myself as a writer, I would sometimes have a concern that I need to follow up on those in some kind of really orderly way. But a lot of this book's power seems to come from a certain kind of freedom from those kinds of concerns.

Salter: Yes, that was what I was trying to say when I answered the previous question. The boundaries of the book seem a little amorphous. It's kind of a dream, and things are real, and they might be on the edge of it—it's not the usual feeling. Naturally, some readers don't like that. I mean, I've heard that, "Why, why, why? What happened to that person, and why did we ever start talking about them if we weren't going to come back?" But I think that just comes from, what can I say—usual expectations. And I say, What can I do? That's not exactly the form here.

DeWeese: Do you feel like over the course of your career your ideas about what a novel is or can be have changed at all?

Salter: Well, no. It should be interesting. That's the main thing. And after that I suppose it has its own terms.

DeWeese: How do you think about structure as a screenwriter who—do you think about structure differently when you're writing a novel?

Salter: Well, you *should* think about structure in a novel. Here I kind of played loose and easy with that, so you might say. I wasn't concerned with it that much in this book—as I said, it began to evolve in a way. You say, "Well, I've either got to do this, and be more consistent with structure, and interweave these people back continually, or not." So in the end I said not. At least not that much.

DeWeese: You also do something interesting with point of view. And it's not unique to this novel. There's a willingness to let consciousness float at times. Bowman's obviously the main character, but there are important moments in which we move from his perceptions to other people's perceptions. Do you do that intuitively, or do you have a sense of when you feel like it's a good idea—

Salter: I don't have a thing that clicks and says, "Here's a good place for that." It just comes out of the writing. I don't know. I've done that—you might say I've gotten away with it—before. It's been commented on before. But in one particular case somebody reviewed this book, but also me, in I think it was the *Atlantic*, or it might have been *Harper's*—it was one of the two. It was back a ways, probably in April. I respected it. I mean, he knew what he was talking about. He complained about that, more or less.

DeWeese: Why complained?

Salter: Because you're not supposed to do that. I don't recall exactly—it wasn't niggling. He was just commenting that this was an irregularity, and then he quoted a little place where it happened, it was three or four lines about sailing on a boat. It must have come from *Burning the Days*. And when I read it, I thought, Ah, that's terrific. It just seemed rather wonderful to me. And I didn't say that at the time [of writing it]—I mean, it was just written. So when you said is it instinct, it must be some sort of tendency, anyway.

DeWeese: It's one of the things that I really admire about the book. There's a certain power and maybe emotional involvement for the reader that's derived from—it's not omniscience, but it's a willingness to move in that direction. And you said you "got away with it." There's somehow this understanding that one should never leave the head of one's main character—

Salter: I don't know, it's one of these things apparently they teach. Like, the same point of view and, I don't know, a lot of clichés about writing—generally with some solid foundation for teaching. But, you know, I know that I can write that way, too, and if you know all the rules, you can—Joan Didion was asked how she approached matters of grammar, and she said, "Grammar is a piano I play by ear." So if it reads correctly, then it really doesn't matter if it deviates in some way. In fact, the deviation is what makes it read well, because it's not expected, and it changed your mind in mid-flight, so to speak—the reader's mind, of course.

DeWeese: It seems to me it's a condition as a writer that you want to feel that freedom to access the material at some other level that doesn't have to do with rules.

Salter: Yeah, when you're not going to get graded, you're free to do anything you like. Of course, that can result in some horrific things, too.

DeWeese: And you write in notebooks, longhand. As someone who has written or been around computers from the time I was young, I often worry there is a kind of material that is accessed through using notebooks, writing longhand, that we can't access if we're sitting in front of a computer. Do you feel like that process of writing in a notebook offers you an opportunity to discover material that you wouldn't find otherwise?

Salter: Well, I write e-mails on the computer, of course. And some e-mails can be long, and you're editing them as you write, or at least I am, deleting sentences and going back, but it's not quite the same process for me. But I don't know if we're seeing the same thing, since you grew up one way, and I another. I'm sure you can write longhand, too, but don't you see it may be different in a different way for you? I don't know. All I can say is I feel a great informality in writing longhand. I feel I'm alone in the house, I'm just wearing a bathrobe, I don't have any shoes on, nobody's going to bother me—I have that feeling when I'm writing longhand. I haven't sat down *to compose*, so to speak. Also, you can write anywhere, you can go out and sit on a—I guess you can do that with a computer, too—but all you need is a scrap of paper, an envelope. And you can attack a paragraph, or jot down a lot of ideas that might let you into something—I mean something you want to do, the thing you're trying to do. It just seems to have an ease for me that I appreciate. I'm certainly not recommending it. I think you should do what feels right to you. It's often been commented that writing is different now, because you can write so fast, so freely, and it gets more word clogged. I don't know if that's true. That wouldn't happen to me in any event, but maybe that's true generally.

DeWeese: Why wouldn't it happen to you?

Salter: I like to cut out words rather than add more words, more description.

DeWeese: I want to ask about a line in *All That Is*. It's in the scene where Bowman is telling his mother that he's going to marry Vivian: "It was love, the furnace into which everything is dropped." The line is written in such a way where I think we're meant to understand that it's her observation.

Salter: Well, it's certainly not his. We know that. And it's certainly not Vivian's. It's his mother, or the narrator, or the author. And I didn't particularly puzzle over it. I just wrote it.

DeWeese: Many of your characters are undone to varying degrees by love relationships, so I'm wondering if you feel that observation is correct, that there is something destructive about love relationships. Is there a danger to love relationships that you feel your characters are encountering again and again?

Salter: I don't think this is a personal feeling, I think everybody knows this, don't they? All literature, all personal experience—I wouldn't say the word is "danger," but the complexity of it . . . and I wouldn't say "fragility," exactly—but the variableness of it, and how close what you feel and what you know conforms to what everybody tells you you should feel or you should know, yeah—I think that makes it a central issue in people's lives.

DeWeese: One of the things that appeals to me about so much of your work is that there seems to be an exploration of this tension between enchantment and disenchantment. I'm thinking about the end of *The Hunters*, where we have a sense that Cleve is trying to remain connected to the beauty of what he's doing, but is becoming more and more disenchanted with the realities of it. It seems to show up in your work again and again, but I don't know if you think about it in terms of enchantment or disenchantment.

Salter: I don't think I do.

DeWeese: How would you describe that tension that your characters seem to be trapped in?

Salter: Well, let's jump to another book, or two, or whatever. Here's *Light Years*, there's not really enchantment in here.

[At this moment, DeWeese spilled coffee on his notebook and the Salters' couch, destroying the continuity of the conversation. The Salters reassured him that this was unimportant, even going so far as to claim they were thinking of having the furniture cleaned anyway. Doubtful. Kind of them to say so.]

Salter: I don't think there's enchantment or disenchantment, either one in

[*Light Years*]. It's the story, really, of the impermanence of a really privileged and perhaps deceptive marriage—I mean deceptive to the reader. And the book even says that—there's what you see, and there's life behind that, the real life. So I don't think that they're disenchanted. She probably, mainly, is an impulsive person, a dramatic person, and self-destructive to an extent, strong-willed, and decides she'd like to turn that page in life. I don't know if that corresponds to this great wave of women finding themselves, dating back to the early '60s, '70s, when all this was renewed with Betty Friedan's book, and then the consciousness-raising, that whole feminist history. That wasn't in my mind—it doesn't really have anything to do with that. It was just a natural feeling I think anybody could have at any time: "I'd like to be living another life," or "I should be living in a different way." And it just happens in this marriage. So something that was really very appealing begins to fade, and what happens to them afterwards, that's really the book. But that's what *I* think the book is. What the reader thinks the book is may be not exactly that. I mean, that's always the case—you don't know what you've written until people start telling you what you've written.

DeWeese: Religion rarely comes up directly in your novels, but I do often sense that there's a kind of spiritual component, or characters striving for a connection to something. Do you think of that striving as a search for spiritual connection, or is it wrong to call it spiritual?
Salter: I would say it's closer to a moral striving than spiritual, though I don't know how close those two words are, really. "Spiritual" suggests something a little different. I think in *The Hunters* there's a moral element. And I suppose—I mean, you reveal yourself through writing, right? Even though you're writing about other people and other things, you have a mask you're behind, you're not obliged to the autobiographical elements, you can alter or conceal to an extent where they're almost indiscernible—but you are writing what you are, all the time. There's really no way of getting away from that. So the element you're talking about, be it spiritual or moral, I suppose is there. It's not put in the forefront. I would say it must be implicit somehow in details, and the observations of things, and the occasional conclusions that the book or the section of the book makes. Also in things that people say.

DeWeese: There's also a strong sense of an aesthetic—a kind of existential aesthetic. Maybe this is what you mean by "moral"—there are better ways to live, or better ways to behave. But in *All That Is*, with Bowman, it's sometimes difficult to tell to what degree Bowman is driven by aesthetics, and to what degree he occasionally floats along, kind of going with a flow, versus at other times pursuing some kind of desire to introduce into the world objects of aesthetic beauty—in his case, literature.

Salter: I think that's right, and that unevenness is part of the book. It corresponds, in a way, to people coming and going, to that feeling—that almost river-like or tidal sensation. I think when you finish reading it, if you liked it, you have a feeling of a whole era having passed, and yet what exactly passed? It doesn't have a lot of solid benchmarks. The president gets shot—that's almost as far as he goes. So I think that's right—he varies. He *is varying*. Some things are more important or come to the surface at times, at times no, he's carried away. He's carried away by love, or what he takes for love—or what I take for love. And sometimes not.

DeWeese: As you said, the frame of *All That Is* is the frame of your own life. Toward the end there's a passage about how Bowman is aware that the novel's place in the culture has been diminished—and *All That Is* ends sometime in the mid-1980s. Have you noticed changes in the publishing industry over the course of your career that you would point to as being fundamental?

Salter: I think these are well known, and very obvious. There are a lot of small presses, but they're mostly, I don't want to say insignificant, but quite small, almost local. And the other publishers have all become conglomerates, and when you go to the publishing offices—somebody said this last night—you go to the Condé Nast office and each floor of the building is an identical floor done the same way, but it's a different magazine with a different mission. So on one floor is *Vanity Fair* and on the next floor is, I don't know, *National Geographic*—that's not one of theirs, but it's like that. And in the publishing houses, it looks different, the architecture is different. They all have modern cubicles. The most important ones have good views. They argue a lot about who gets which office because that one looks out at a wall, this one looks out at the river. The rest of the people are in a pen—as in television, whenever you see a business there are always people in these little enclaves, they have a computer, a picture of their dog and wife on the wall. So it's not the same. Publishing used to be a good deal more idiosyncratic, a good deal more old school, naturally, and was owned by individuals in many cases who were able to exercise their instincts—what they wanted to publish. That's not quite true anymore. It is true you can publish what you want, but the bottom line is very, very important—these are big corporations, so the financial people have a lot to say about what's going on. That was always a consideration in publishing—you can't go on just publishing books nobody buys, who's going to pay all the salaries?—but it's different, it's just done in a different way. Just as I think probably Wall Street is different than it used to be, although I know less about that.

Yes, so I would say it's changed. For instance, Pat Strachan the other night, she said that if I brought in a book of fiction, male fiction—she said I couldn't propose a book of mid-list fiction. This is an experienced editor, and she happens to be at Little, Brown, I believe. They don't want to hear that. They're publishing, naturally, young people's fiction. The readership is largely women, always has been, but I think more significantly now—my impression is that it's more definitive. Men will read books about politics, history, sports, movies, all of that, but the fiction generally belongs to women. I don't know—that may be wrong, but that's my impression.

DeWeese: Do you feel like these changes have affected your own writing career, or are they only affecting younger writers?

Salter: Well, they can't affect me now, because mine is over, or virtually. I think young writers are affected by this, naturally. You're inclined to take your own experience and use it as the norm, even though it may be really very far from everybody else's. Somebody said to me, I think a schoolmate, said, "My uncle's an agent." So I went to see an agent named James Brown. I mean, I was twenty-one years old and I'd written something. And he saw me. He said come in, and talked to me. Now, I don't remember whether he read it or not. In any case, it wasn't published. And the next agent was very much the same. They read manuscripts that came over the transom, as they say. They were a couple of former magazine editors who'd become literary agents, so they read stuff and he read this and said, "Yeah, all right, let's see"—he was an old school fellow, it wasn't that casual, he was smoking a pipe—he said, "So-and-so might like this." That kind of thing. But it seemed quite easy. Now I constantly hear, "How do I meet an agent? How am I going to get an agent?" So my impression is it must be a little more difficult than it used to be. But again, I'm only going on my own experience.

DeWeese: Another industry that I feel has changed in similar ways is obviously the film industry. In other interviews you have somewhat dismissed your years writing films, which hurt my feelings a little bit.

Salter: [Laughs.]

DeWeese: Because when I saw *Downhill Racer* I thought, This was written by someone who understands me. And then when that someone later said,

"Oh, it was all a disappointment . . ." You worked in film during an era that is now considered one of the more important eras in American filmmaking. Are there positive things you took away from that work? Or do you still mostly feel it was a frustrating time?

Salter: Well, I've adopted a tone of bitterness. Of course it was important to me at the time. I thought it would turn out better than it did, I mean for me personally. And having decided, "It's not going to turn out any better," anything—

DeWeese: By better, what do you mean?

Salter: I wanted to make a good movie. I guess everybody does, there's nothing significant in that, nobody starts out trying to make a bad movie. But I wanted to make a movie with a terrific director and have people say it's a knockout, simply wonderful. And it never happened. It could have been a number of things. It just didn't happen, luck didn't fall your way, or it could be from my own shortcomings as a film writer, it might be a combination of both—whatever it is, it didn't happen. I guess I wouldn't still be doing it now, because nobody would hire me at this point, you have to have a pretty solid reputation to keep writing when you're past whatever it is—forty, probably. No, I love films, not as much as I did. And I don't see them as much as I did. And the more I don't see them, the more important they seem to be.

DeWeese: There's this popular narrative of American film from mid to late '60s up through mid to late '70s, that this was a golden era that was then squashed by studios becoming corporate or part of international corporations. As someone who was working in the industry in those years, are there aspects of that narrative we are getting wrong, or oversimplifying or overlooking when we fetishize this period as a beautiful moment?

Salter: I think you have to wait a little longer. Wait another twenty years and see how all that goes. Films go in kind of cycles. Before *Star Wars* there was no *Star Wars*, and there was no multibillion-dollar Lucas industries—in fact he made a couple of failed movies—so that changes everything right away. Before *The Godfather* there was no *Godfather*. I think it's incidents—they change everything, and they change the wave of what's going on. But it seems to me there are always big films and small films. And it's the balance, the attention of the public is shifting a little bit. There's always an audience for big films because there are all those people who like to see the car chases and so forth. But then there is always a sophisticated audience, so to speak, for a different kind of movie. I think that's going on pretty much the way it was. The numbers have gotten, it seems to me, frightening—I can't imagine. I talked to Steve Gaghan, he was the writer of *Traffic*, he's a literary kind of guy, and of course his connections came through Sundance—a lot of people's early movies, the scripts were worked there, they made connections there, then maybe Telluride or one thing or another, that's the way he started. So now he's trying to make another movie, he won an Academy Award for the script [for *Traffic*], he's seeking to make another movie that he wrote, and he needs thirty million dollars. Well, I know that there's been inflation, but even cutting it to ten percent of it, that's not what a film cost then—it didn't cost three million dollars. And the big films, of course, cost a hundred million, or whatever they cost. So in that league, that seems a little different to me. But of course people are always sneaking in, in the gaps between this and that, some clever guy—like Soderbergh, I guess. It's the same story, retold with different examples, different figures. As far as being golden, well—it had its films, but today has today's films.

DeWeese: To get back to *All That Is*, you have an ability or willingness to follow characters into dark places—to have characters occasionally make decisions that might upset readers. There are times I felt a tone that almost moves toward something a little bit gothic. I'm wondering what kind of role you feel . . . The words I wrote down are *malevolence* and *revenge*. But what kind of role do these darker impulses play in your fiction?

Salter: Well . . . I can't think of any particular dark impulses. There are infidelities. There are some smarmy people—not often. But I don't think they have big significance. They're just—that's what I was writing about.

DeWeese: I guess I'm thinking in *All That Is*, when Bowman takes Christine's daughter to Paris. And then there's a short story, I'm sorry, I can't remember the title, there are two men traveling through Europe together, and one of them—

Salter: "American Express."

DeWeese: Yes. These are darker stories—maybe it's wrong to call it darkness. These moments often have a sexual element. I guess that's what I was thinking of, but maybe you don't think of it as dark.

Salter: Well, I knew in "American Express" what is happening. But of course it's not just sex, that was just the ultimate incident, that's where we last saw them. When we first saw them, all they had done was a highly irregular, immoral act of stealing a client from the firm they were working for. One is no worse than the other, in a sense. I just meant that to be a picture of two men and what happened to them when they took the wrong road, so to speak. They took the wrong road but it wasn't that bad, which is what happens, yes? If you're the first one stealing and get out the door, you'll be all right—which is essentially what happened in that story. They were lawyers and sons of lawyers. And I guess, I don't know, lawyers seem a logical villain to me.

DeWeese: [Laughs.] But Bowman's not a lawyer.
Salter: No.

DeWeese: The episode in which he takes Christine's daughter to Paris, it's not quite the same as "American Express," but it's similar in terms of taking a young woman in a way that I think most readers would say, This is not the right—
Salter: Not the right way to behave.

DeWeese: Yes.
Salter: Well—I don't feel that strongly about it. I'd say it's the way people behave, and whether it's right or proper doesn't have much to do with it. [Pause.] Also, it has some voltage.

DeWeese: What do you mean by voltage?
Salter: The situation has voltage. As you said, the impropriety of it, the feeling that a lot of people—I don't know how many instinctively—have about it, it has some power. It's not just a casual incident. That's one thing. And secondly, there's the question of what is your reaction, and how much of that is what you feel *should* be your reaction? How much are you really thinking, and how much is what you are "supposed" to be thinking? This is an element that is in play all the time when you're writing. Are you writing what you really know and what you really feel? Or are you writing the "correct" thing, are you obeying social and literary norms?

Rachel Greben: When I was reading *All That Is*, right up until that incident I was thinking, What's going to happen with Bowman? And out of the blue he does that. And I remember saying, "I don't know what to think about this character now. He just made me really mad." But I love how you give the reader opportunities to be puzzled sometimes, and to make their judgment on their own. And you give it time.
Salter: What did you finally decide?

Greben: At the end?
Salter: No, I mean after the dust settled a little bit.

Greben: With Bowman, I understand what he did. Also it made me mad, because I understand what she would feel like. And the whole situation with the mom's daughter, on a whole different level—you know, I have a daughter too, so it makes me—
Salter: Naturally.

Greben: The hair on my neck rose. It did make Bowman interesting there, because you didn't expect it, and you were ready for something. So although I don't approve of what he did, I really enjoyed not having it carved out exactly what I was supposed to think about this character. I think another character says that about Bowman at some point: "Watch out for him." And we're like, *What?* A lot of that resounds with normal experience—you don't know everything about people, you can't know them. That's part of what makes it interesting and scary. I enjoy the challenge as a reader.
DeWeese: Do you ever worry that you're challenging readers too much? Or is that not something you worry about?
Salter: Well, if you go too far—I don't know. I suppose I should feel that's their problem. But when you hear comments and you realize the story didn't come through, they didn't understand, they didn't read it carefully enough—skipped over a very important phrase here, or a word—I suppose you have to think about that. Are you assuming too much about the ability or interest of the reader? I'd say it crosses your mind, but I don't know how important it is.

DeWeese: When you say the ability of the reader, what kind of abilities are you thinking of?
Salter: Well, the ability of the reader to read the words, and not just to be going down the page. To be listening. A reader who enjoys reading—I feel that I can do well with such a reader. The readers who put less into it and who are a little deaf, really, to the sound of things, and the nuances of things—I feel they're missing it a little bit.

DeWeese: There's a certain kind of novel that presents a character's behavior and then quickly explains the character's behavior psychologically.
Salter: Yes.

DeWeese: Your writing avoids that in ways I think are very compelling. What I wondered is whether drafts you write have some of that and you excise it, or whether you conceive of stories in a way that doesn't involve this contemporary style, where the story exists for me to psychologically analyze a character.

Salter: I try not to write those things to begin with. And if they show up anyway, I'm likely to take them out. I prefer not to have that—I prefer to have the story and the people speak for themselves, and neither to judge nor explain them too fully, too energetically.

DeWeese: I teach, so students sometimes ask this, but it also comes up among writers—what the word "literary" means. The term's obviously baggy, and yet it's important. I guess I'm asking because I feel it's related to the ability not to explain the story, to excise the psychologizing. I'm wondering what you feel the difference is between a literary exploration of the world versus something we would decide is not literary.

Salter: There's not a good dividing line. Because nonliterary stuff may turn out to be very literary, you just didn't know it—because that's the way it came in, so to speak.

DeWeese: What kind of qualities would it have that would make it literary?

Salter: The quality of enduring. People like it and want to read it. In its essence, what makes it literary—well, it never really becomes "literary," but it does become part of literature. It may not be "literary." Is Henry Miller literary? Not really. I mean, he's carrying on, he's got a great poetic gift, he's very full of energy, he's a little batty—not really, but he's out there. I don't think it would have been called literature when it first came out in the early '40s, I suppose, and was smuggled in as pornography—not really pornography, but steamy, or whatever the word is. But now we don't think of it that way. I don't think we do. We say, That's remarkably good. People still—I assume this is true—people still like to read it. I do, I think he's a wonderful writer.

You know, there are three writers whose books are not on the shelves at the Harvard Book Store. They don't keep them on the shelves, they keep them behind the cash register, because they kept being stolen by the students, shoplifted: Burroughs, Kerouac, and Charles Bukowski. So that's a literary statement, in a way—they want to read this. They continue to want to read it. It's never disproven or demolished.

DeWeese: Are there writers you value that aren't part of the contemporary conversation about literature, that you think have been overlooked?

Salter: Oh, yes. But I mean, I like them, but there may be very good reasons for them being overlooked. There's a French writer, fairly well known to be on the lunatic fringe, called Pierre Guyotat. He served in the army in Algeria, and he's a wild and feverish homosexual, and his books, I think, are incredible. But nobody would ever read them, and I wouldn't give them to anybody that I didn't know would like them—I wouldn't propose it. There are others, he's not the only one. He comes to mind immediately because he's a singular writer. Destined to never become known.

DeWeese: Any others you can think of?

Salter: Well, the thing is you don't often come across them, because often they're not published. I've had writing students who I thought had a real gift, but nothing became of them. They didn't go further. Or they didn't realize it themselves, they didn't know what was really good about themselves. It's hard for them to know. What I always found is they'd written something really pretty good, but sections of it or something in it was a mistake. And they'll correct it for you if you point it out, but something goes out of the story—it's not as good. It's not in their original voice. It's following your instructions, and somehow, it's gone.

Greben: In class, if you're trying to guide a student and the end result is that the story loses its power, would you say a good editor can fix that problem, and walk the line between guidance and—

Salter: Well, I was trying to be a good editor, so I have to say probably not. But a writing student is a little different from a writer who has submitted a manuscript and an editor who's working on it. The writing student is fresher, less sophisticated—whatever they are, they're fresh and malleable, and what essence they have belongs to them. I don't want to make it too poetic, but it's like the petal of a flower—in a way, you bruise it by messing with it too much. Some of them write really very well.

DeWeese: There's an image early in *All That Is* of a house or mansion that Bowman believes he saw when he was a child. And there's this repeated search for a home—we often follow his attempts at a new place to live. It doesn't seem specific to *All That Is*, either. A book we haven't talked about, but *Solo Faces*—there's a sense that many of your characters are looking for the place they believe they belong, and not quite finding it. I'm wondering whether that theme of looking for a home is something you think about overtly, or whether your characters seem to become interested in that as you're writing them.

Salter: That's what I think. The second of those.

DeWeese: Because that has been an element in more than one book, have you changed your thoughts about what this home is that they're looking for? Does this place exist?
Salter: Naturally, I think they're searching for the kind of home that I would like. Usually it's not specific. In *All That Is*, it's quasi-specific. He's talking about he wants a beautiful room in one episode, in another he's admiring the house of one of his writers up in the country, it describes that house. When he finally buys a house, it describes that house. So it's fairly specific about what he would be satisfied with, what he's looking for. Does that correspond with what I would like? Yeah, I would say so.

DeWeese: Do you have a sense that he finds it? The novel is episodic, and it ends with an episode—
Salter: I don't think he found the house, but the implication is he found some hope of being happy, being settled. Of course, that's happened to him before. But I think it ends on a touching note, myself. Here's a case of—you mentioned, is it written enough? Is this written enough for the reader to see? In that particular instance, maybe not. Maybe I should have written a little more there. But I thought it would be gotten, that it was apparent. No, there's no indication he's going to buy a house, or is looking for another house.

DeWeese: You said he's probably looking for the kind of home that you would like. Do you feel like you found this at some point?
Salter: Well, I never found the perfect house. How are you gonna do that? It's not easy.

Greben: From a reader's perspective, I think the end is written plenty. Because again, the reader will take away what he or she wants. If he or she wants to have hope in Bowman's future, they can have that. If he or she is just, *No way* . . . as a reader you can fill in the blanks.
Salter: But is that good? I didn't intend that, really. I intended to end it more hopefully, a little more decisive, but I didn't want to go into sentimental— you know, a lot of romance-at-last kind of thing. Anyway, there it is. For me, I understand it.

DeWeese: There's one other line in the novel—it's when Beatrice [Bowman's mother] is getting older and she's losing track of things, of reality. Again, I marked it because it's one of the few moments when religion or spirituality is directly addressed. She asks Bowman what he thinks happens after death, and he responds by asking her what she thinks happens. She says, "I think that whatever you believe will happen is what happens." And the next line reads, "He recognized the truth in it." It's a little bit of a magical statement.

Salter: Well, of course that's an ironic and incomplete answer. It's just saying that after the last thing you were thinking, there's no more thinking—so that's the final thought, and that's what happens. That's what I meant by the truth.

DeWeese: I want to thank you for your time—you've been more than generous. Are you working on something now?

Salter: I'm not working on anything at the moment. But yes, I'd like to write something more. I think there are plenty of possibilities. I don't think I've used up even my own limited possibilities.

Life and Everything That Happened: An Interview with James Salter

Andrés Hax / 2014

An edited version of this interview appeared in Spanish translation in the cultural magazine *Revista Ñ*, a weekly supplement of *Clarín* newspaper (Buenos Aires, Argentina), Issue 560 (June 21, 2014), 4–6. Printed with permission.

I went to see James Salter as one goes to see the wise man of the mountain. In fact, I was going to meet him in my professional capacity as a reporter for Argentina's largest daily newspaper, *Clarín*. *All That Is* had just been published in translation by Ediciones Salamandra. But my secret intent was to receive a blessing from Salter. I can't explain this rationally. What kind of blessing could this be? Even I didn't know. I revere Salter. His words haunt me and his fictional worlds have become a permanent part of my imagination. In my mind they are real places. As real as any place from my physical life that I can call to memory.

At 10 a.m., I knocked on Salter's door. There he appeared with his wife, Kay, by his side. His courtesy and friendliness were disarming. I must say, however, that if Salter was generous with his time and with his answers, he was also stern and demanding. He took occasional notes during our conversation. Before the formal interview took place, seated at his dining room table, classical music playing in the adjoining kitchen, he asked me tough questions in his sweet voice. For example: "Have you written books?" It was like a gut punch. "No. Just newspaper articles," I answered. "Ah, just articles . . ." he said, nonjudgmentally, like a doctor listening to a patient's heart.

In the end, however, I did receive my blessing. After the recorder was turned off, I told Salter of my admiration for him. Fumblingly, I confessed to him my love of literature and how I wanted to be *inside of it*. "You mean, you want to be famous?" he asked, genuinely confused. No, that was not it.

I explained to him that besides life itself, reading fiction—novels in particular—was the core of my life. Or rather that it was like a parallel life that I
wanted to be my real life. That I wanted to be *inside of literature*. He looked
at me and was silent for a moment. And then he said: "Well. *You are.*"

The following interview took place in Salter's home on June 4, 2014.

Andrés Hax: In terms of process, how do the creations of *The Hunters* and
All That Is compare? They are completely different books, but what are the
continuities and differences between those two books as they stand now?
James Salter: This is not a usual question, if you're afraid of that. Well, as
it happens, there is going to be a book auction at Christie's this December. They have selected a number of authors, I guess about twenty-five, and
asked them to annotate the first edition of a number of their books. I guess
they try and pick a book of some significance. I don't know who all the other
writers are; I know DeLillo is one, because he mentioned it to me. This is all
a fundraising auction under the auspices of, or for the benefit of, PEN. There
was an identical auction at Sotheby's in England last year, which was a big
success. The book that they selected for me was *The Hunters*, my first novel.
And I just have finished, two days ago, three days ago, annotating it. So it's
very fresh in my mind.

AH: You annotated literally on the page?
JS: On the page. All of the authors are doing that, and then as you'll see,
some people have done an incredible job. The Hunter Thompson book—
he's dead—was annotated by Ralph Steadman, who is his illustrator. He
drew a lot of original drawings on the pages.

AH: Before this, when was the last time that you had read *The Hunters*?
JS: Maybe eighteen years ago when I revised it for an edition that Counterpoint published. I'd been thinking that I would like to write something about
all this, life and everything that happened and everything that it brought to
mind for me, and things that it emphasized for me, and issues that had nothing to do with flying but were issues of relationships. Well, relationships is
not the right word. Issues of personality and moral questions. Even though
they are, in a sense, trivial—these are not deep, moral questions—but they
were issues to me personally. And so I'd been trying to think of a way to
write about them, and one day it just happened that they came to me. I
wrote down quickly in the back of the only available paper I had right then

what I thought the book should be. I outlined it very, very quickly. And then I sat down and wrote it chapter by chapter. I didn't give one chapter precedence or put one aside because it was difficult to write. I think I just wrote them. As I look back over it, I see that I was very uncertain and, to my mind, very amateurish in trying to get into the book. But I am criticizing myself here. I am not going to suggest that the reader notice that immediately. When *I* read it again, I noticed it.

AH: You noticed that when rereading *The Hunters* for the Christie's auction? And also when reading the novel for the Counterpoint edition?
JS: Well, I wrote that in the annotation of *The Hunters* for the auction. That's what I now see as a writer.

AH: You were hard on yourself.
JS: Well, I tend to be hard on myself. Did I know that at the time I was writing the novel? As I read it, I seemed to remember that I really didn't feel I was into the book yet. I had some difficulty getting into it, but I wrote it anyway. At a certain point—maybe chapter three—the book began to assume its own life, began to tell itself. I don't feel that anymore.

Let's go forward now to *All That Is*. I started many times on the book, but I didn't really start. I was writing down proposals to myself of certain people and writing, not outlines, but putting together what I thought a book might be. I was obviously interested in writing about an individual, and I couldn't settle on who that individual was or how the novel was going to take form. I began by writing about failed individuals and then about what became of certain people after the war. I did this over a number of years. For some reason it wasn't urgent to me, but it was present in my thoughts and I never could come to any real decision about it. I've often been asked: Why was it thirty years between one novel and the other novel? It wasn't a question of working for thirty years; it was a question of waiting. And for about twenty-odd years until I was satisfied, to some extent, with what I was going to do. When I finally reached that point, I reached it because of intermediate things I had written. I wrote a chapter for *All That Is* before I ever wrote the book. You probably know what chapter it is.

AH: I don't, I'm sorry.
JS: Well, it's the one called "Virginia" [published in *Paris Review* 203 (Winter 2012); the chapter is titled "Christmas in Virginia" in *All That Is*]. I was working on that without being sure where it was going. And I reached a

point where I finally decided I was going to write about an editor in a publishing house. It spanned the era of the book, for me. That is to say, the era where small publishers and private publishers began to either be taken over by or to become corporate. I was old enough to have known the editors who worked for some of the publishers in that period, and I also knew the era itself. So I finally drew a chronological line, and on that I began noting what might happen to the main character, Philip Bowman. It's a book of a personal life about men and women after the war and what became of them. But it's essentially a book, it finally turned out, that says: if you don't have love in this life, you've missed the whole point of it. After "Virginia," I began to write the chapters successively, but some I had to put aside and go on to the next one and then come back and fill in the spaces. There are a lot of personages in the novel, some who appear again, others who never appear again. It's a book that proceeds by appearances and interruptions.

So there's a difference in the way those two books were done. And, of course, there's a difference in the authority that I felt when writing them.

AH: Was *The Hunters* more fun to write than *All That Is*? Was it more exhilarating?

JS: *The Hunters* was more fun to write, but a lot more uncertain. I didn't know whether it was any good or not. You know, you waver. You think you're writing something interesting, but somebody can demolish that in a moment by looking at it and saying: What are you writing this for? By the time I was seventy-five years old, I knew I could write, but the question remained: Am I writing the right thing? You have to be devoted to it. You must be interested in it, or you can't write well. I can't anyway.

AH: Correct me if I'm wrong, but in terms of your complete work, there are some books that were written, in part, because editors encouraged you to do so. I was thinking of the rewriting of *Cassada, Burning the Days*, and also *Solo Faces*. As opposed to others that maybe were written *on spec*, so to speak. Is that a fair division?

JS: Well, spec!

AH: I don't know if I'm using that term correctly . . .

JS: Well, you're right.

AH: Do you have a different affection for those two categories? Or is it the same for you?

JS: Well, that implies a certain lack of inner impulse and direction, which I accept. It's also quite true. I would not have written *Solo Faces* had I not been urged to. I would never have written an autobiography, at least a partial autobiography, unless the editor had said: This will be wonderful once you write more. As for the need to revise *The Arm of Flesh*, I immediately was in agreement, but I didn't know whether I wanted to take the trouble to do it. Eventually, I agreed. The editor wanted to publish it with *The Hunters*. I said, well if I'm going to revise *The Arm of Flesh*, I'd also like to revise *The Hunters*. I didn't object to writing *Burning the Days* because the memories were fresh. Whether the suggestion that I do that rather than write something else during that time was good or not, I don't know. I think the book was good. I think it reads like a novel.

AH: The motivation of the question was more along the lines of what you write to Robert Phelps, which appears in *Memorable Days*: "Don't lose your courage. Finish this book. Believe in it."
JS: Oh, I urge him to believe in his book?

AH: I was wondering about this notion of encouragement and courage as a writer . . .
JS: I was referring to *Heroes and Orators*. It was not a very good book. And there, in that letter, because I like him very much, I'm trying to tell him all this.

AH: You had this enormously courageous life in the war, and then—I've heard you mention in an interview you did with the Canadian Broadcasting Corporation—the idea of the difficulty of getting to the writing. Actually you said, "There is a certain reluctance to sit down at the desk." There's this idea of courage as a writer, of the fortitude necessary to write.
JS: That's probably laziness I was referring to more than courage. I think it takes some courage to put yourself out there, unless you're writing something to amuse people. But even then, to put yourself forward requires a little courage. It's stepping on the stage, and people are going to boo you. The depth of the courage depends on what you're writing and how much you reveal and how much you tear up your life, so to speak, to write.

AH: While reading *Memorable Days*, I was thinking that if I were a powerful and charismatic editor and I had you under my spell, one thing I would love for you to write is a book on the practice of writing. I mean on the art of the novel, on what a writer has to do and has to be. You write about this in fragments in your works. In *Light Years*, for instance, you write about Nedra: "I'm going to describe her life from the inside outward." I feel I could put together an anthology of your philosophy of writing, but could you write that book? Do you have a firm set of values and of rules and of knowledge?

JS: Well, I mean, after a while you know some things about writing.

AH: And what are those things?

JS: [Laughs.]

AH: It's an impossible question . . .

JS: No, it's not impossible. I mean, you know some technical things. How to do certain things, how to introduce things, how to link things, how close to get to things and when. I'm just speaking generally. So you know all of those aspects that are part of the craft, I suppose, of writing. Beyond that, you're going into the deeper level of writing, which is to say, how to break through and say properly what you're trying to say, how to find out, and what is the appropriate vehicle for saying all that. It's not pedantic. You're not teaching anybody anything, but you are telling them something. And why are you telling them this? What is the impulse to do this? Well, in my case the impulse is that I like to write about things that wouldn't exist if I didn't write about them. So, that means you have to write about these things in a certain way that makes them memorable.

AH: And you teach yourself that? Is that something that you could teach to a student?

JS: Well, some of those things you can suggest to a student or somebody who appreciates what it is to write, someone who understands how to read. You read other writers maybe with appreciation, but certainly with a sense of critique. You're saying, Do I really like this? If I like this, what's going on here? And if I don't like this, why am I—like a cat—turning up my nose at it? I'm not really interested in it. I'm reading it dutifully because I'm supposed to read it.

AH: I very much enjoyed seeing online the conversation between you and Richard Ford at the 92nd Street Y. And I asked the question in that spirit because it was very nice to see what you could say to each other that someone who has not written a novel could not ask you in fairness. I'm asking you unfair questions. For example, when you spoke to him about wanting to write longer and he wanting to write shorter, or talking about the length of sentences, there was a communication between the two of you that was pure craftsmanship that you both could understand.

JS: Well, that's what I'm speaking about now. You don't have to really be at that level of a writer to be talking about craft. But, of course, with him it's sort of batting the ball back and forth. The problem with that discussion was he had the topical questions. I didn't know what he was going to say.

AH: You were ambushed.
JS: Yes.

AH: Are you as fond of, or as close to, your short stories as you are of your longer narratives?
JS: Some of them.

AH: Was it Faulkner who said that writing short stories is more difficult than writing novels?
JS: I think he said that if you fail as a poet, you become a short story writer. And if you fail at that, you become a novelist. I don't think he's telling the truth. He said a lot of—well, everybody said a lot of things.

AH: Why did you write short stories? Are they truncated novels?
JS: I think there are sometimes a lot of short stories within novels. A short story may simply be conceptual, or a conception, something not big enough to write a book about. It's more anecdotal. But it can contain a great number of things. I mean, there are short stories that could never be anything else; there are others that simply could have been a novel. Flaubert's long story "A Simple Heart" is practically a novel. It's long, it's deep.

AH: Imagine if you were at a dinner party or an intimate gathering, and there was a gentleman or a woman to whom you were very drawn but who didn't know your work, someone who was not a reader. In the course of the evening, that person says to you, genuinely: What do you write about? What is your writing about? How would you answer that question?
JS: Well, I used to answer the question formulaically by saying: What I'm essentially writing about is what it is to be a man. But I'm a little embarrassed to say that now, because men are held in such contempt and women have seized the stage, so to speak. And to say such a thing immediately labels you as a masculine or even an ultra-masculine writer. Well, I am both of those

things. Not ultra, but I do write from a masculine, and probably an outmoded, or now unfashionable, point of view. However, the writing is the writing and if it's true it's true. There are things that I think are immutable that are not subject to changes in energy, which is really what has gone on here.

AH: What do you mean by changes in energy? Cultural energy?

JS: Yes, I think cultural and social energy have become more feminine. Maybe not worldwide. I'm speaking of America. When I say "what it is to be a man," I'm not speaking from a chauvinistic point of view. I'm speaking from a philosophical and physical point of view. That's what I think that I'm writing about. Do I have a deeper subject? Well, I guess I'm writing about human desire and the physical world. And as I said previously, I'm tempted to write about things before an epitaph has to be written about them. I'm writing in lieu of an epitaph.

AH: I like the biography in the film that Open Road Media made of you. That was the first time that I saw you mention this notion, as you write in the epigraph to *All That Is*: "There comes a time when you realize that everything is a dream, and only those things preserved in writing have any possibility of being real." I have this sense that part of what you write about also is that there's a part of existence, of consciousness and of life that is dreamlike. Not only when you write does it have a chance of becoming real, but you write about the dreamlike quality of existence somehow. Is that a correct intuition?

JS: Dreamlike. You know, I don't have any idea what my writing really looks like. It sounds funny, but I know when I have written something that I'm satisfied with. It's hard to know what people get out of it. I believe you, I believe what you said, and there are people who say other things and I believe them. But what I think myself, well, I really don't know. I can get lost in the writing myself. Not a dream. But it can include me. It can envelop me. Even though I wrote it, it can still do that. Does that sound like I'm fooling myself? I don't know. But when I read it, I understand it. It convinces me. Is that what we were talking about? Am I creating a dream? In a sense. Dream is the wrong word here. That implies an unreality, and I'm really writing—generally speaking—about a palpable reality. The physical world. The world that—I said *love* a moment ago—but if you don't get the world while you're here, you're missing it. So I don't know if that's what you're talking about when you say you can reverse it.

AH: I mean that your writing is vivid and palpable, and yet these places have disappeared. The planes in *The Hunters* don't exist anymore. That manner of combat will never return. Everything is slipping away and in a constant state of mutability. You fix it for a moment through writing about it. In that sense, maybe it's not that it's your mission as a writer, but I feel like I am entering a shared dream of existence through your work. Everyone talks about how you are a master of the sentence, but there's a sense of your prose rhythm that is in crescendo. You have said about *All That Is* that you were trying to get away from the idea of "Salter is the master of the sentence . . ."

JS: Well, I was trying to not draw attention to my writing. I don't know why. That seems a curious thing to do. I think it was a misconception, and I'm sorry I tried to do that. I didn't succeed. There's a lot of writing in there that draws attention to itself.

AH: What are your ideas about prose rhythm?

JS: I'm talking from a writer's point of view. If you don't have a sense of that kind of music and that kind of rhythm, if you don't respond to it, you don't write or think that way or read that way, then forget it. This is not important for you. But if you have a feeling for it, then I think it comes into the writing without any planning. I don't think you say: Let's get it going, let's have some drums here. But on the other hand, you know this intuitively. You think: This is a long section of whatever it is, let's go to some brass here. We've been in the violin section—or whatever it is—for a long time. Or, we've gone a long way without dialogue here. Could this be better said in dialogue? Would this be more affective or would it be better reading if it were done that way? Or, let's make it a little easier on the reader, here, more pleasurable. Because, after all, the pleasure of the reader—pleasure here is not the right word—but the entertainment, the willingness of the reader, the affection of the reader—you want to make the reader like the book. If you haven't done that . . . That's not the book I'm trying to write.

AH: Do you read your work out loud? Do you put it up on the wall and look at it? Is it the shape of the words or the sound of the words that you notice?

JS: I read it aloud to myself.

AH: In your voice?

JS: Yeah, but when I'm writing it, the look of the words matters to me, too. What is that look I'm striving for? Who knows? You're either pleased with the way it looks, or you say: This is rather impenetrable here. Or, this has some very disagreeable words in it. Unnecessary. Or whatever fault you're finding with it. Because, after all, you are finding fault with it all the time. This is a problem that the writer always faces because you imagine there are some superior writers who are simply writing and it's coming out of them like a spring. And you're not writing that way, you're writing only confronted with difficulties, continually. The image of that writer who is writing effortlessly is always threatening you. You want to write that way, but you simply can't do it.

AH: You have written about meeting Nabokov and doing his profile for *People*. In that encounter, did you go to him trying to get any wisdom for your own writing life?

JS: No, I didn't expect to. I was merely going to see this man who wouldn't give interviews and trying to find something human to write about him. He wasn't going to talk about writing with me. He didn't even know me. Why would he do that?

AH: What had you published by that time?

JS: That was 1976. I felt he should know about me.

AH: He hadn't read *A Sport and a Pastime*? You didn't take him any of your books?

JS: No, I wouldn't do that. I was posing as a journalist there. I'd be very cautious myself about another writer.

AH: When you're writing, do you stop and look and then write what you see, or does what you see appear as you are writing? Does it appear in the flow of the writing of the words?

JS: No, the flow. That's what I was saying, the flow. That's your demon. That people are writing with great flow. Occasionally you do, of course. You're writing about something, you know just how it should be, and you try to get it down. I would say that writing generally is more construction than flow. Every good writer haunts you. You're trying to get them out of your consciousness completely when you write. But it's hard to destroy them. They creep back on you. Just looking at the bookshelf may cause you problems. A lot of writing is written just washing dishes or whatever you are doing because you're thinking about things. You try to get a purchase on them, or a beginning on them. Or maybe you write a section of them in your mind, or think of a name, or an attitude. You're turning it over all the time. Then a certain amount of time is spent writing it down. And, of course, a lot of time rewriting it. Evelyn Waugh, a writer who wrote very well and who I feel wrote with fluidity—he's English, they all do that—said once, People have a notion that writing a novel is simply a matter of standing behind a screen somewhere and writing down what people say. He said, It's nothing like that. It's more like going around a vast and indescribable rubbish pile and looking for things that might be of use. Ah, here for instance, you find a dented piece—this could be a candelabra if it were polished up a little and set right. Well, I understood what he was saying.

AH: Would you ever look back and ask, "Am I a part of literature?"

JS: Part of literature? Well, I'm part of writers. I'm part of the world of writers, I would say. Literature? It depends how you describe what you mean by literature. In the broadest sense, I'm part of the world of literature. In a more narrow, and I would say in a more elevated sense—the heights of literature—I've never felt I had the authority to make that claim.

AH: And do you feel that that could be validated externally, for example, if you were to win the Nobel Prize?

JS: The question is unanswerable in a way because that's not going to happen.

AH: If you are not sure, then who could be sure?

JS: That's good of you to say, but I haven't had the validating book. It's been pointed out to me. I don't mean at the dinner table. Critics have said that, and I think that's true. But the books themselves, there are some of those books that I think are quite good. In a sense, it doesn't matter. I always wanted fame. But when you get fame, in whatever degree, it's immediately burdensome. You didn't know it weighed that much when you wanted it.

AH: Because of the demands it imposes upon you to keep achieving fame? Or because of people like me who come to pester you at your home?

JS: All its aspects are bad.

AH: And also because it's not enough? You want more?

JS: Everything you've mentioned. You want more. Others have more. It incites envy. It's socially undesirable. People expect you to be something. And who is that person that they expect you to be? You're not interested in the personage that they have conceived. Your privacy is invaded. Don't worry, there's no invasion here. Very few people come here. But they're invading your privacy, really. It's a bad thing to have. Yet you wanted it more than anything and you were right in wanting it and striving for it. In addition to wanting to say things, that's one of the reasons you write, at least in the beginning.

Entretien avec James Salter : "J'essaie de me préserver des autres voix quand je travaille." [Interview with James Salter: "I try and keep away from other voices when working."]

Arnaud Laporte / 2014

Published in French translation in *Le Magazine Littéraire* (7 August 2014), 20–23. Original English transcript printed with permission.

Arnaud Laporte: We could build this interview on three axes, which are also the founding elements of your life, always found in your books: writing, war, and women. But I do not know if that order suits you? Ladies first?
James Salter: There is no ladies first anymore. Women now are in line with everyone else.

AL: What do you remember of your first text ever written?
JS: The first story I ever wrote I copied from a magazine because I had no idea how to write one. It was a short story, I don't remember by whom.

AL: Your first real fight?
JS: The one I remember was in the park with some tough Irish slum kids.

AL: Your first sexual intercourse?
JS: I can't imagine anyone is interested in hearing this. In any case it's told in some detail in *Une Vie à Brûler* [*Burning the Days*].

AL: You often said that war is the central event in your life. You wore the uniform for seventeen years and a hundred dogfights. How has this changed your outlook on the world, on life, on men?

JS: I would say that the war was *a* central thing. Its importance has faded. The men who were in it are gone. So it's probably still a part of my personality but covered over by other things.

AL: You read Saint-Exupéry, with whom you share many passions, but you say that at the time of St-Ex, there were real dogfights, and in Korea, it was murder. Do you have the feeling of having been a legal murderer?

JS: It was actually Saint-Exupéry who said, when he was a reconnaissance pilot in World War II, that fighters don't fight, they murder. He meant that they came up behind you and in a couple of seconds it was over. It was a figure of speech, not an indictment.

AL: How many red stars under your cockpit?

JS: One—the minimum, although there is such a thing as one-half, a shared kill.

AL: What do you think of the high use of drones today and, in particular, by the US military?

JS: Drones are only a step in the continual development of weapons. I don't think they're inhumane. Their use is part of a bigger question and certainly no more savage than flying an airliner full of civilian passengers into a great building filled with thousands of other people. The question is, what does one think of that?

AL: Your writing thrives on life, on what you experienced, and your latest novel opens with an evocation of the war. You write from your experience. Is it a quest for truth, or a distrust of fiction?

JS: Fiction is reality in another form. We know it's not true, but that doesn't matter, it feels like truth. That's what I write.

AL: In *All That Is*, you write, "What the joys of music were to others, words on a page were to him." Did you read a lot before writing?

JS: If you mean, did I read books before sitting down and writing, no. I try and keep away from other voices when working. Almost anything you learn from someone else's book is useless to you anyway.

AL: Critics always talk about the accuracy of your writing, the fact that there is not a word too much. In a book, we sometimes want to underline a sentence. In yours, I would like to underline every sentence, or almost. Does this mean that what we would not have wanted to underline is what you had removed, eliminated?

JS: I don't know how to answer that. I think of the reader, yes, but it's myself I want to satisfy. I don't feel I'm writing poems or anything perfect. In a paragraph, I like to have a good sentence or two, and on a page a good paragraph. Sometimes there's more than that. You take out what's unnecessary.

AL: I guess you rephrase ten times, a hundred times, each sentence until its shape suits you. Is this the case? Do you rewrite a lot?

JS: Writing is rewriting. I think it's hard work. The opening is important. If that's right, everything is easier.

AL: Gustave Flaubert, in a letter to Louise Colet, 16 January 1852, wrote: "What seems beautiful to me, what I should like to write, is a book about nothing, a book dependent on nothing external, which would be held together by the internal strength of its style, just as the earth, suspended in the void, depends on nothing external for its support; a book which would have almost no subject, or at least in which the subject would be almost invisible, if such a thing is possible." Did you have, at some point in your writer's life, the same desire as Flaubert?

JS: What could he have meant by this? Perhaps Louise Colet knew.

AL: Flaubert had his "gueuloir," but your writing is closest, it seems to me, to Marguerite Duras's, John Cheever's, or Virginia Woolf's. It seems made to stay in the reader's brain, to soak sensitive layers and layers of understanding in the same gesture. Is this what you want to happen?

JS: I want the reader to have pleasure, both sensual and intellectual pleasure, and to remember it. The pleasure also of having certain things confirmed.

AL: I mentioned two women writers. What is the importance of gender in writing, according to you?

JS: Everyone is equal on the page. I love Colette, Sybille Bedford, Marguerite Duras—*The Lover*, especially—Anne Carson and Joan Didion. Simone de Beauvoir. They write from a woman's point of view, but that's one of the reasons to read them.

AL: Talking about women, you have often said that the main focus of life is sex. Reading your books, I think about this sentence of the Marquis de Sade: "Every man is a despot when he has a hard-on." Is it the seeking of this (fugitive) sensation of power that dominates the life of a man, according to you?

JS: I said that the sexual axis is the principal one in life. The sexual act, I think George Sand said, is the holiest act in life.

AL: France has a special place in your sex life, as shown in *A Sport and a Pastime*. How do you explain this erotic air you breathe on the Old Continent?

JS: France has always had a central place in my emotional life. No other country except my own comes close. Traveling in France, in the days that I did it, living in France was wonderful. The old hotels are sacred to me, certain towns by rivers. France was the place I came to first, Paris, when I first came to Europe. Paris scorned me but later made up for it.

AL: In Europe in the nineteenth century, artists were making their Grand Tour. You too, in your own way, you have made your Grand Tour?

JS: I've made a number of Grand Tours. I never had the time for just one. There's the cultural Grand Tour in France and Italy, the monuments, cemeteries, pictures, and so forth, and there's the noncultural one where you wake bruised—I think I wrote this—after indelible nights, your pockets empty.

AL: What are, according to you, the relationships between sex and love? Is it that men only think about sex, and women about love?

JS: Sex and love. . . . Let's say they can live perfectly well without each other, but they're finer together.

AL: However, to describe a sex scene, you wrote once: "she saw the ceiling, he the sheets." It's terrible, and at the same time it's so funny. What is the truth in it? What do you want to say about sex with this sentence?

JS: I was just writing a description of something ordinary, a pencil sketch. It doesn't have more depth than that.

AL: The publication of *A Sport and a Pastime* was quite difficult because the sex scenes were very explicit for that time. Since then your freedom has been praised. But today, some accuse you of sexism in *All That Is*. Yesterday or today, there is always a problem with sex, right?

JS: Yes, although as you suggest it's not the same problem. The social confine today is that the writer is now free to describe absolutely anything regarding sex and use any words so long as it does not seem like disrespect.

AL: Back to writing, you told of your admiration for Gogol, and your regret not being able to read Russian. In this regard, do you read the French translations of your books?
JS: I can read French fairly well. I haven't read this book yet.

AL: What do you think the French readers lose in the translation of your books?
JS: Even with an excellent translation, even a superb one, there is some distinction that always exists. I try to write in a way in which, if a word were changed or was in a different position, the sentence would not be quite as good. So something, some tone or suggestion or bit of style, can always be gone. I think I was lucky with Philippe Garnier.

AL: Your writing has often been compared to Impressionist painting, but I think that each brush stroke tells a whole world in your books. And thus we see many individuals pass by in *All That Is*, some will be there for a few lines, a few words, others remain in the environment of your hero, but all fully exist.
JS: This novel is perhaps the most impressionistic of all because it really works as a memory, with its associations of ideas, its absence of a clear structure, his digressions, his ellipses.

AL: Have you built it so, or is it a narrative structure that is imposed on you?
JS: The structure became clear as I was writing. I had a painting of Kirchner's in mind. Bold figures, some of them only intimated, the crowded street.

AL: "There comes a time when you realize that everything is a dream, and only those things preserved in writing have any possibility of being real."
—*All That Is*

To write is to be stronger than death. Writing from a memory is a way to make it become eternal. Conversely, what is not written disappears. This is a great belief in literature, in books, that you have?
JS: Nothing lasts longer.

AL: But your hero, Bowman, after a lifetime in the world of publishing, believes that the "power of the novel in the nation's culture had weakened." Is this what you think yourself?

JS: I think it's evident. The publishing houses are changing. They may even disappear completely. There may be democratic anarchy, a great sea of texts, long and in spurts like the previews of movies, with writers both known and anonymous. The novel will take too long to read.

AL: You are often said to be an atheist. In *All That Is*, the question of Judaism seemed to have a larger share than in your previous books. Is it just an impression, or is it a subject that concerns you more today? Does James Horowitz want to take a little space in the life of James Salter?
JS: Well, I wouldn't call this a voyage homeward or anything like that. The publisher is Jewish, actually a couple of them are. This is just reality.

AL: To seek the truth, is it a reasonable goal in life? Is there a truth, or different truths for each person, and different truths for every person at every moment of life?
JS: There's a fundamental truth that exists for everyone: We are here with the earth, stars, time. The rest is morals, religion, politics, philosophy—some of it may be inborn—and the truths of science. People claim they have discovered the truth. Other people have never discovered it. I'm actually a little afraid of people who know the truth. I think you can only know something that seems like it.

AL: And in every moment of life, as is the case for Bowman, the choices we make close the door to other possibilities. Yourself, you say you spent too much time writing scripts for Hollywood. But we only live once. That's all there is, and nothing else. Is the title of your book to be heard as a form of wisdom or a form of despair?
JS: It's neither. It's certainly not despair. It's more a form of embrace.

AL: "It is all one long day, one endless afternoon, friends leave, we stand on the shore."—*Light Years*
If writing is made of experience, so one could think that publishing a novel at eighty-six or eighty-seven years old makes this book even richer, closer to the "truth." What do you think about that?
JS: I think we've already discussed truth.

AL: You have often said you wanted to write to be famous. You are, and are admired by most major American and British authors. Has fame brought you some kind of satisfaction?
JS: Yes, but it didn't come at exactly the right time.

AL: *Burning the Days* ends with these words: "Great desire to live on." There was also a great desire to continue to write, to publish a new novel, thirty-four years after the previous one. Do you still feel these great desires?

JS: I still feel a desire to write.

Index

www.ingramcontent.com/pod-product-compliance
Lightning Source LLC
Chambersburg PA
CBHW020651030726
47498CB00002B/468